RECREATING
MAINE'S FIRST SHIP

Photo Essay by
PAUL T. CUNNINGHAM

Cunningham, Paul T.
Recreating Maine's First Ship/ Paul T. Cunningham
1. HISTORY / United States / State & Local / New England
2. Transportation : Ships & Shipbuilding - History
3. TRANSPORTATION / Ships & Shipbuilding / Pictorial
I. Title.

p. 96

Hardcover ISBN: 979-8-3302-6323-3
Softcover ISBN: 979-8-3303-5245-6

Published by:

Boat Building Books
Brunswick, Maine

Dedication

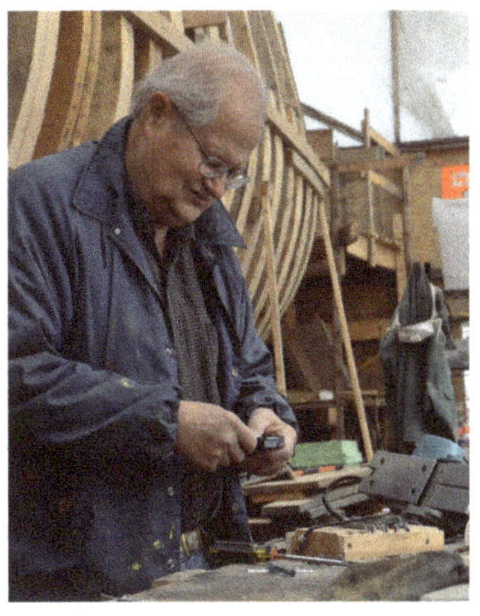

Jane Stevens (1920-2008) founding member of Maine's First Ship, historian, photographer, author, artist, and musician. During World War II at Bath Iron Works, she photographed and drew ship building techniques—used around the country to develop and improve war-time manufacturing efforts. After WWII, she worked as a photographic colorist, a reporter for the Bath Daily Times, and as the Sagadahoc County Registrar of Deeds. Later she moved to "Hossketch" in Popham immersing herself in the history of the community, especially the Popham Colony of 1607.

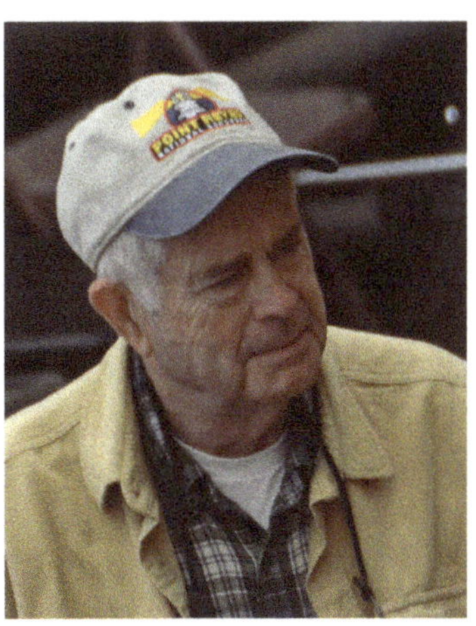

RB Omo Jr. 1936-2023. RB enjoyed a long career in mechanical engineering. In 1980 he moved to Bath, Maine, and to work at Bath Iron Works. He later served as the Chief Design Engineer for Chamberburg Engineering in Pennsylvania. In 2010, RB retired back to Bath, becoming deeply involved in the Maine's First Ship project. He and other volunteers built a replica of the Virginia, the first European ship built in North America. "If it was dull RB sharpened it, if it was broken, RB fixed it, if a plan was needed, RB created it."

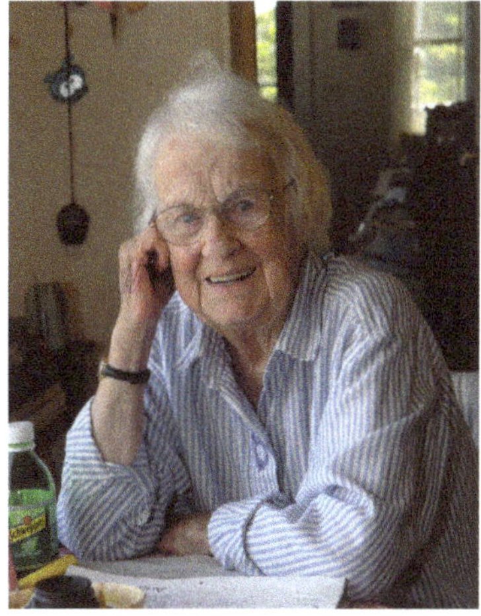

John Bradford 1938-2016, another founding member of Maine's First Ship and a 1956 graduate of Cape Elizabeth High School and a 1961 graduate of Bowdoin College. After retirement, he enjoyed a new career involving his interest in Maine history and archeology. He volunteered at the excavations of the former Fort St. George. Consequently, he researched 1600's English wooden ship design. This led to publishing a book that served as a guide to the construction of the 21st Century *Virginia*.

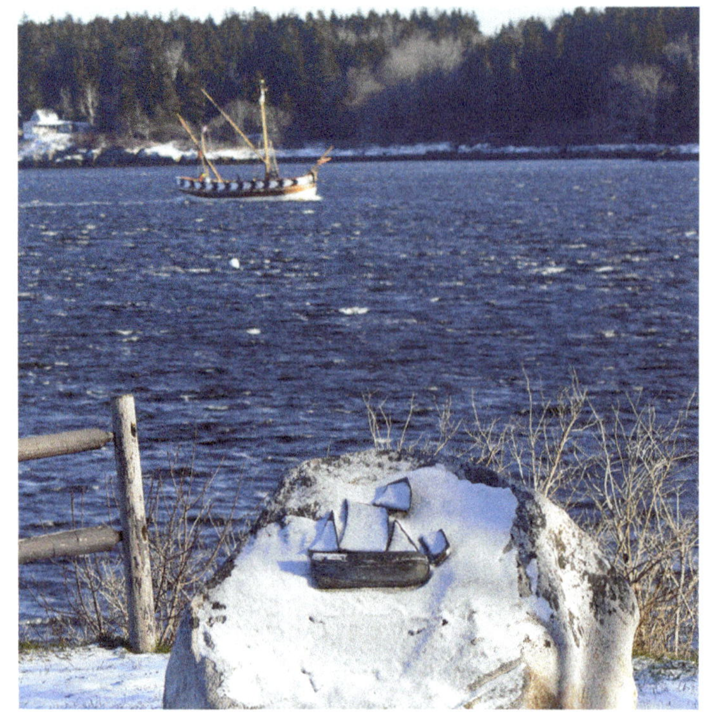

*Professor Jeffrey Brain, third from the left, ovesees an archeological dig at the site of the original
Popham Colony.*

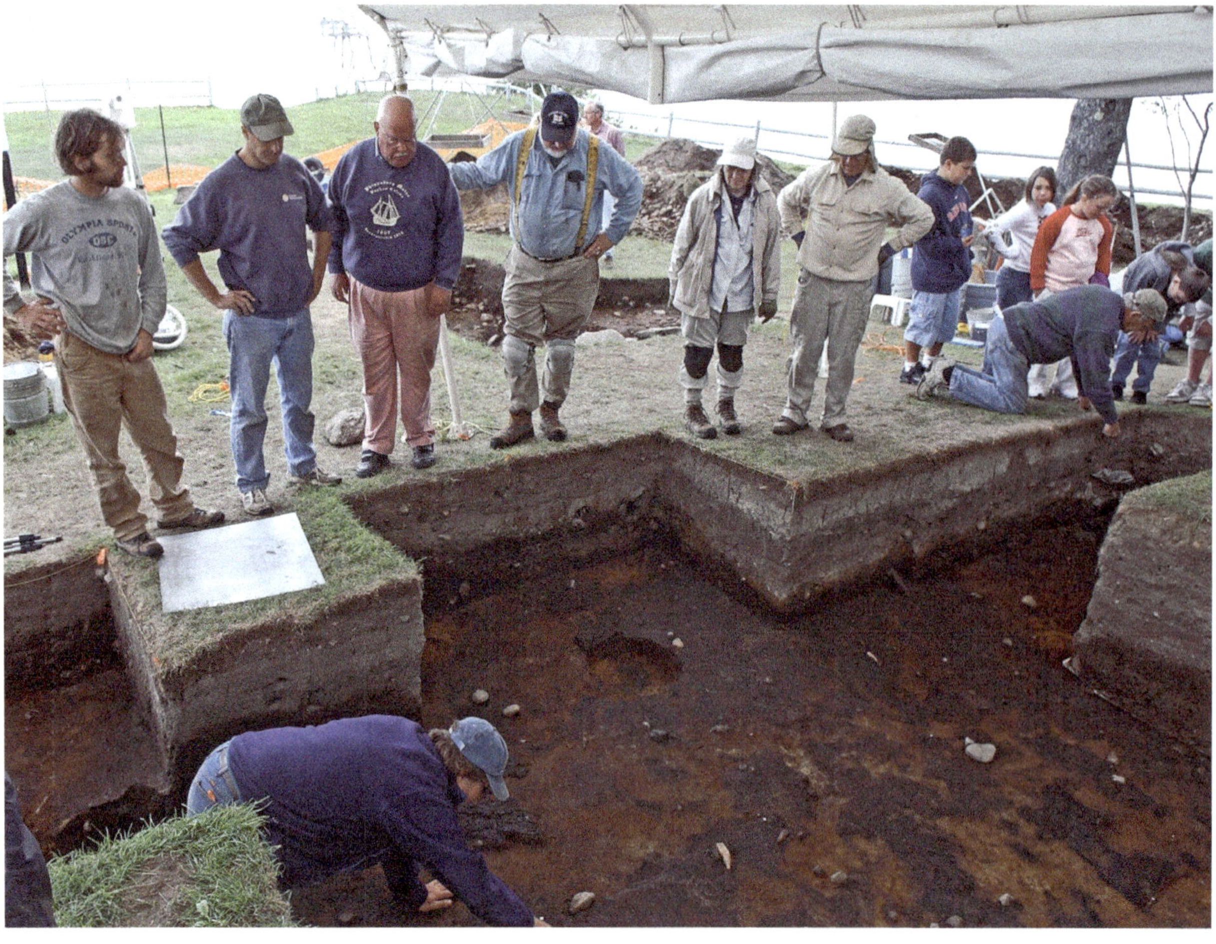

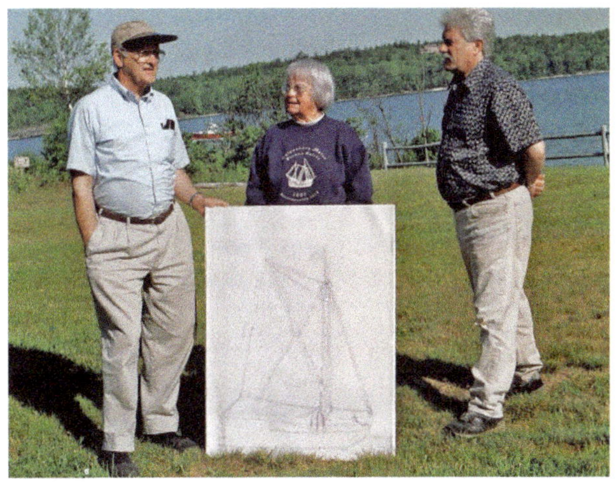

Bud Warren, Jane Stevens, and Rick Cromwell

Foreword

During the summer of 1607 a group of approx. 100 men landed near the mouth of the Sagadahoc (now the Kennebec) River in their vessels, the *Gift of God* and the *Mary and John,* They were sent by Sir John Popham, and others, to explore this part of "Northern Virginia" to search for a Northwest Passage and to see what resources and riches might be available. The construction of Fort St. George and the building of a small ship for exploration were among their first projects. Under the guidance of a shipwright by the name of Digby, a pinnace style vessel, was built. Named the *Virginia of Sagadahoc* this ship is now remembered as Maine's First Ship, and was the first European built ship in North America.

After a very difficult winter the colony was abandoned and some of the surviving members returned to England in that same *Virginia,* while others sailed back in the *Mary and John.*

In 1609 the *Virginia* sailed across the Atlantic again landing at Jamestown. From that point on there is no further mention of the ship.

For several centuries the exact location of the Popham Colony was unknown. In 1994 however, Dr. Jeffery Brain, of the Peabody Essex Museum of Salem, Mass., led an archeological dig that uncovered a 700 cm post hole and and a 25cm hand-hewn post in the Hossketch Point area of Popham. Then, from 1997-2013 he continued his work with more teams of volunteers discovering many artifacts from the former Fort St. George.

Also in 1997, Jane Stevens, Bud Warren, Rick Cromwell, and Sharon Drake began working on ideas to celebrate the 400th anniversary of the Popham Colony. Part of their plan was to raise funds for the reconstruction of the wooden ship *Virginia*, Maine's first ship. In July of 1997 a meeting was held at Popham Chapel to discuss the projects. With nearly 100 people in attendance, The Celebration of the Popham Colony and the Virginia Project began.

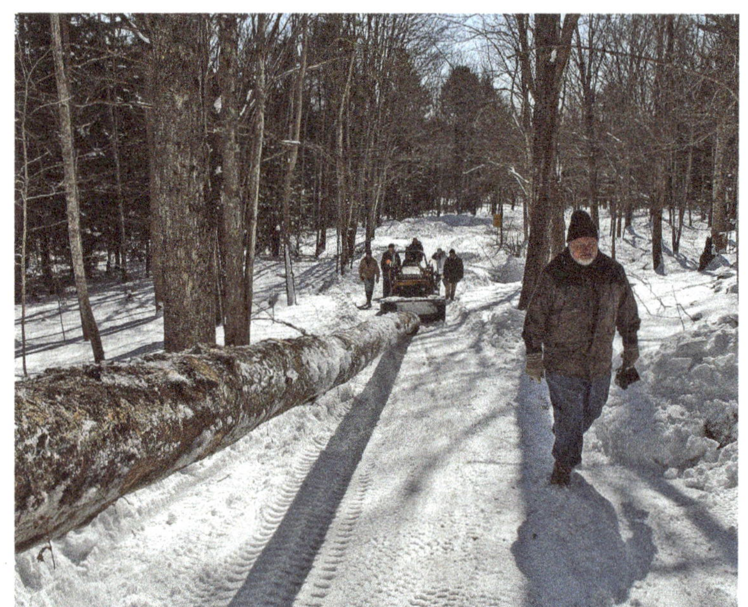

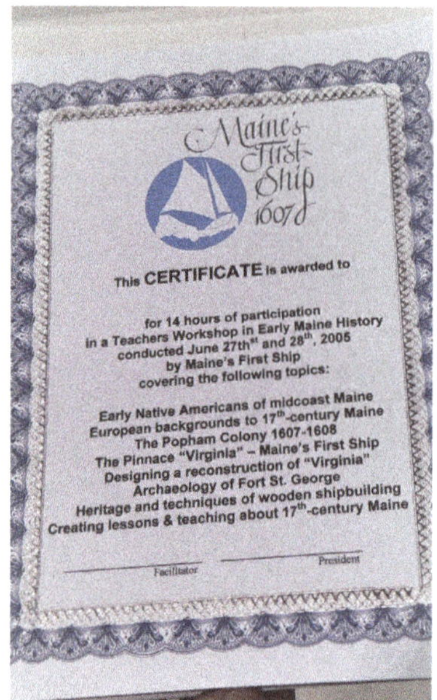

(Clockwise from upper left) The team of volunteers harvest a "mast." The First Ship project was able to offer continuing educaiton credits to teachers, Rob Stevens teaches teachers about Maine's First Ship. Rob displays a half model of the Virginia.

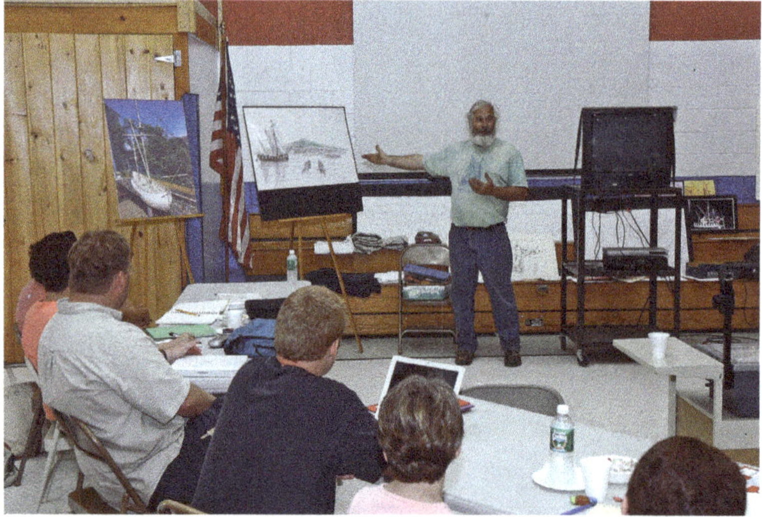

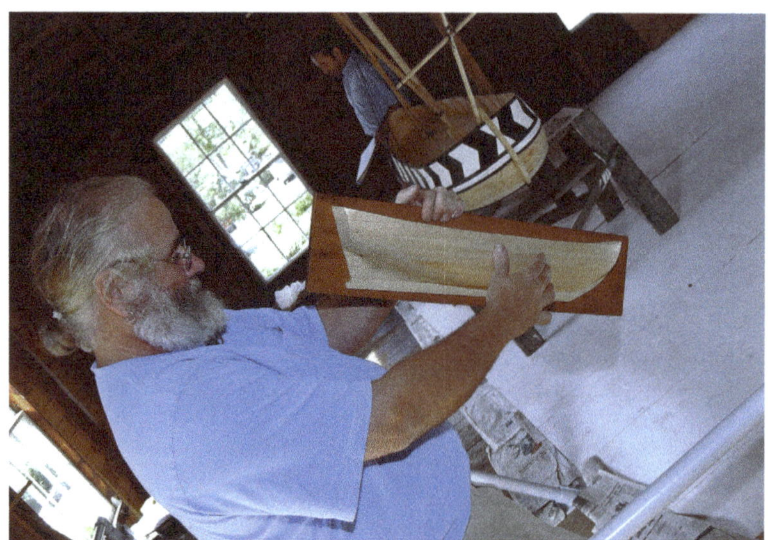

Virgina Beginnings

In March of 2012, I was at the Maine Boat Builder's show in Portland, Maine. As I wandered from one exhibit to another I met an old friend, wooden boat builder Rob Stevens. He informed me that the Virginia Project was finally underway at the freight shed in Bath, Maine.

A short time later, I had the opportunity to drive to Bath and check out the project. Inside the old freight shed on Commercial Street, volunteers, Richard "Dick" Forrest and Dr. Dan Wood were busy lofting frames. Outside I found Orman Hines (another volunteer and one of the leaders of the project) who showed me the oak keel and bow stem that had been prepared for the vessel. These were inside a wood and plastic structure erected behind the freight shed to provide an area where work could be done away from the weather.

I visited the project several more times that year as work progressed. The bow stem was mounted onto the keel. Rob's huge bandsaw was put to service cutting frame pieces (futtocks) from white oak.

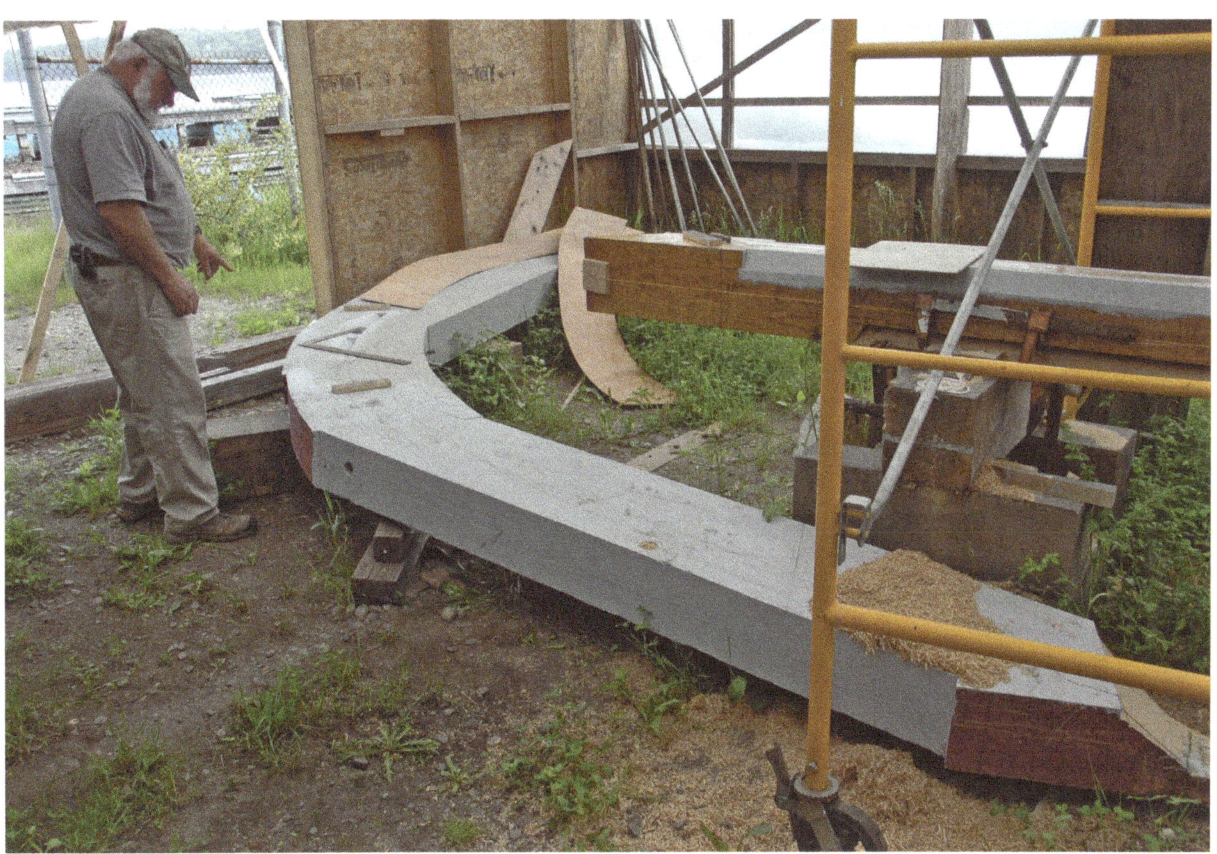

Orman Hines examines the bow that had been prepared for the vessel.

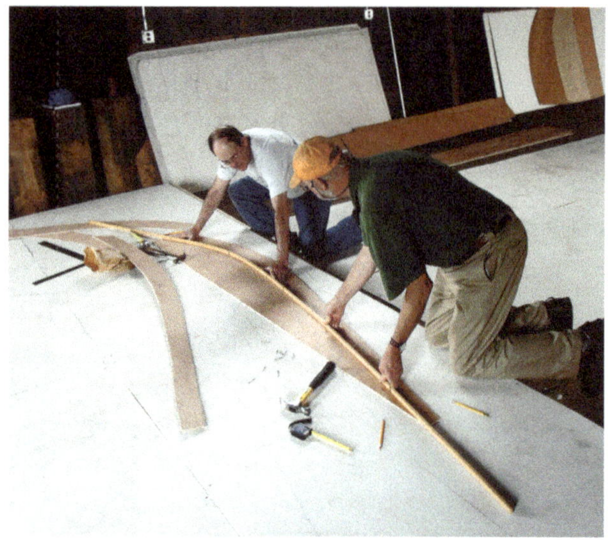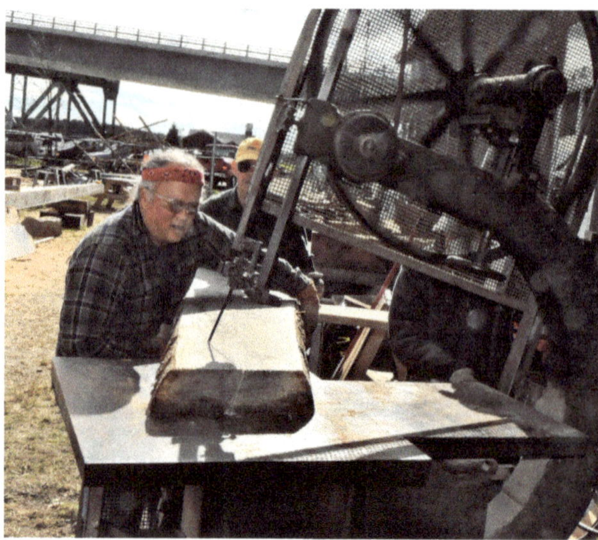

On my first visit to the project, May 2012, I found volunteers Richard "Dick" Forrest and Dr. Dan Wood lofting the frames.

Later, volunteers cut more frame pieces "futtocks."

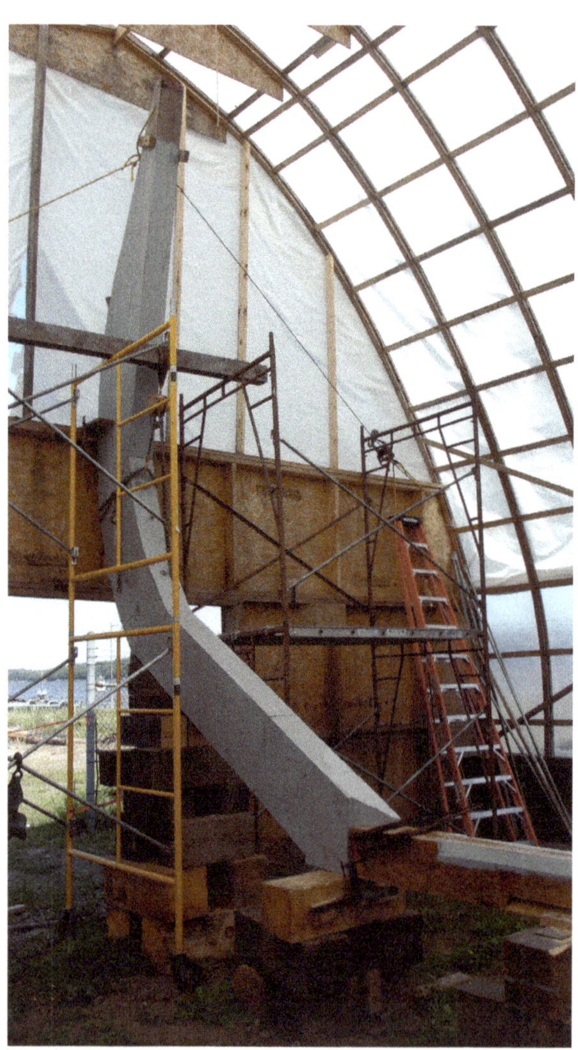

Later that year, the bowstem was mounted to the keel.

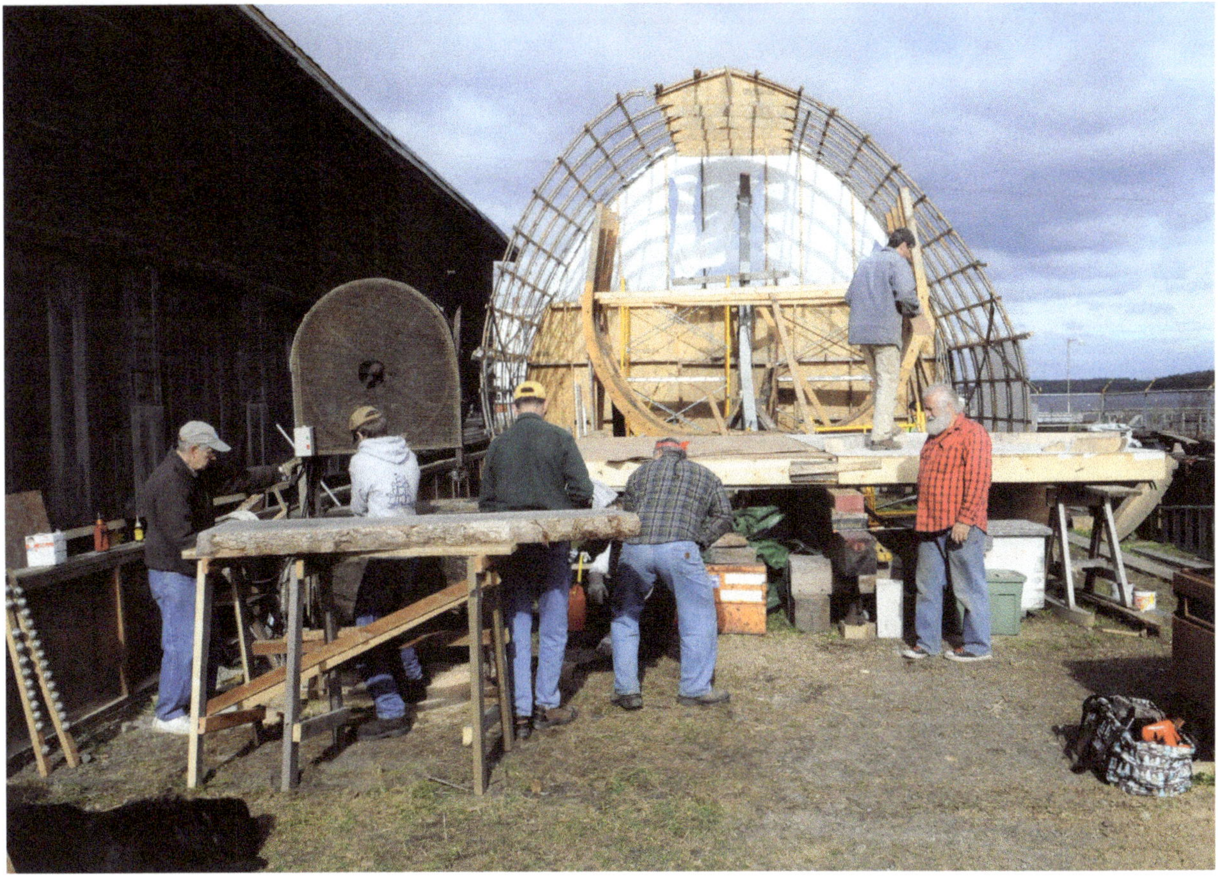

A wind storm during November 2012 brought down part of the enclosure. Quick work by volunteers had the structure back in shape for the winter ahead.

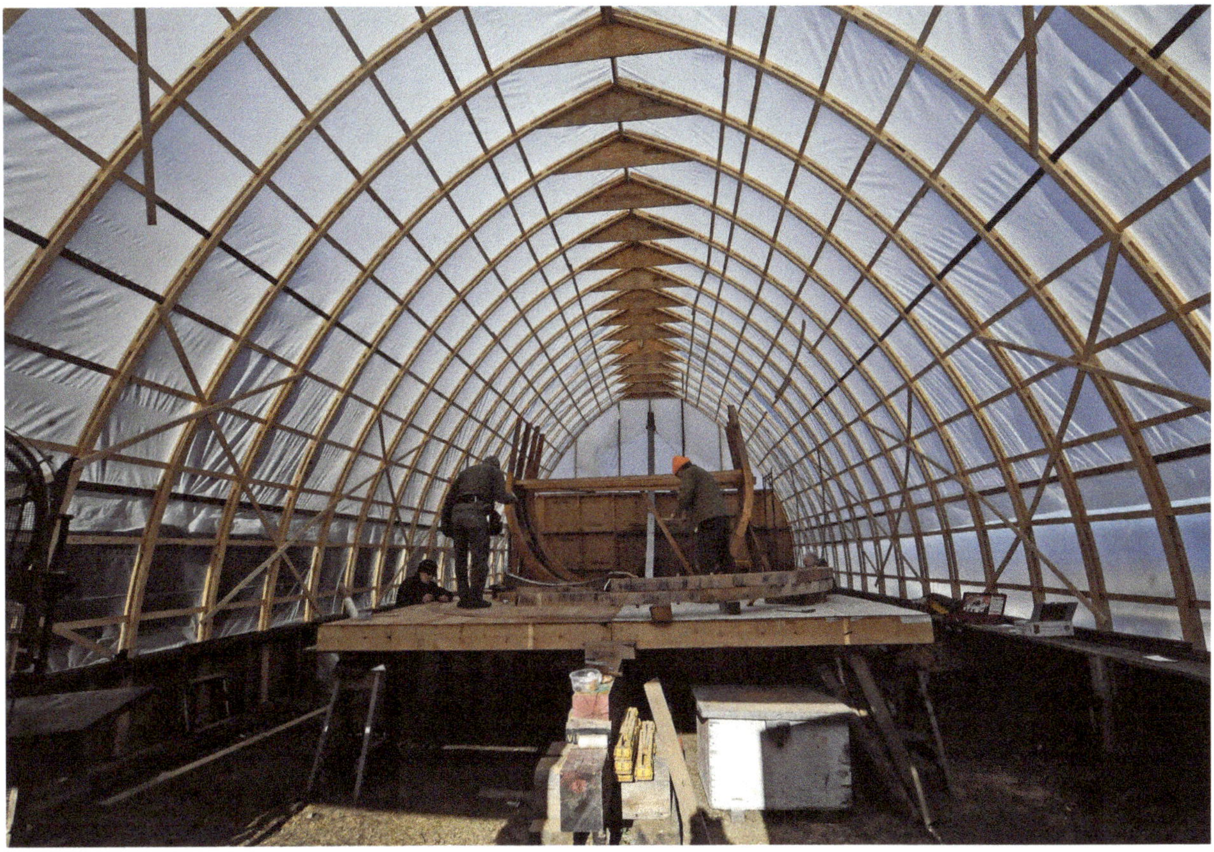

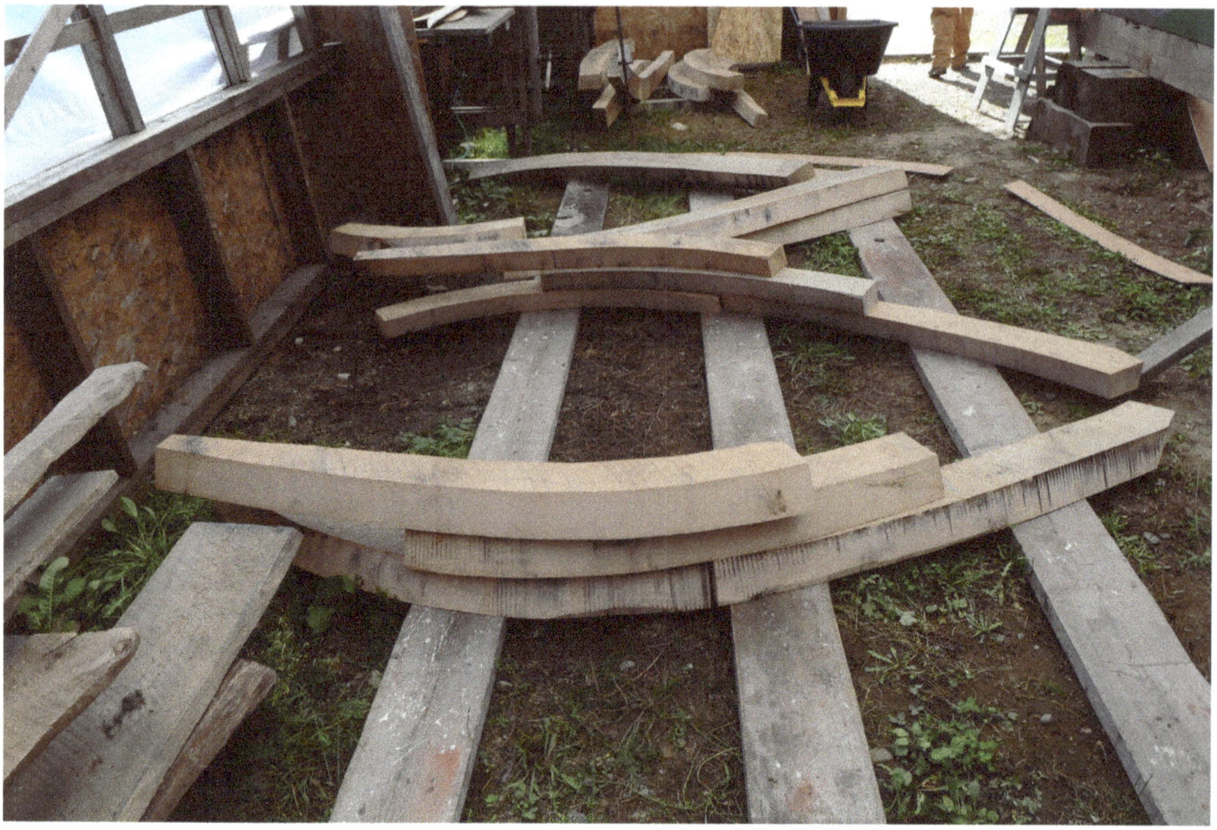

(Above) Futtocks (frame pieces) await assembly into frames. (Below) Drilling the futtocks and using trunnels to create the frames. Left to right: Orman Hines, Roger Barry, Dr. Dan Wood, and Dick Forrest.

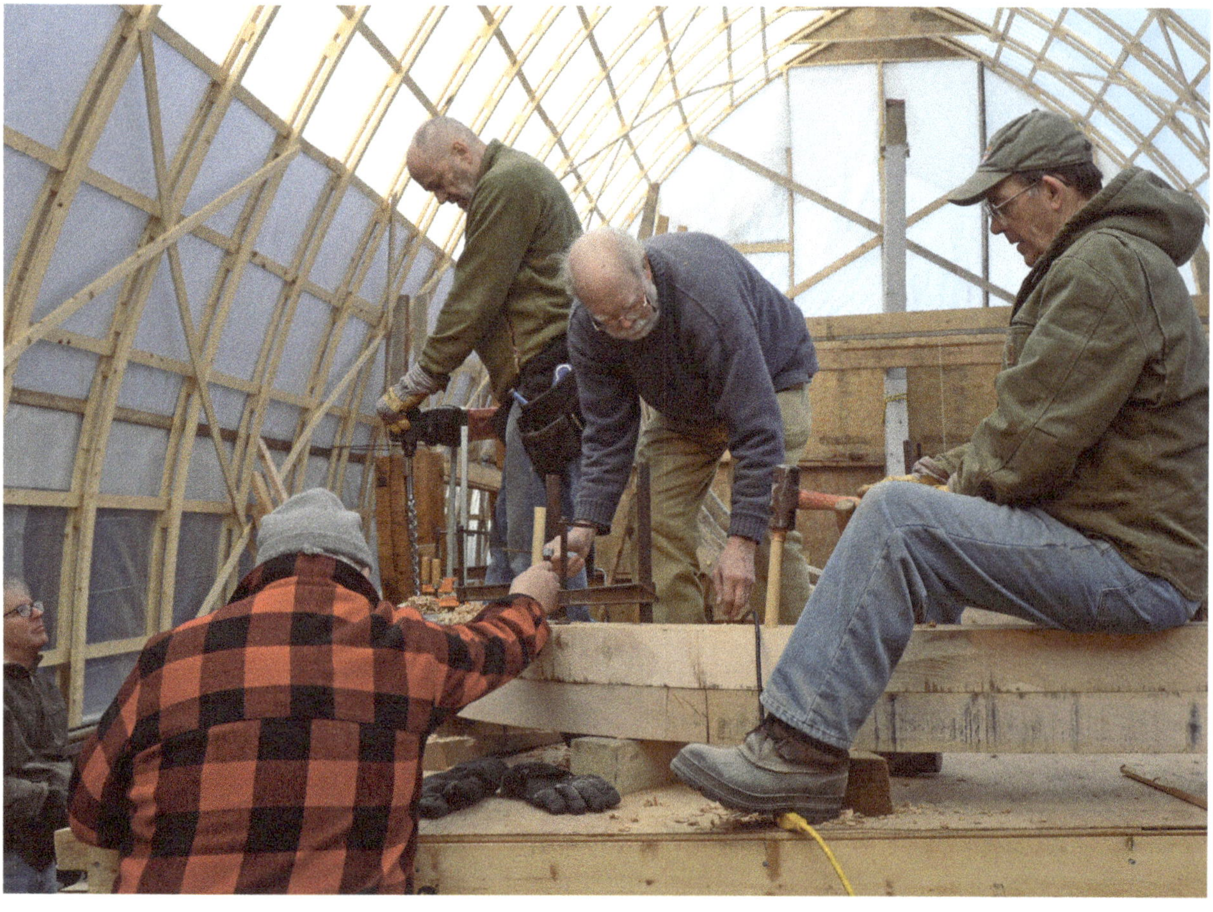

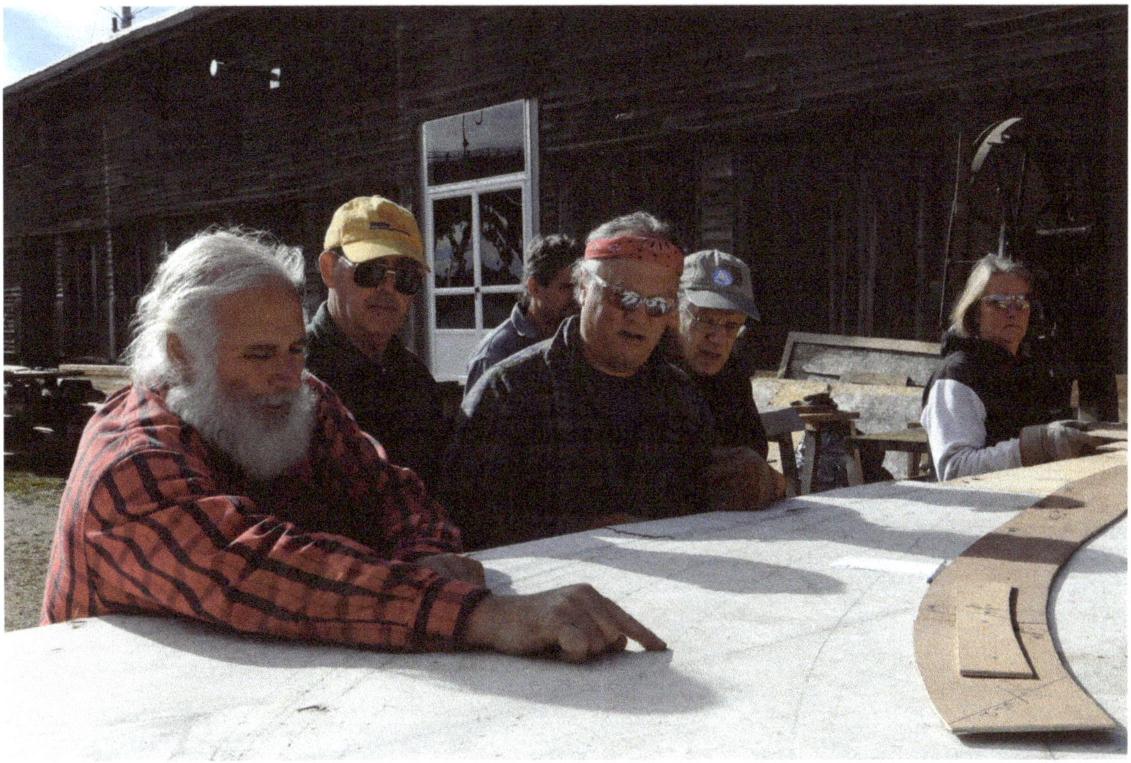

Rob Steven's "Monday Morning Meeting" with volunteers.

Moving an assembled oak frame into place.

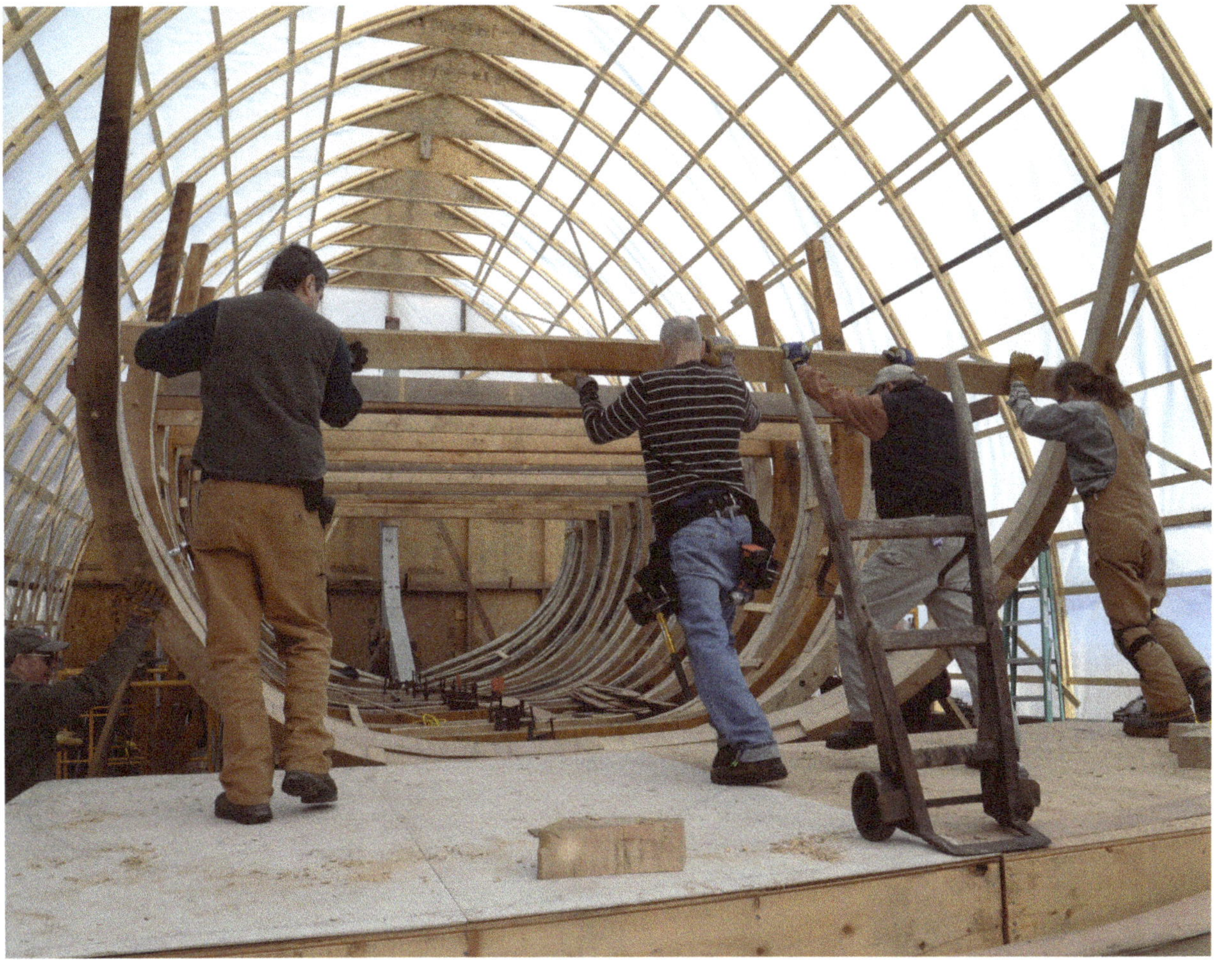

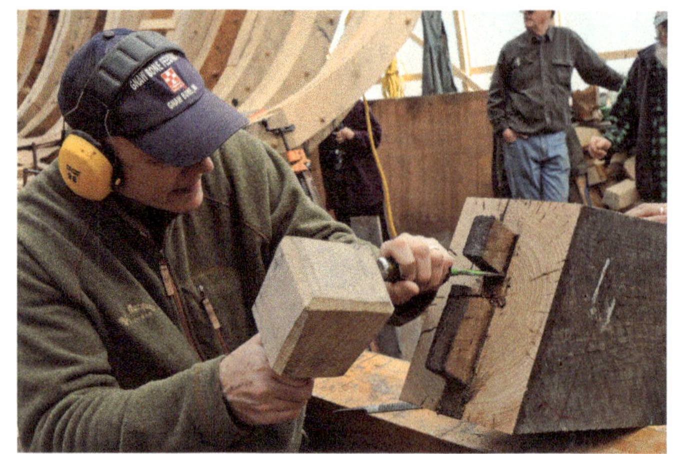

Roger Barry prepares the stern post.

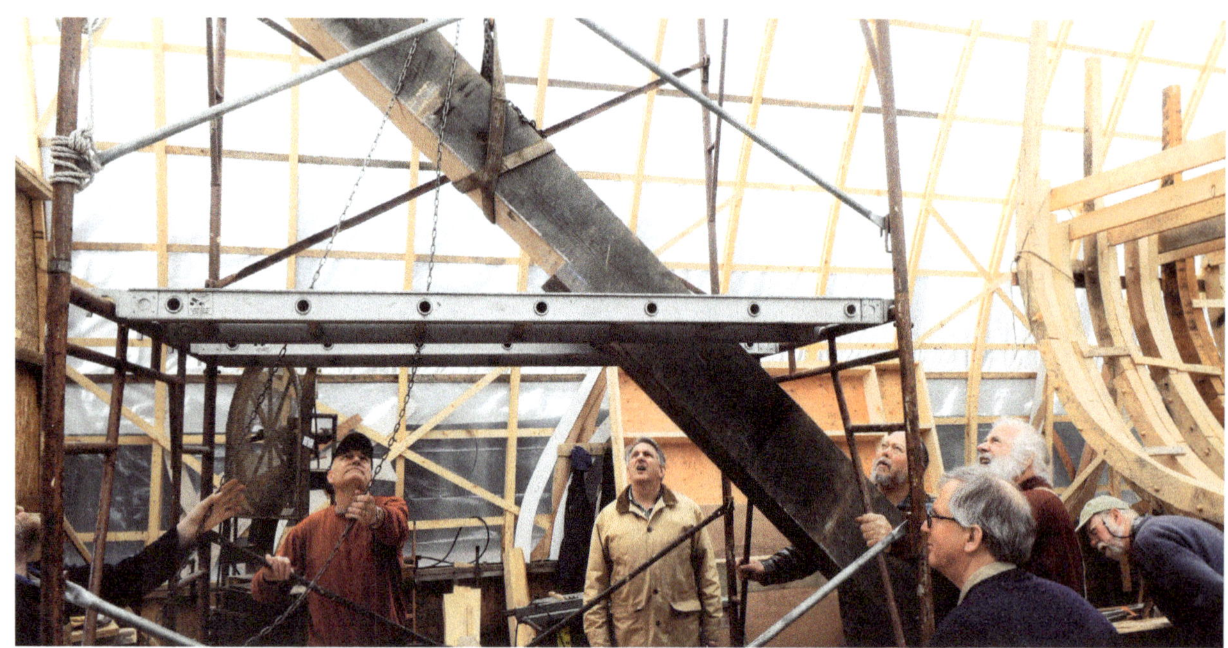

The oak stern post is lifted into position using pulleys and ropes.

(Below) Half frames prepared for placement on the vessel.

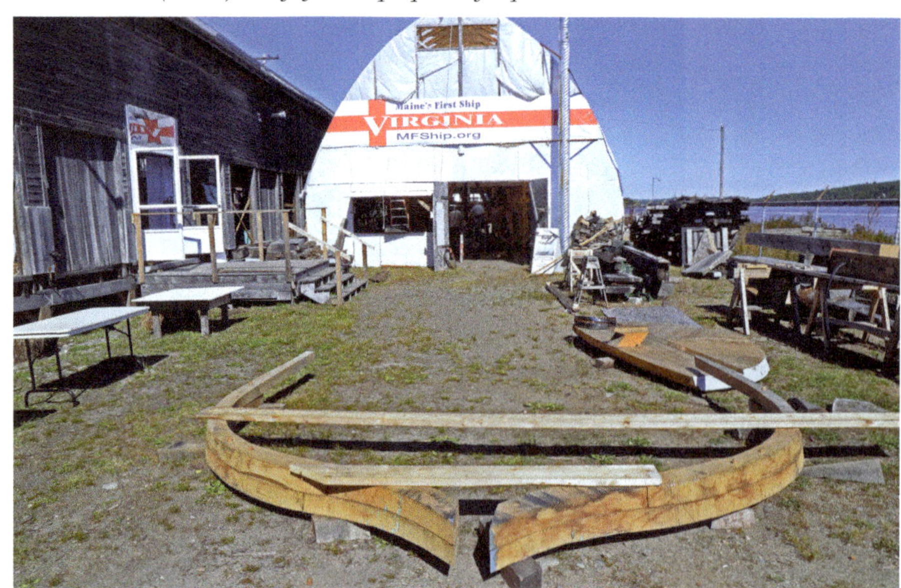

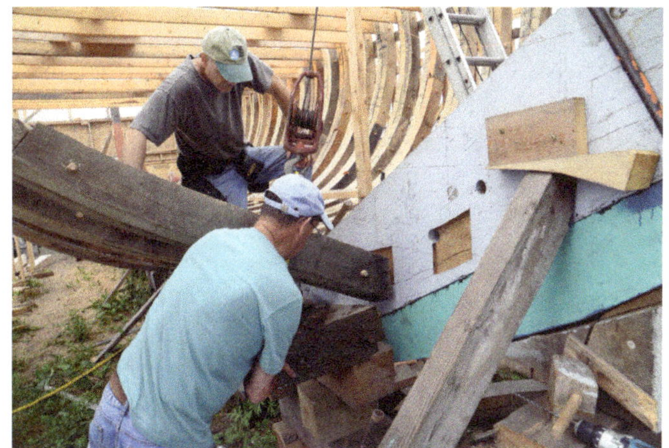

Roger Barry and Dick Forrest securing a half frame into a mortise near the bow.

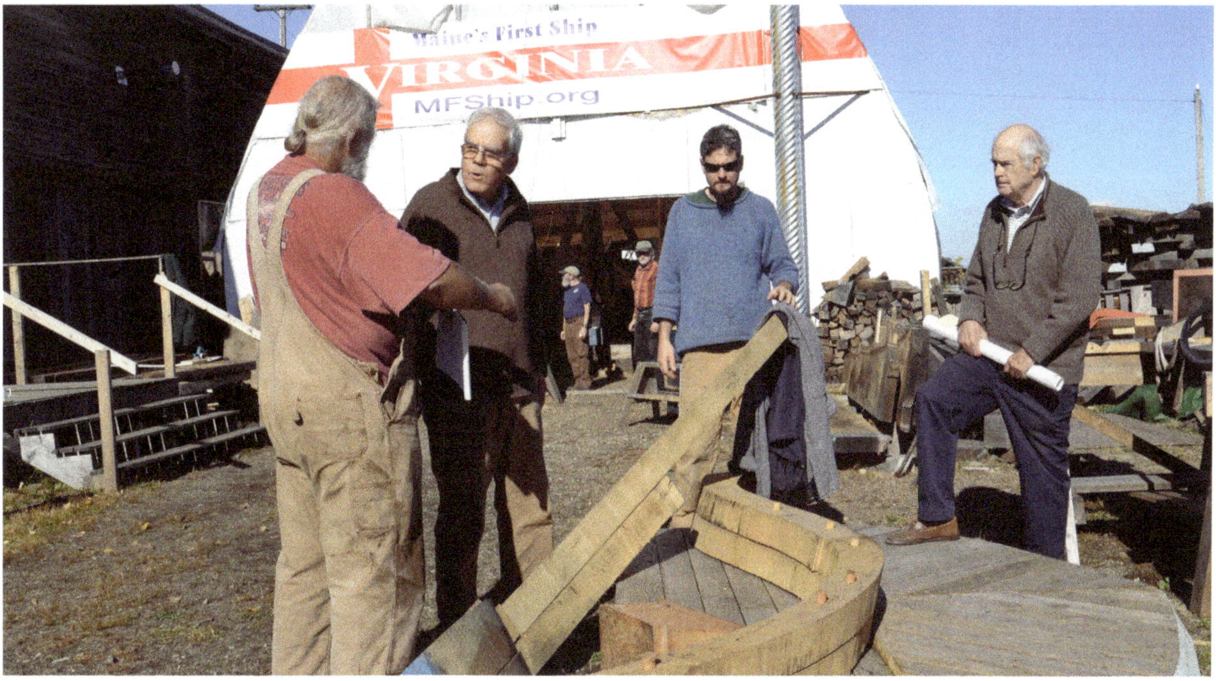

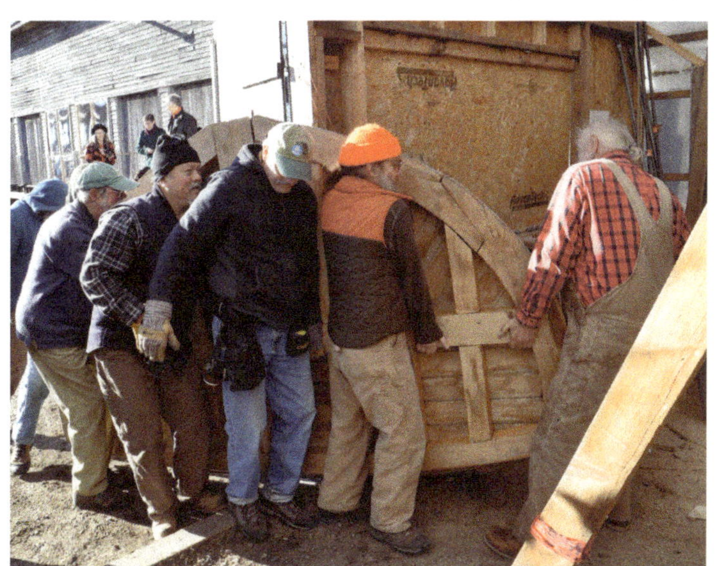

Rob Stevens, David Wyman, Jeremy Blaiklock, and John Bradford discuss progress on the build.

Moving the transom.

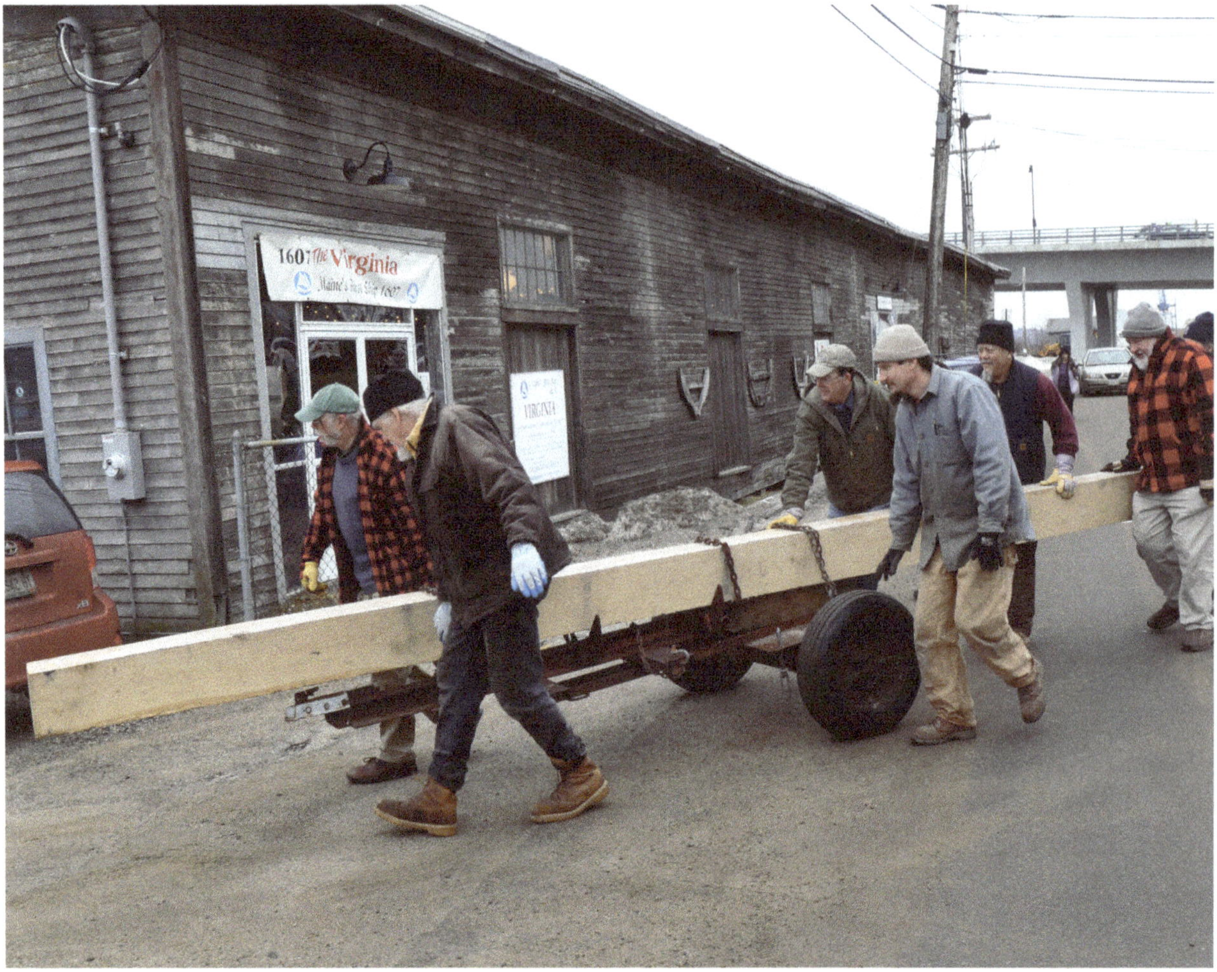

The future keelson is moved to the construction site.

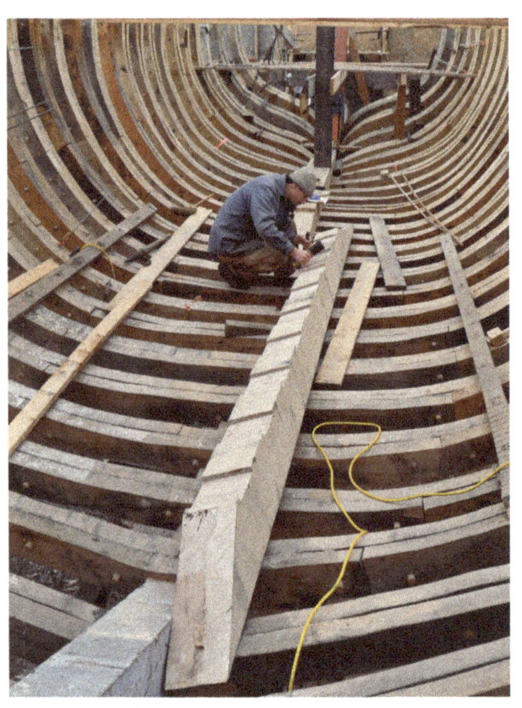

Jeremy shapes the keelson.

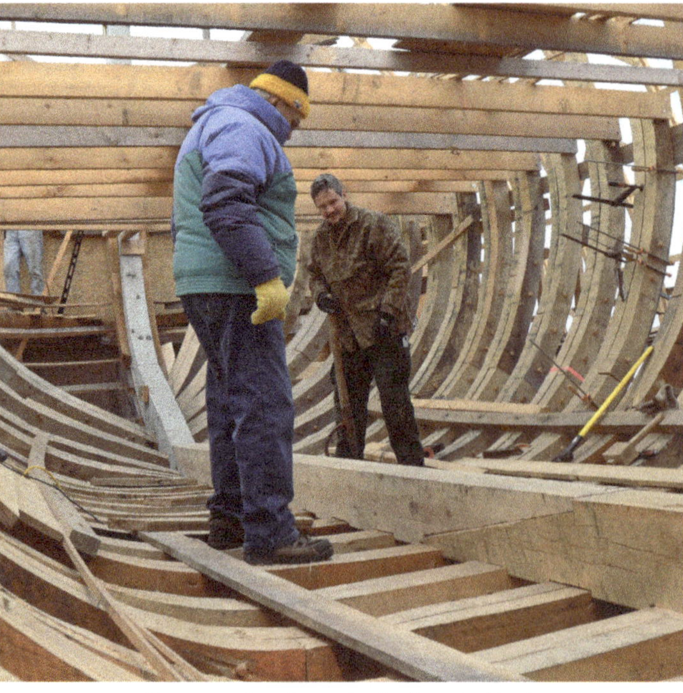

Once put in place, the keelson holds the
frames in position.

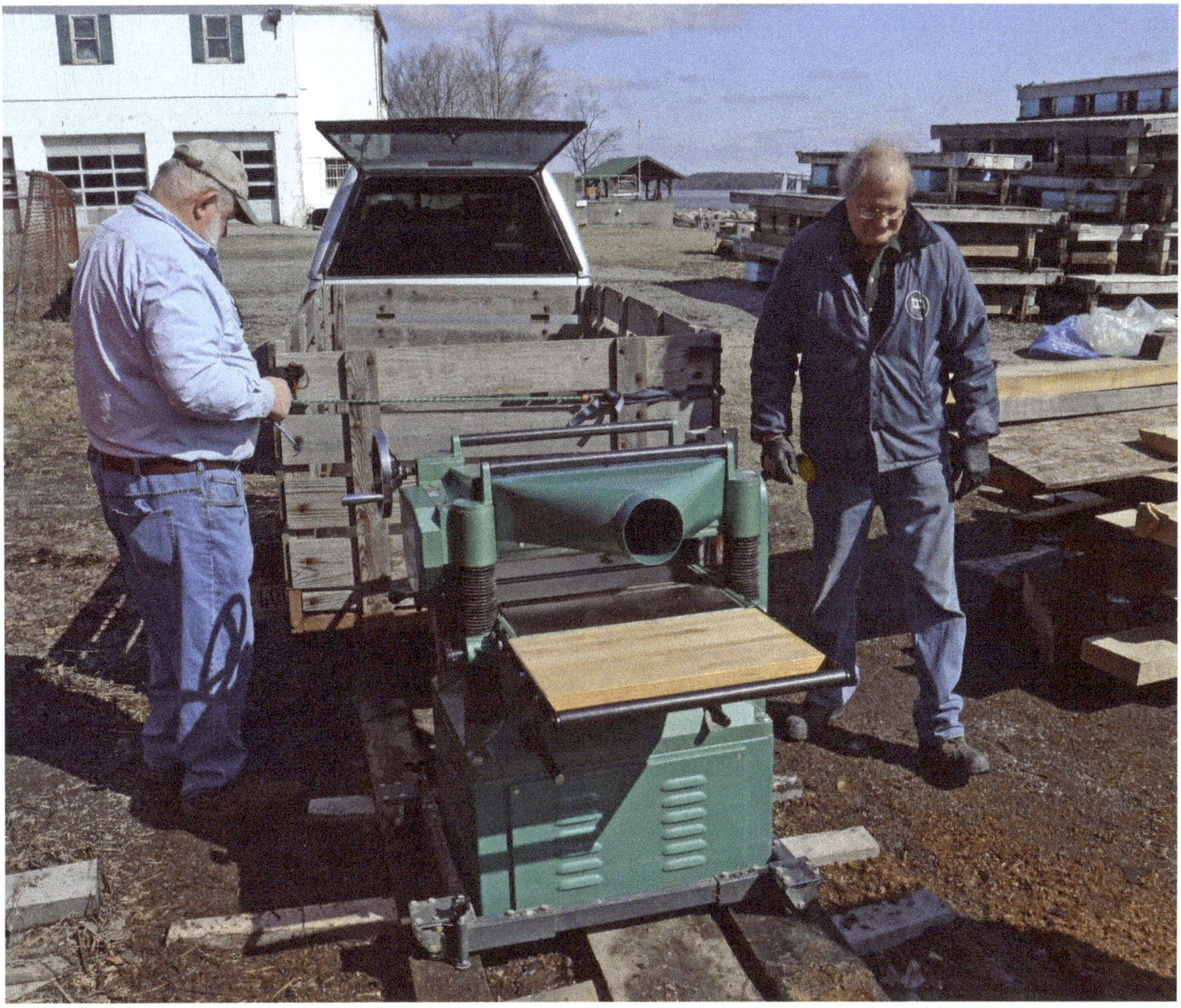

Orman Hines and R.B. Omo welcome our "new" 20-inch planer.

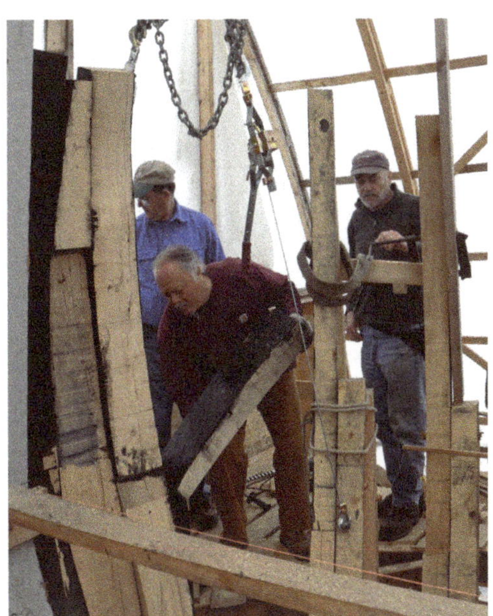

Dick Forrest, Aaron Park, and Roger Barry.
(l-r) install cant frames into place.

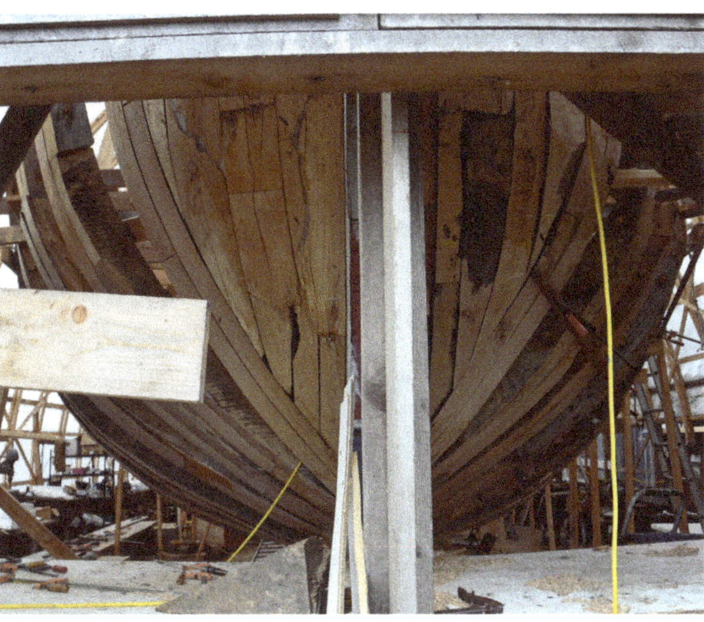

From the outside nearly all the bow (cant) frames are observed.

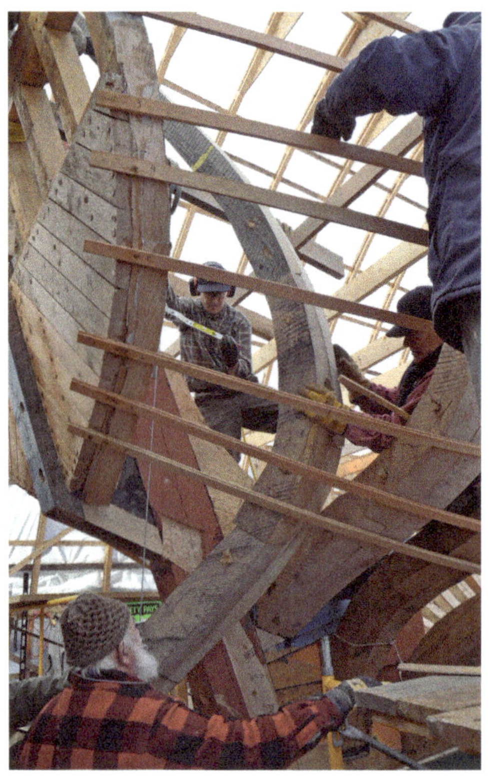

A half-frame is positioned at the stearn.

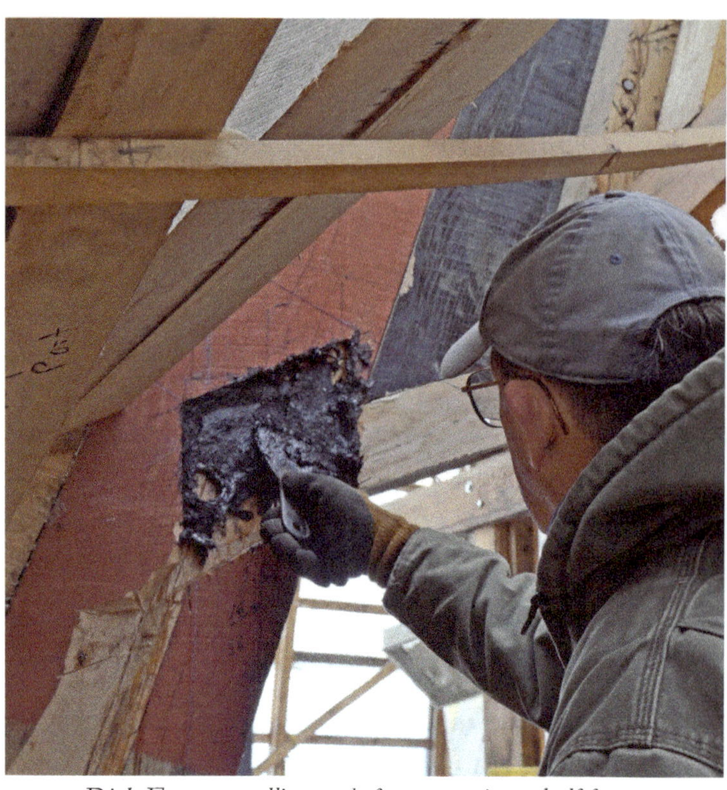

Dick Forrest appllies tar before mounting a half-frame.

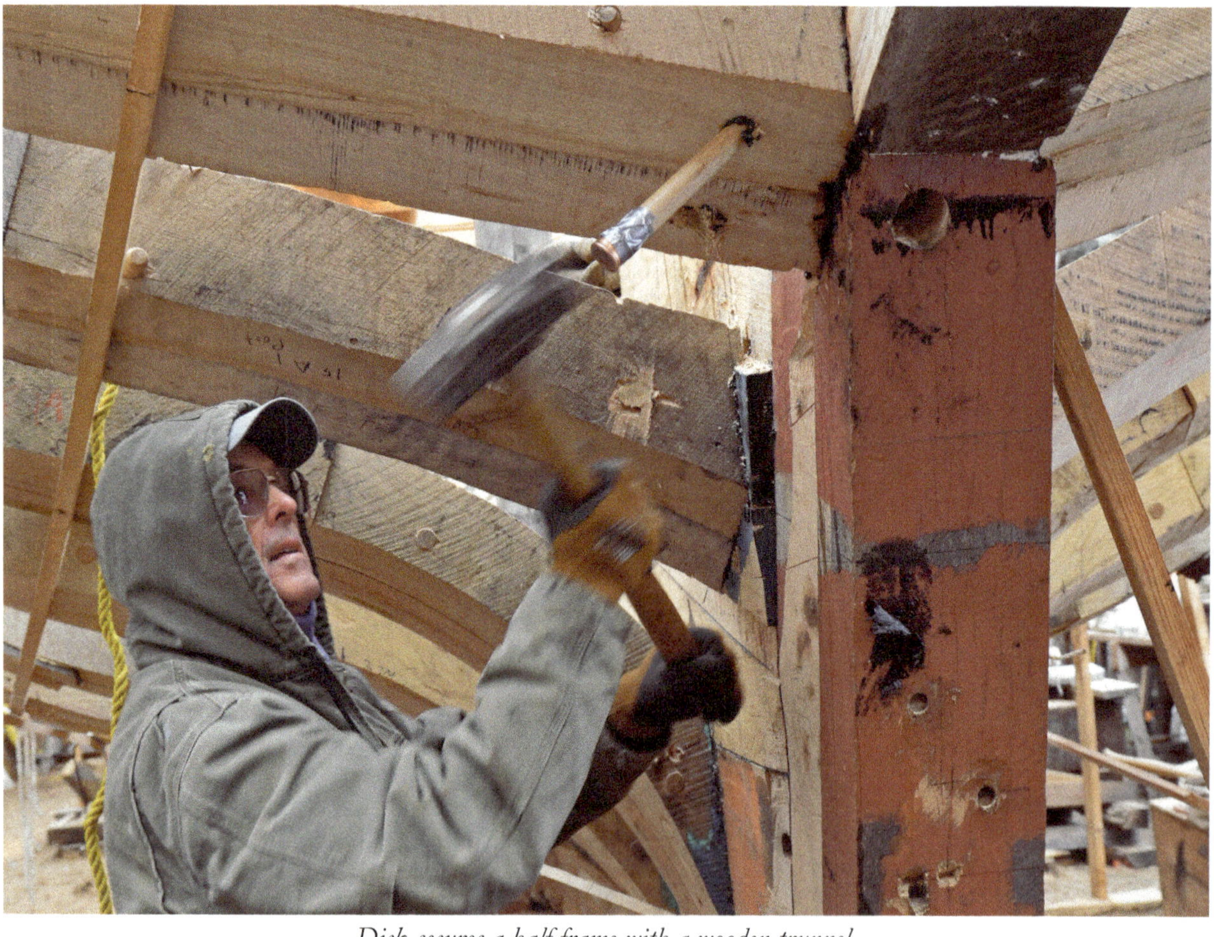

Dick secures a half-frame with a wooden trunnel.

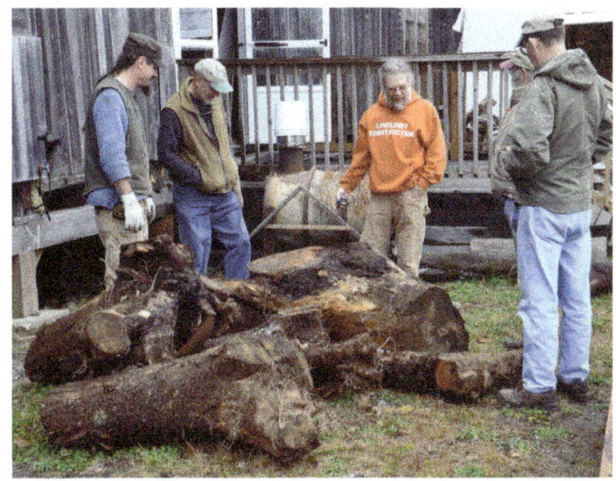

(l-r) Jeremy Blaiklock, Roger Barry, Tim Teague, and Dick Forrest examine the first hackmatack knees to arrive.

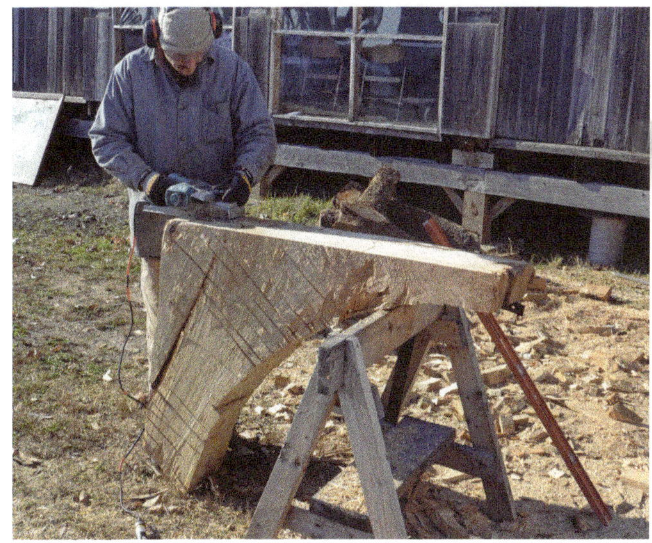

Jeremy shapes a stern post knee from the hackmatack.

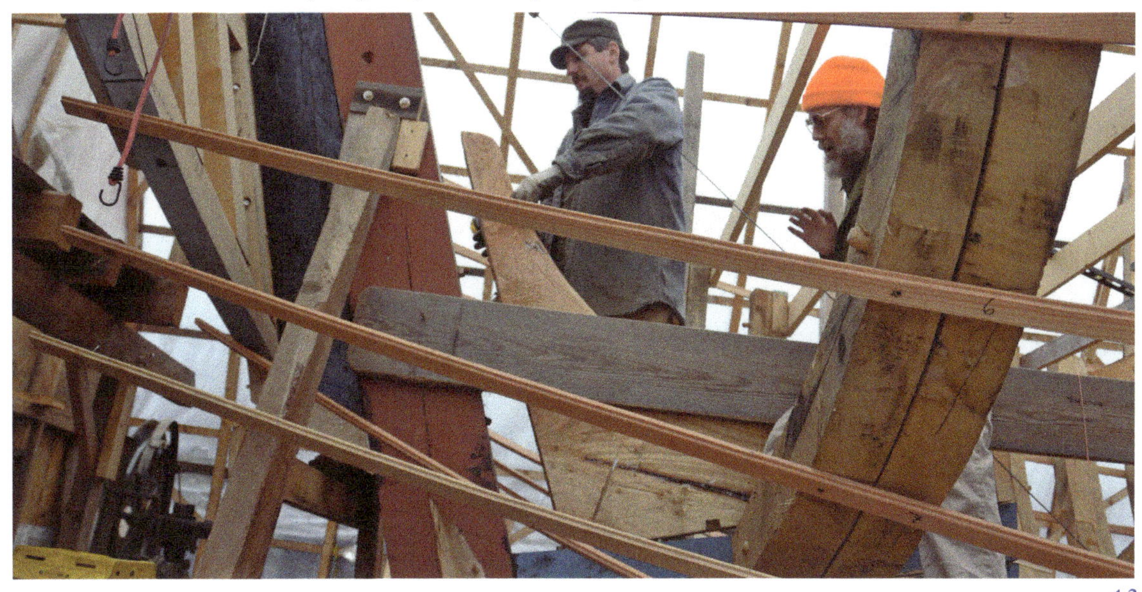

Jeremy and Tim install the knee.

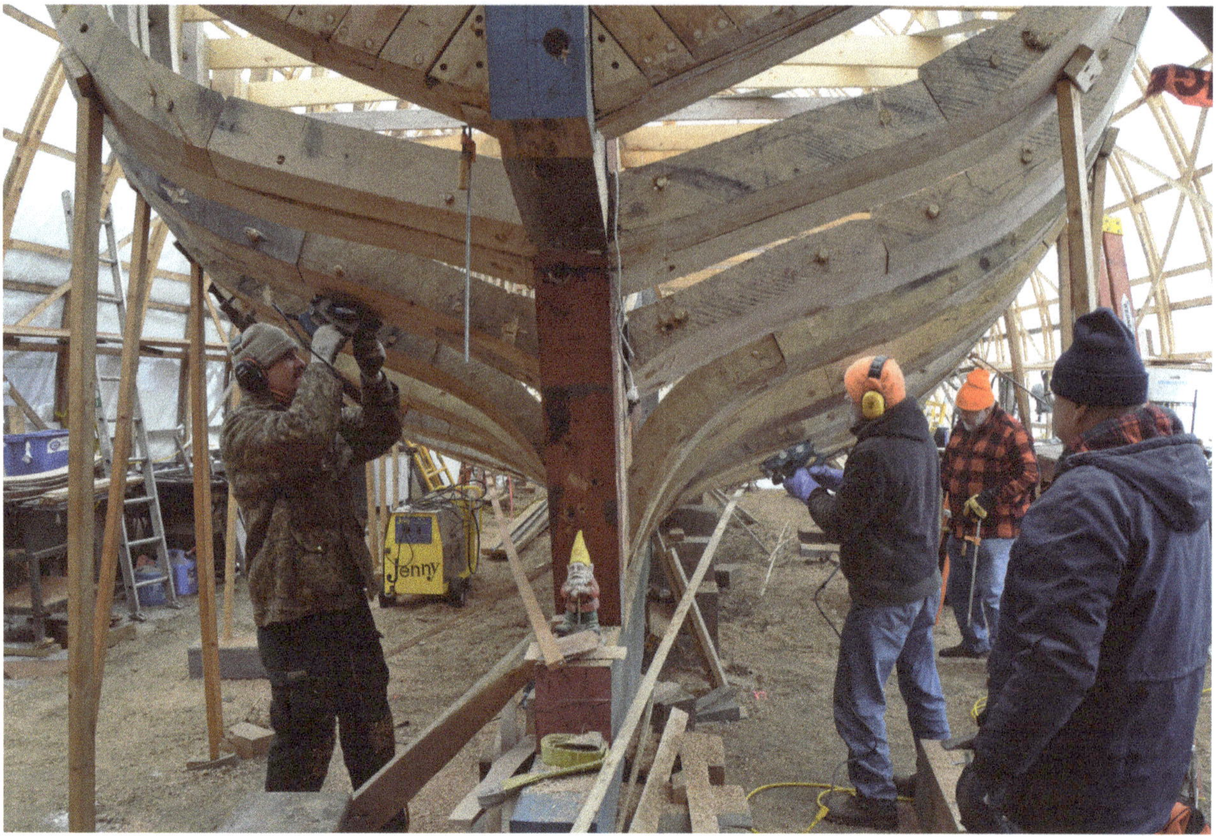

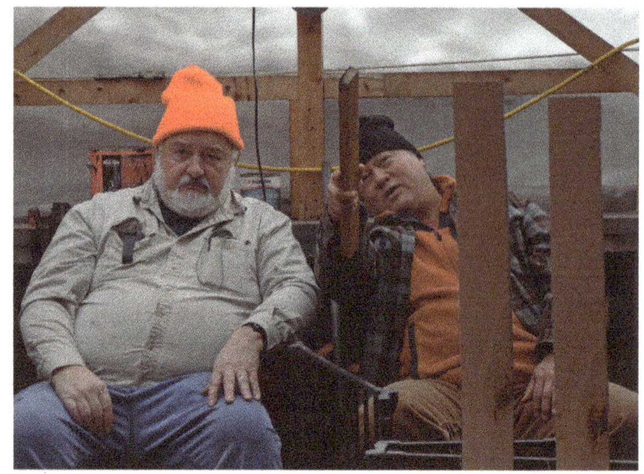

Counterclockwise from the top.

Volunteers fair the frames in preparation for planking.

Dr. Dan Wood uses a hand planer for fairing.

Boat Builder John Gardner teaches volunteers fairing techniques.

Orman Hines and Aaron Park "supervise" the work of the day.

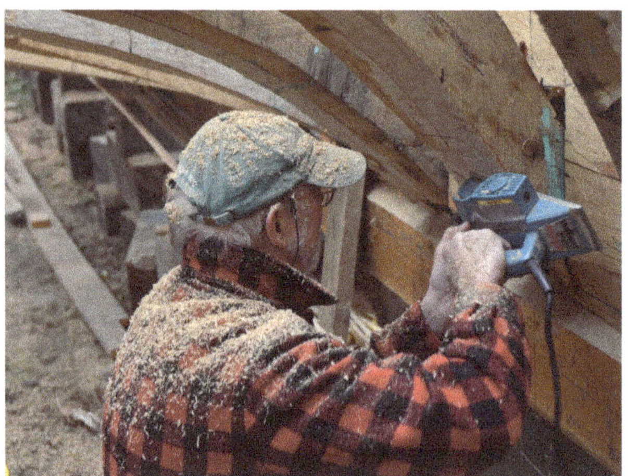

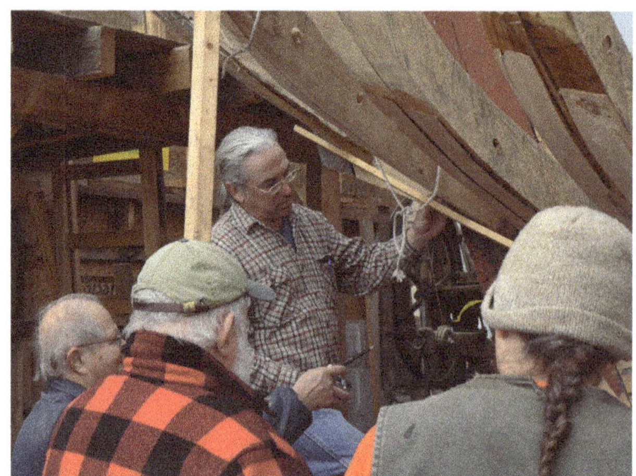

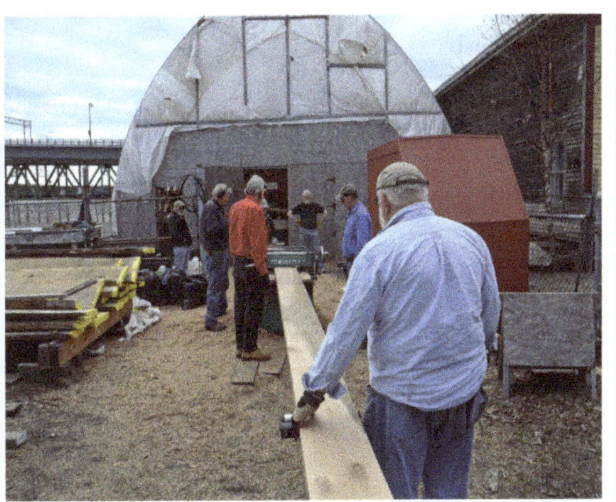

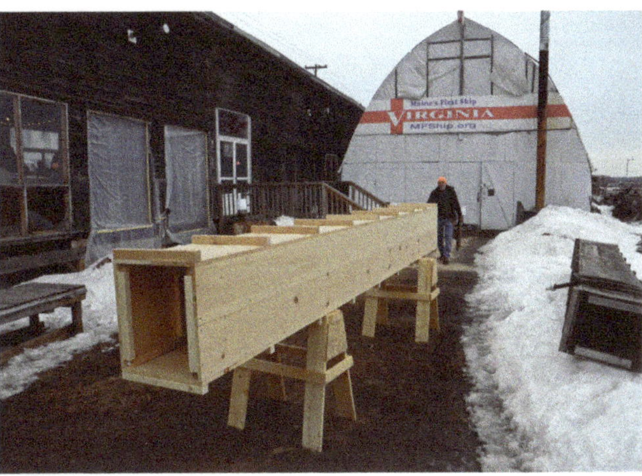

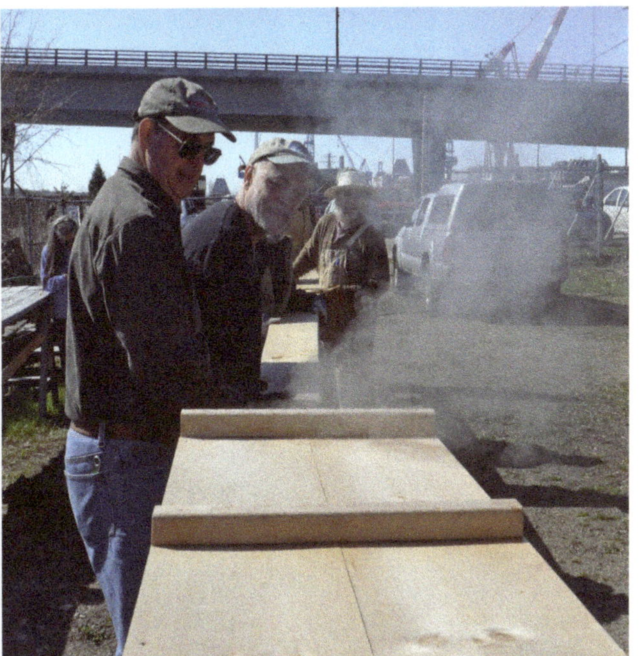

Clockwise from upper left:
Orman Hines amd others plane a piece of oak.
Roger Barry constructed a new steamer capable of receiving the long planks needed for our build.
Dick Forrest and Roger Barry guide a plank into the new steamer.
Gail Smith (right), Dick (left) and Rob Stevens (center) position a bilge clamp.

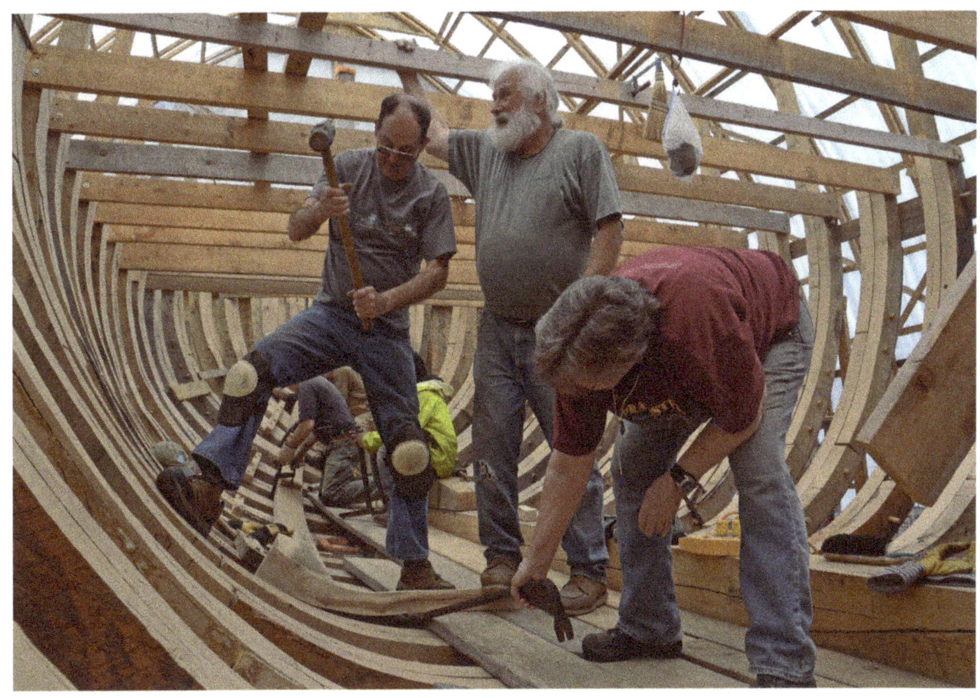

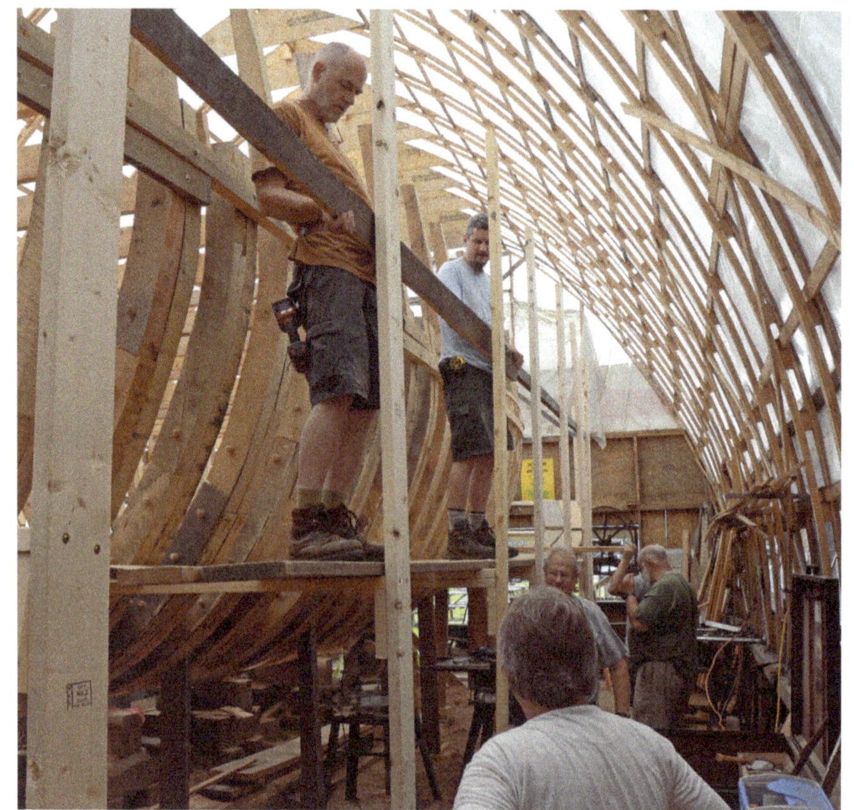

Above: Roger Barry and Jeremy Blaiklock assemble a scaffold to use when fairing and planking the hull.

Below: Bilge clamps secure the hull.

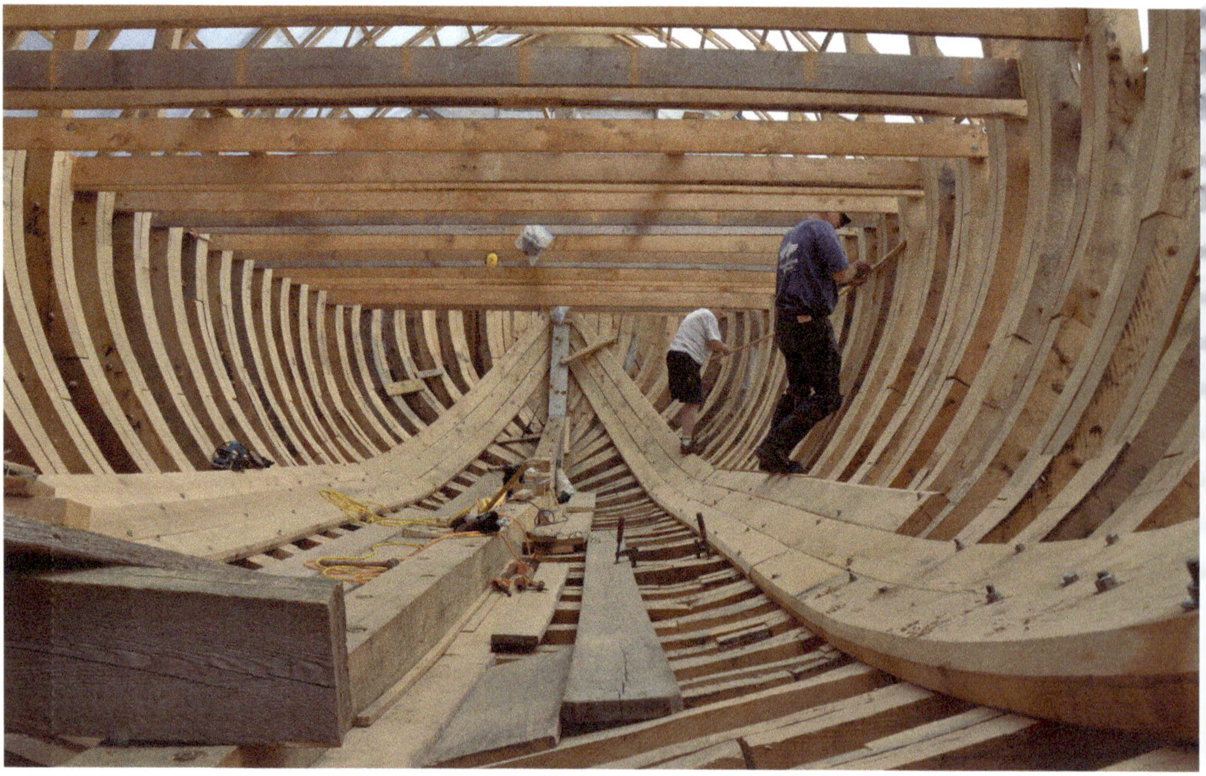

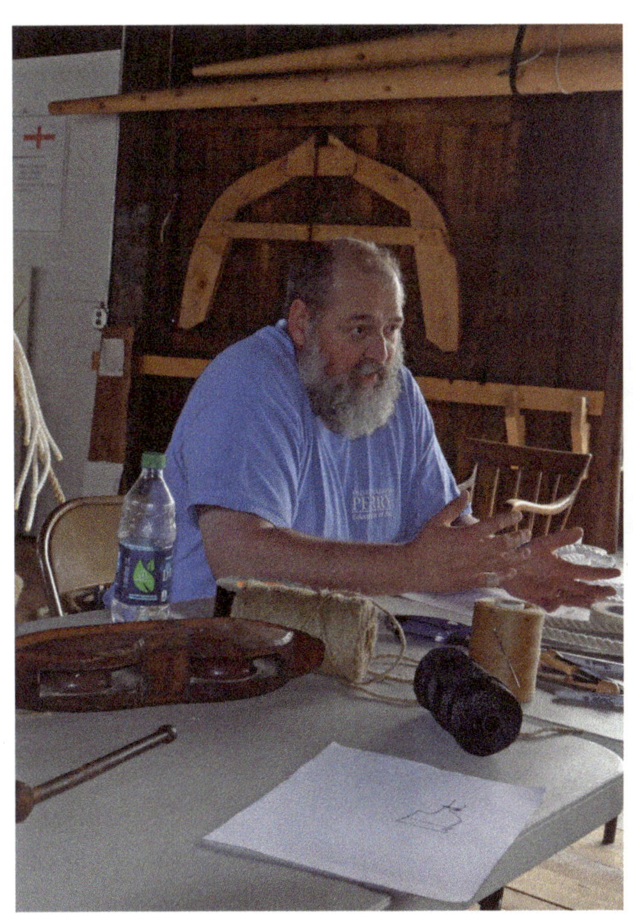

Jim Nelson, head rigger, teaches a class in rigging.

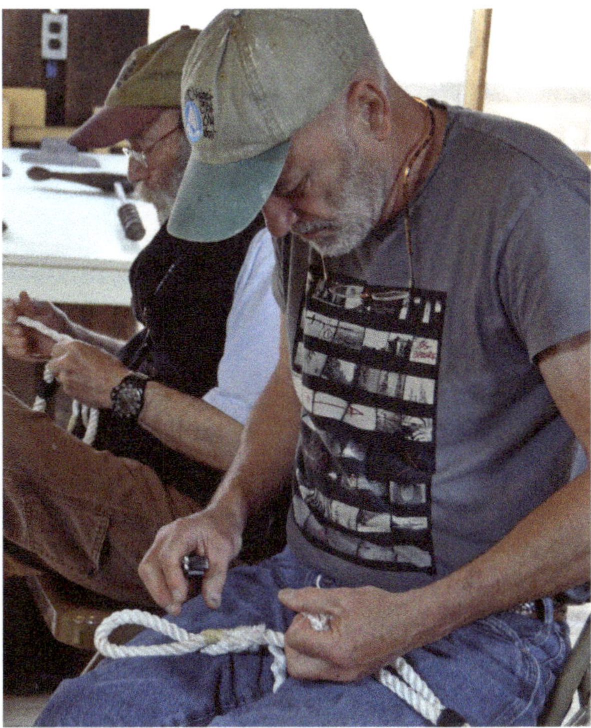

Long-time volunteer, Roger Barry learns to tie rigging.

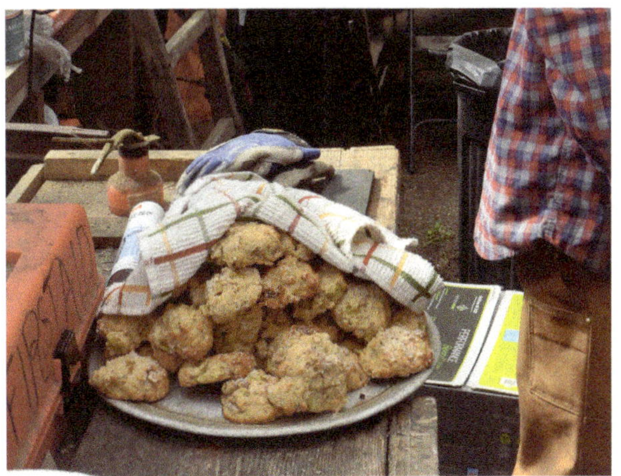

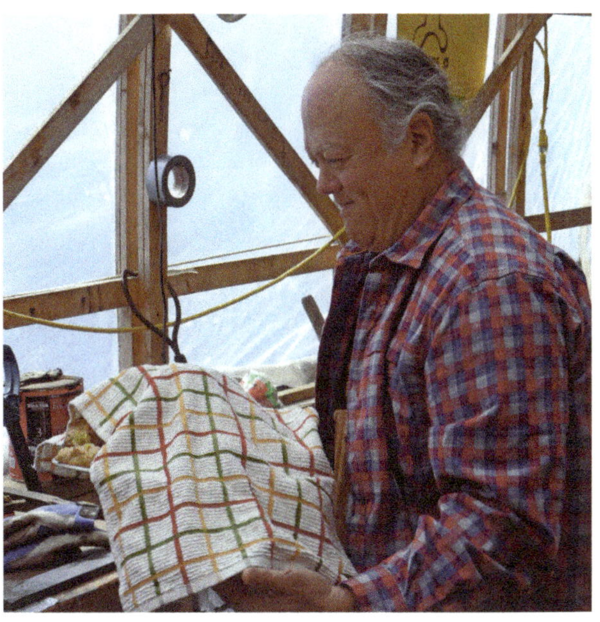

Aaron Park delivers scones to keep the workers going.

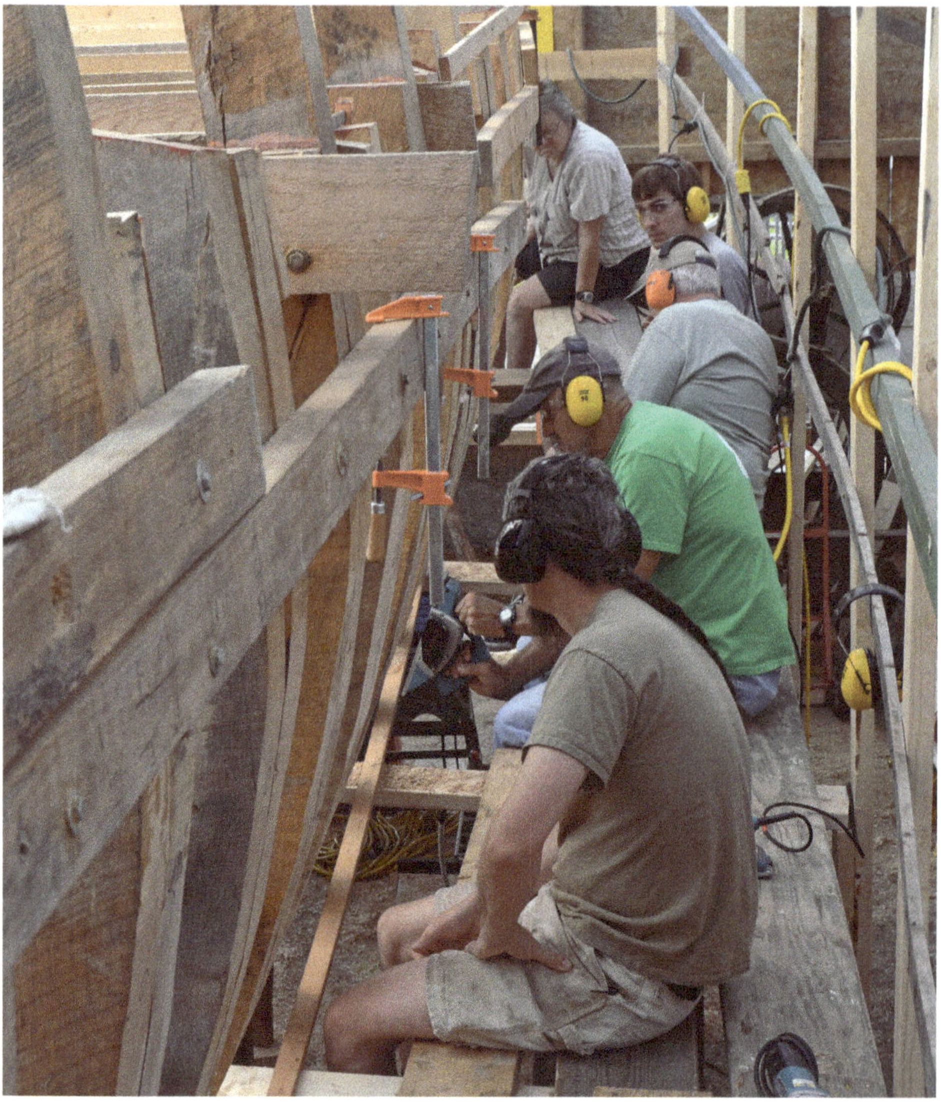

Volunteers line up on the scaffold and continue fairing.

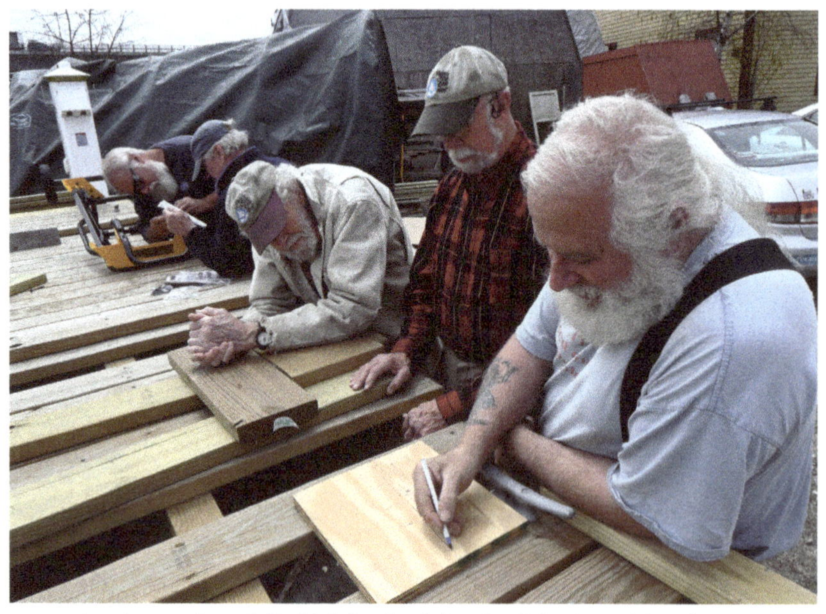

Another session of Rob's Monday Morning Meeting with volunteers.

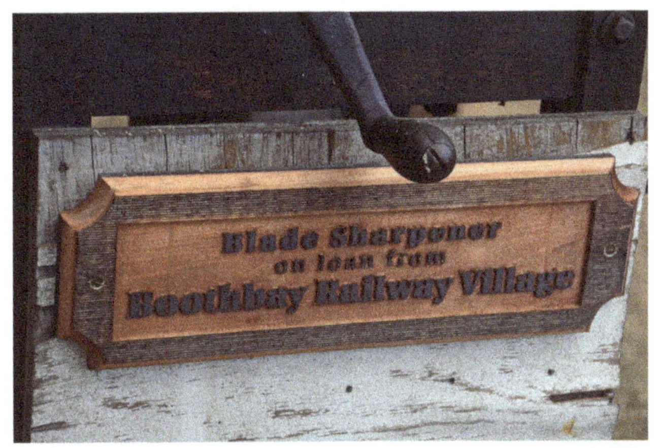

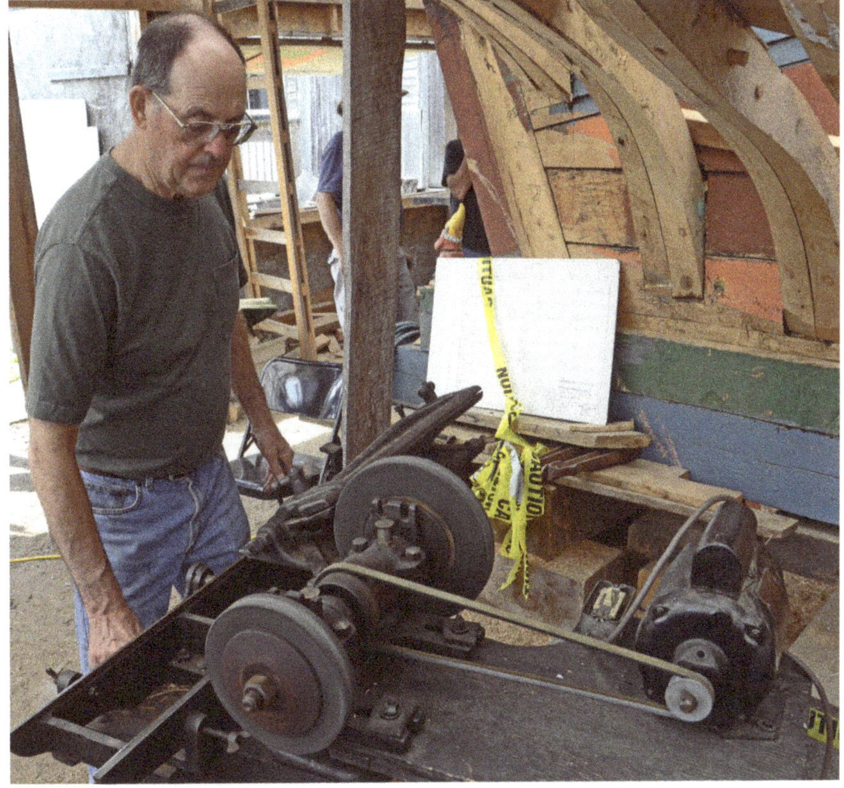

Dick Forrest sharpens an extra set of planer blades using a blade sharpener on loan from the Boothbay Railway Museum.

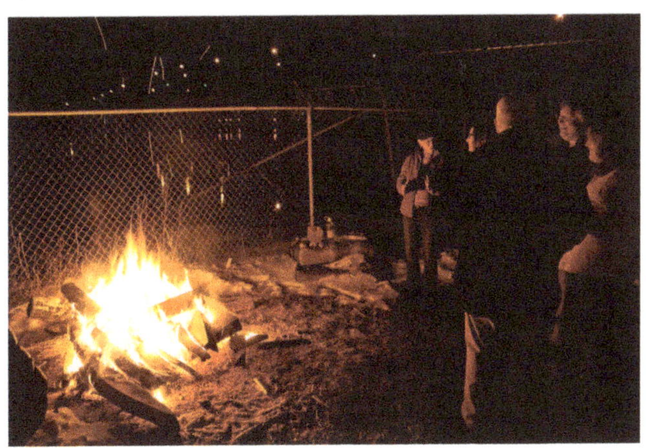

Volunteers gather for a Year's End bonfire.

19

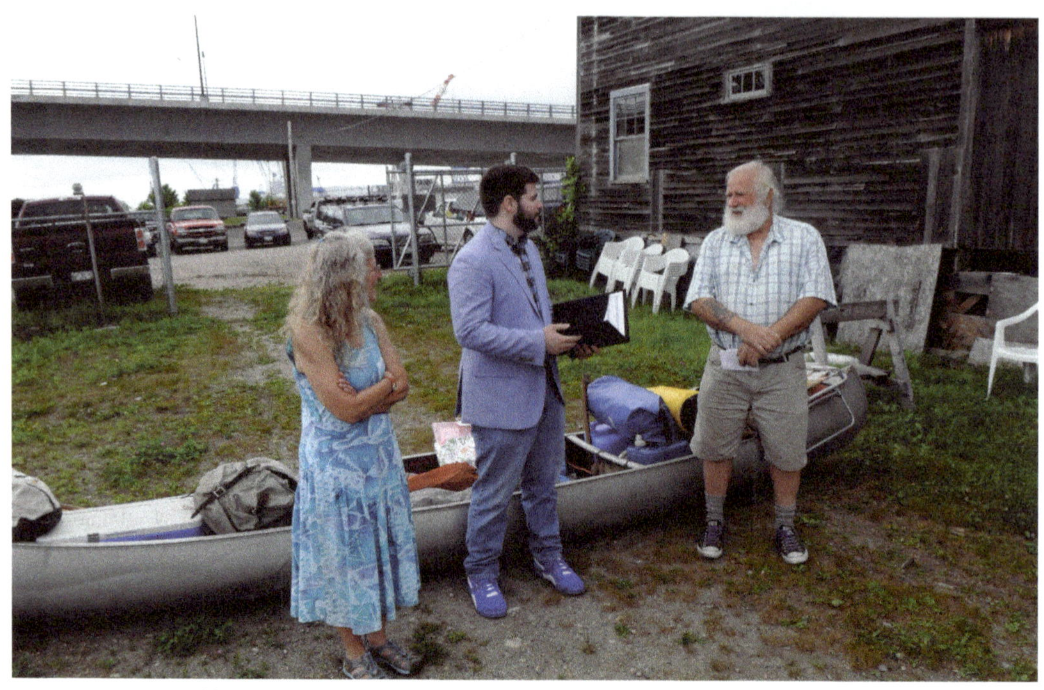

Shipwright Rob Stevens and volunteer Allison Hepler's wedding.

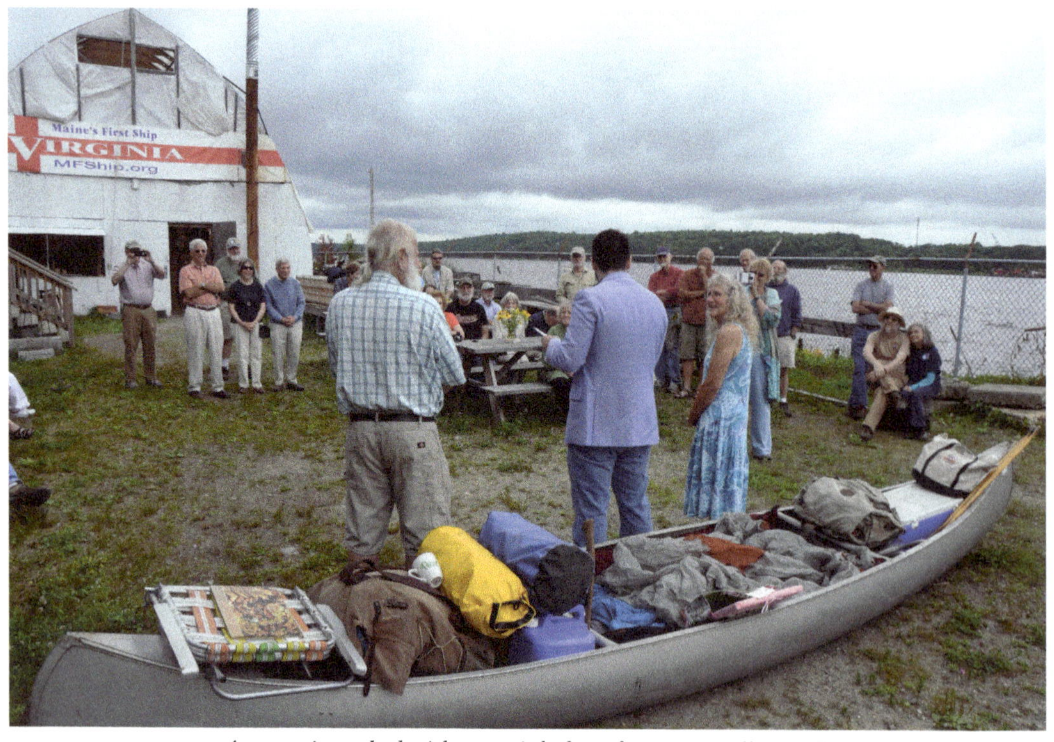

A canoe is packed with essentials for a honeymoon "cruise."

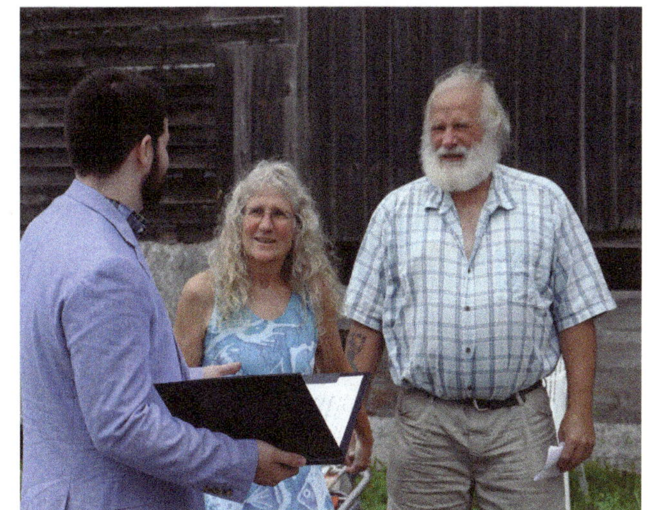

I do, I do. You may kiss the bride!

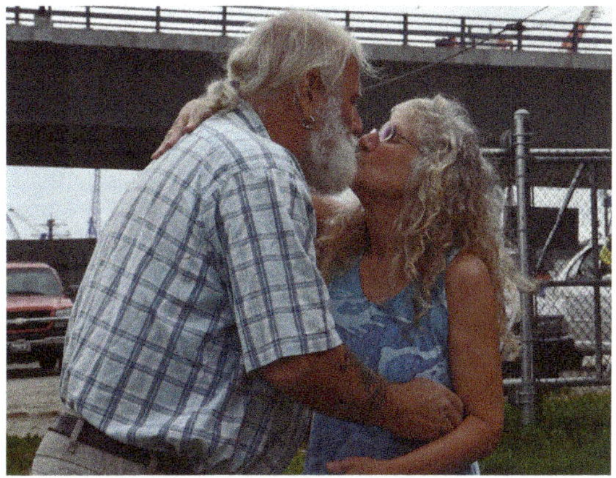

The happy couple and their relatives.

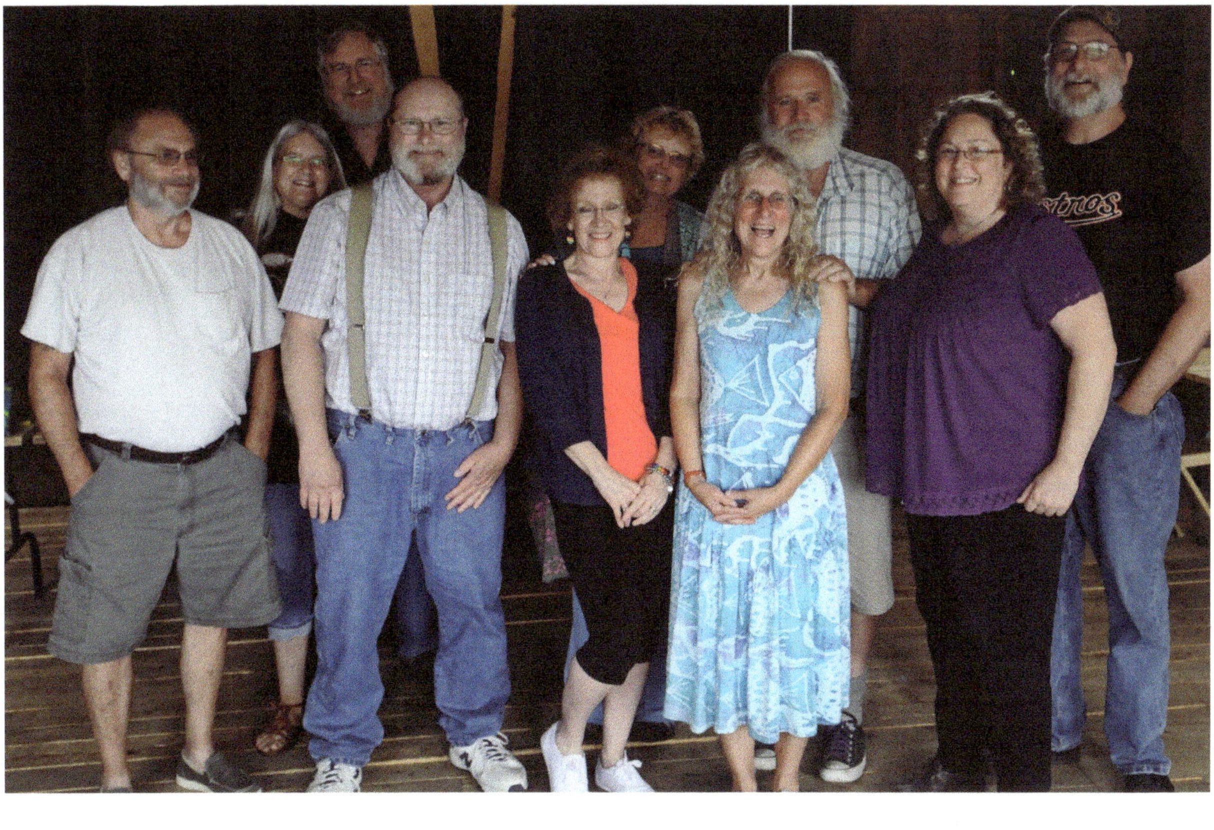

More Fairing. Planing & Planking

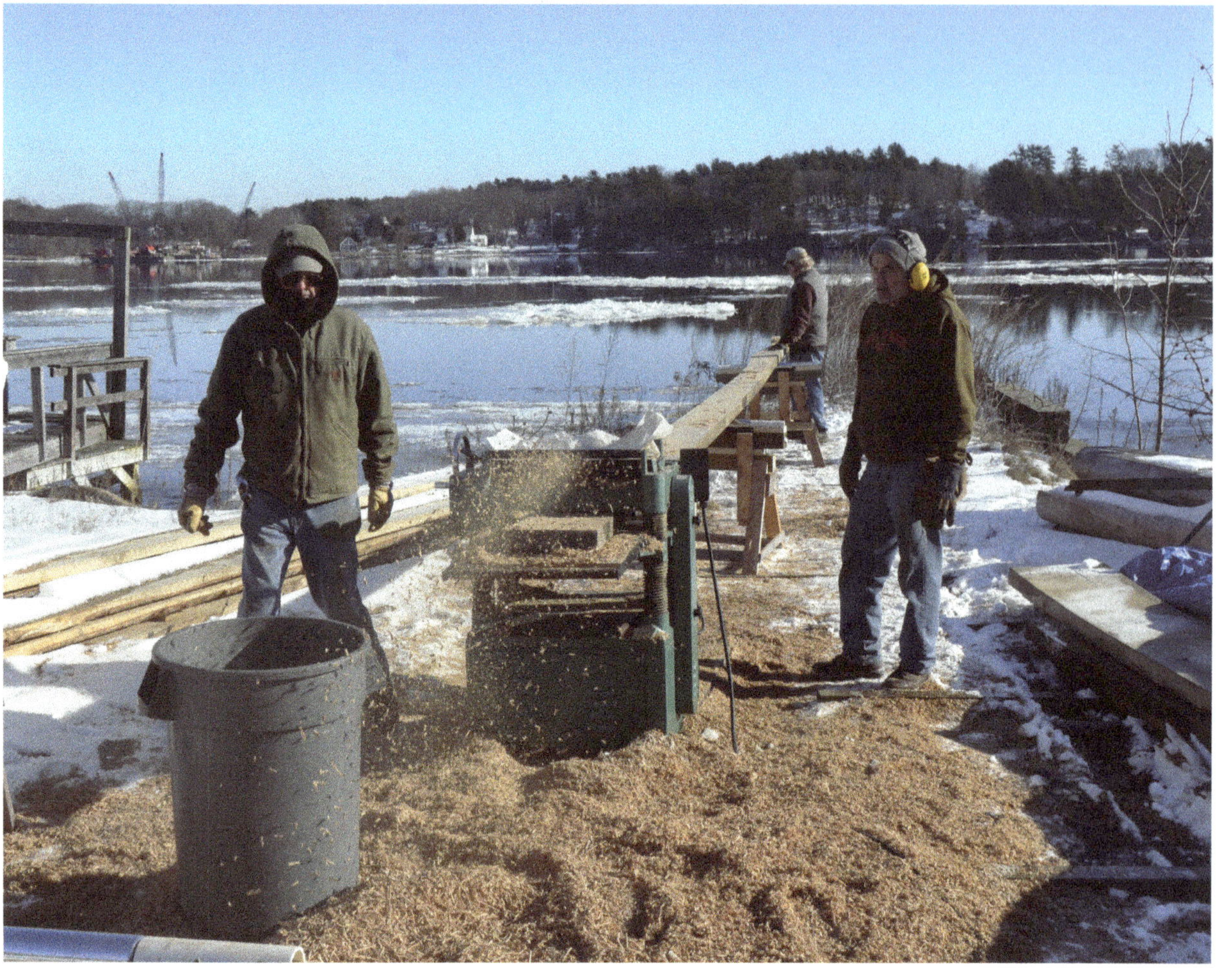

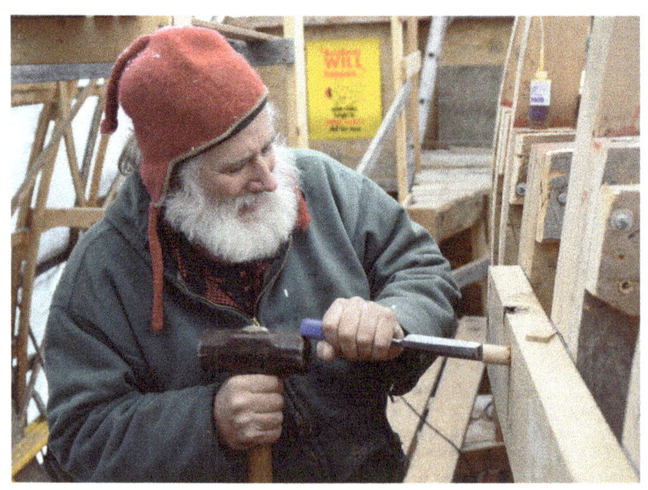

Dick Forrest and Roger Barry planing the first hull plank.

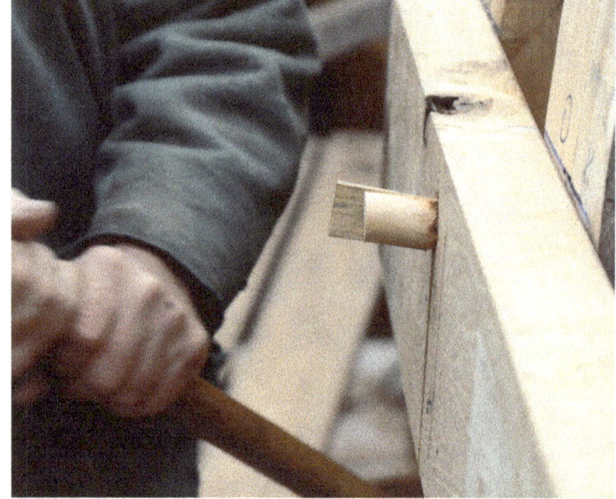

Rob Stevens uses a chisel to split a trunnel before driving a wedge to secure it.

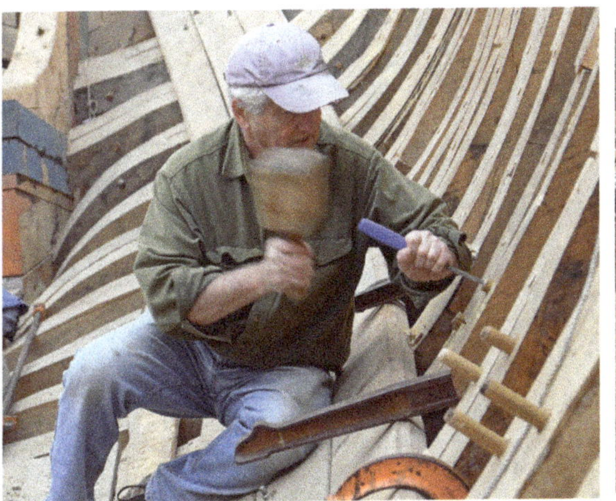

Art Charles wedges trunnels inside the hull,

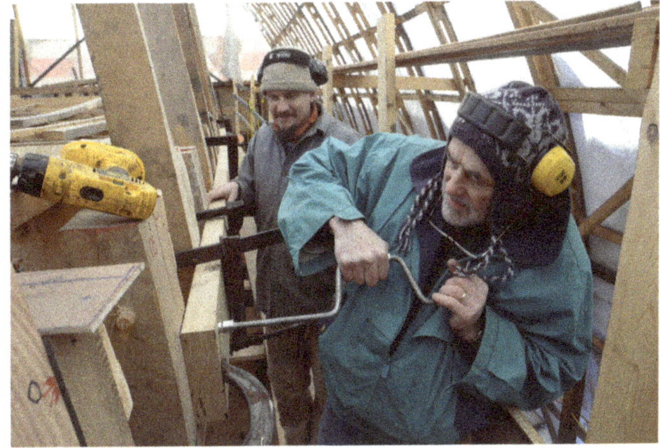

Roger Barry with Jeremy Blaiklock looking on, secures the end of each plank with a lag bolt, rather than a trunnel.

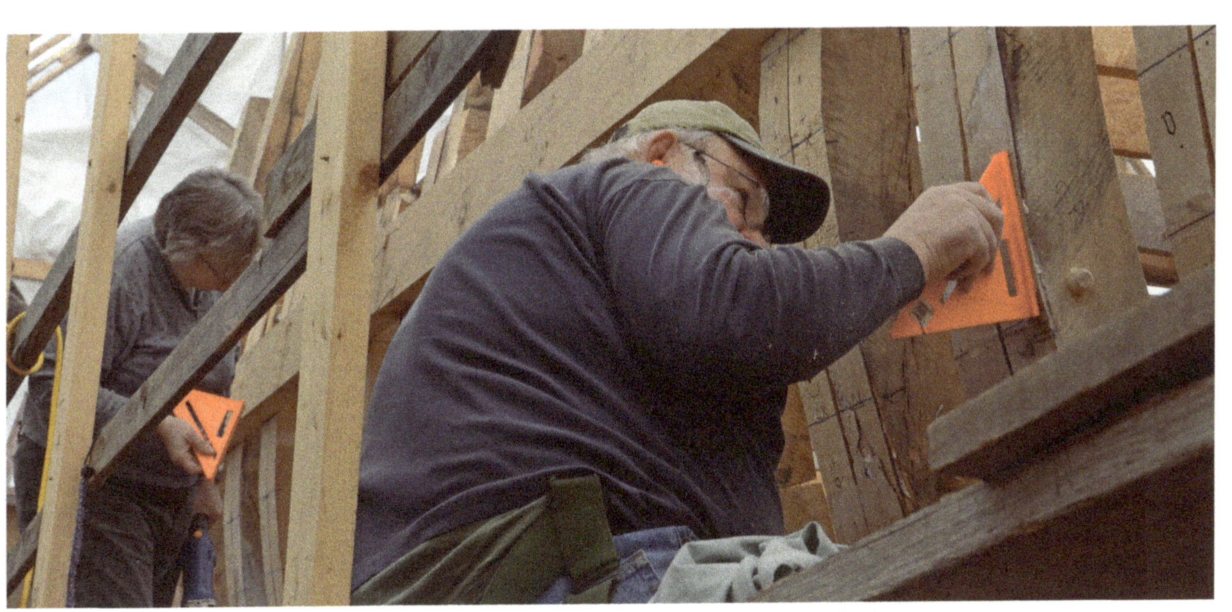

Gail Smith (left) and Orman Hinds continue fairing the frames.

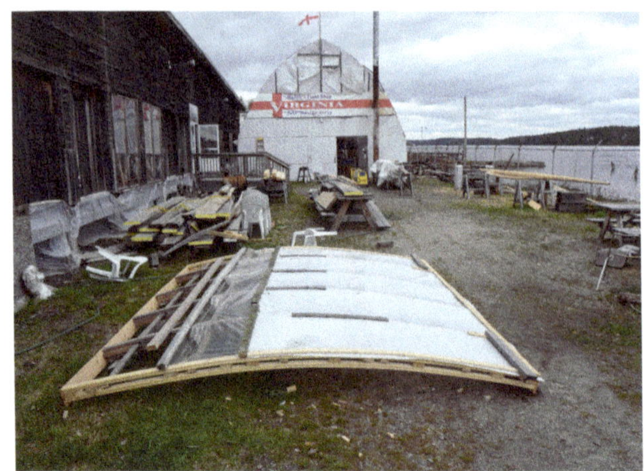

Removable panels were created to allow bow planks to be moved into position.

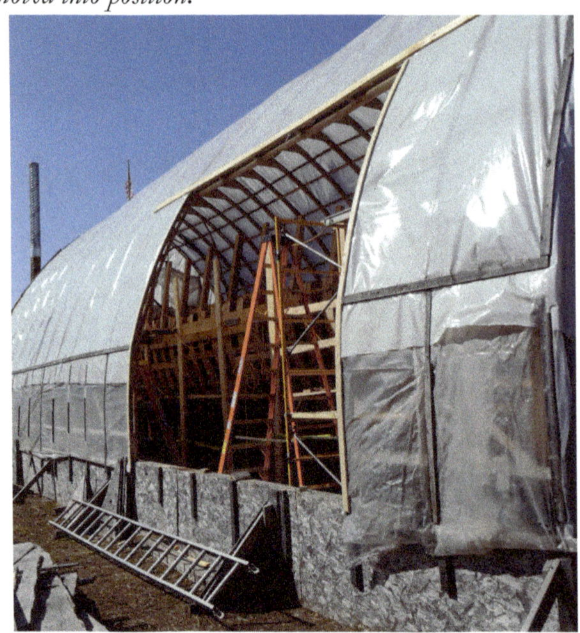

Panel removed to allow plank placement.

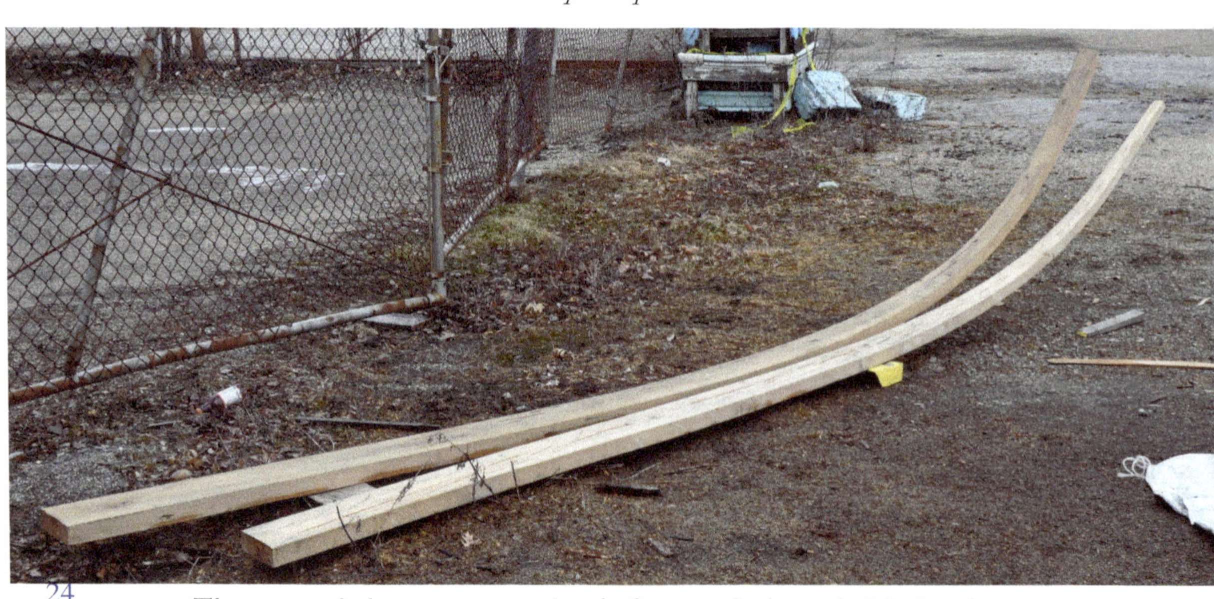

The curve at the bow was so great that the first two planks cracked during placement.

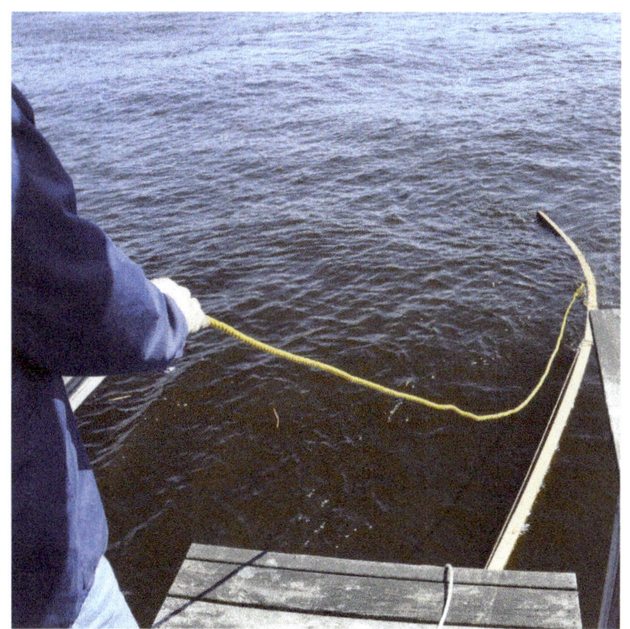

After soaking in the river for several days and steaming for several hours, the plank accepted extreme bending without cracking.

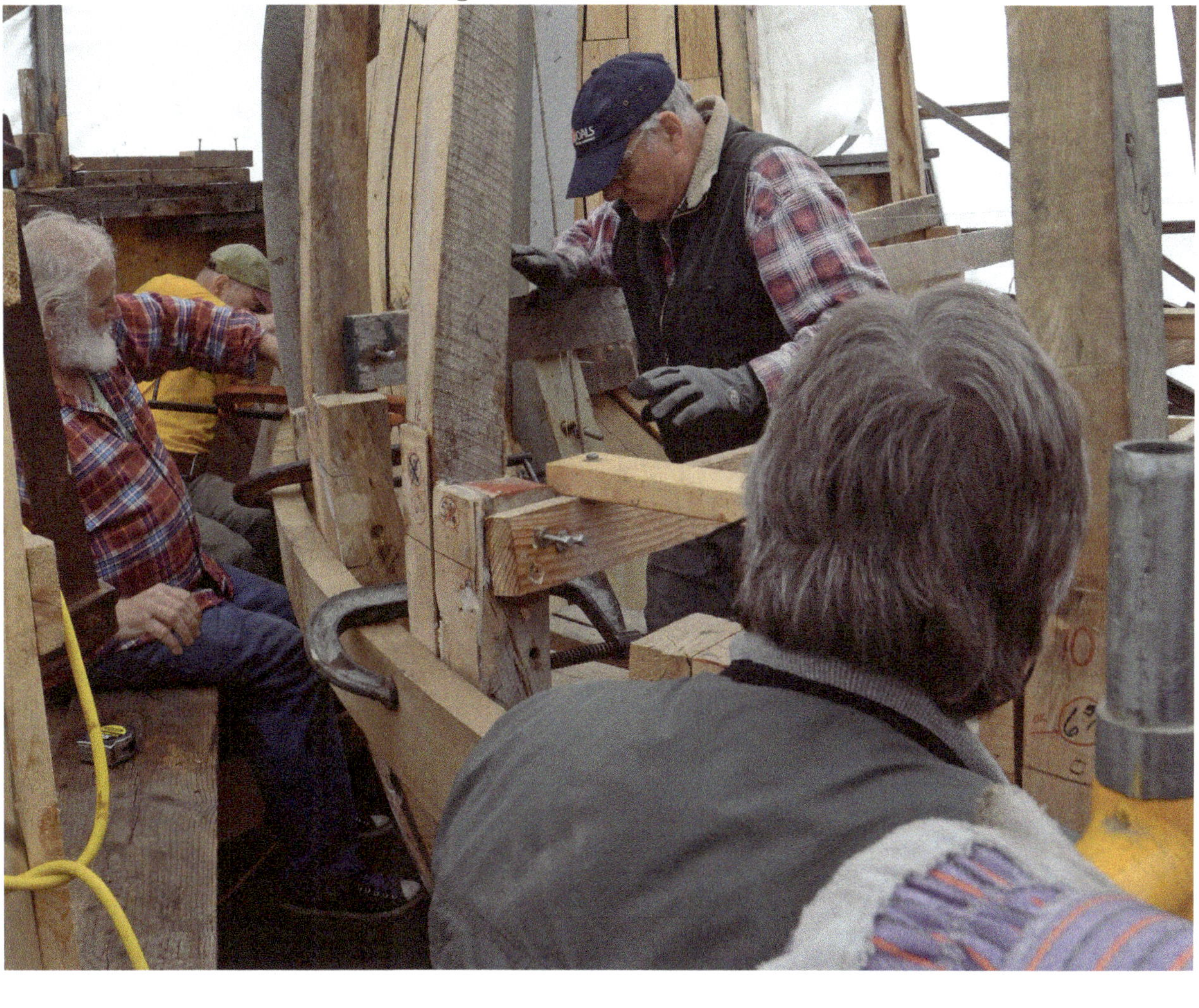

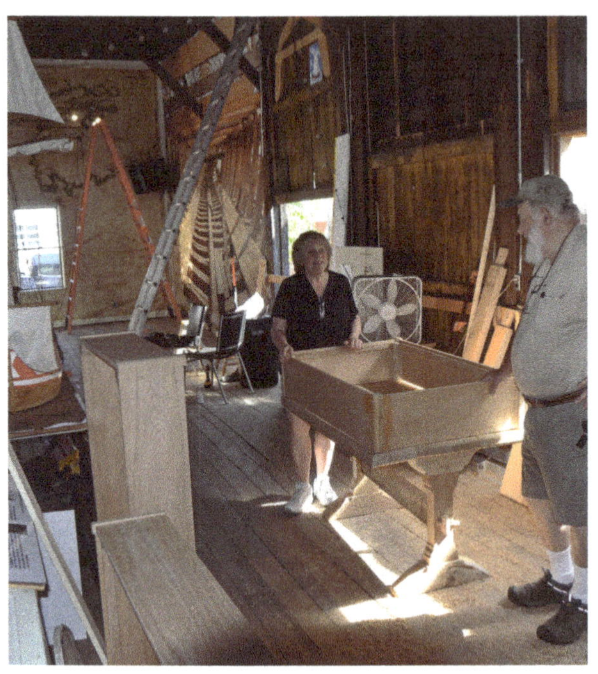

Lori Benson and Orman Hines check out new display cases.

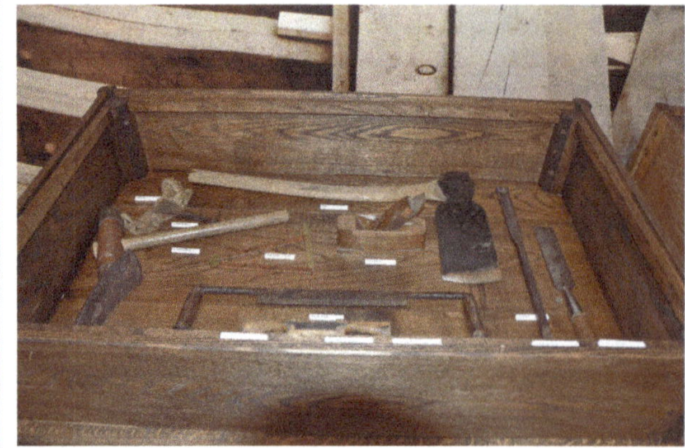

One of the new display cases for our project.

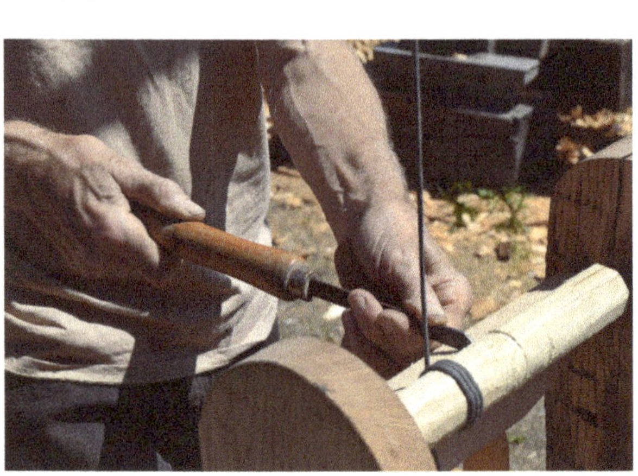

When Fred Gosbee needed a wood lathe, he made one, much to the delight of visitors.

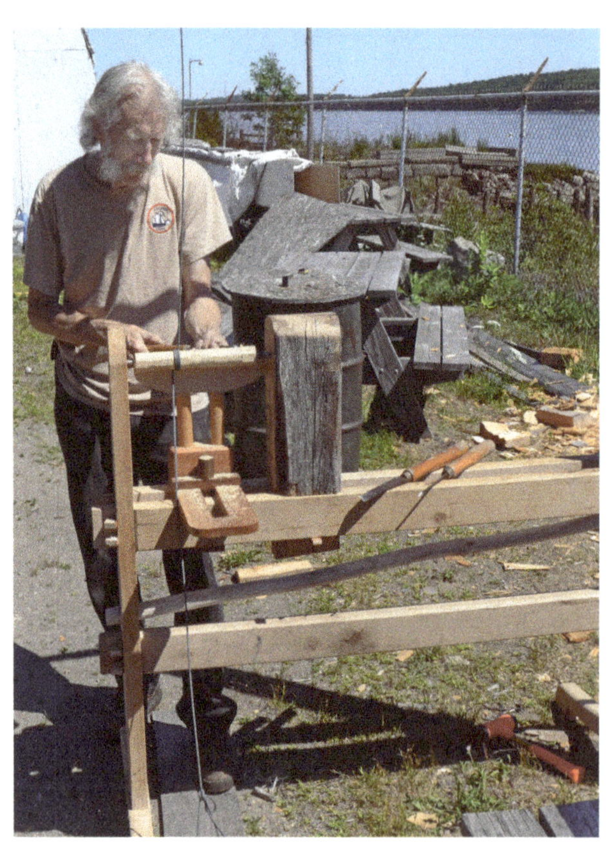

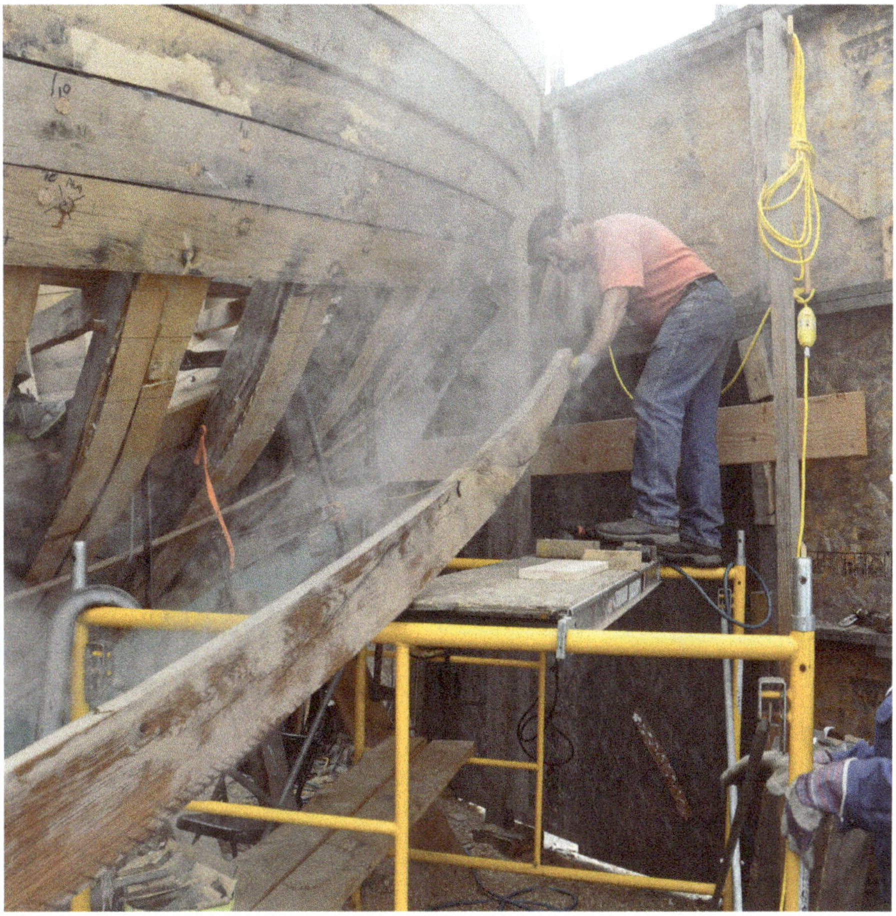

Fresh from the steamer, a plank is bent and attached to the hull.

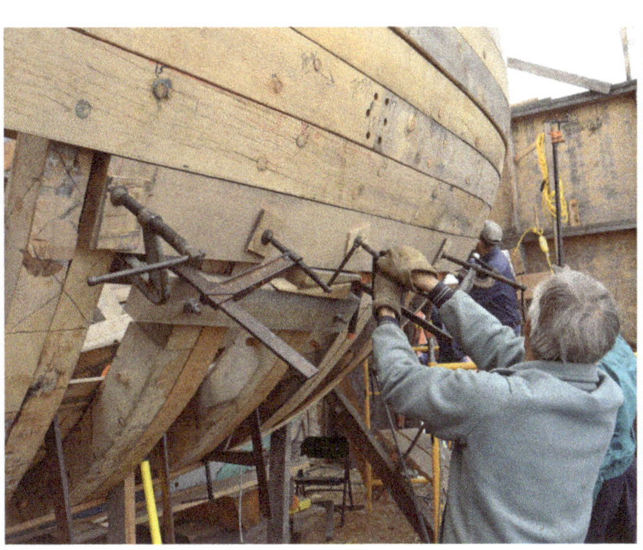

Clamping the plank into position.

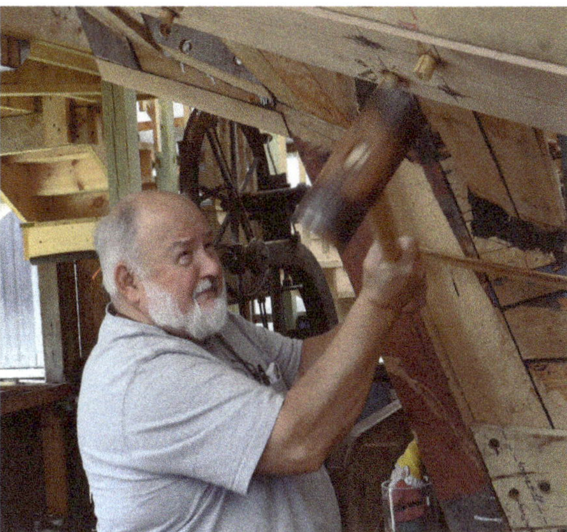

Orman Hines drives trunnels to secure a plank.

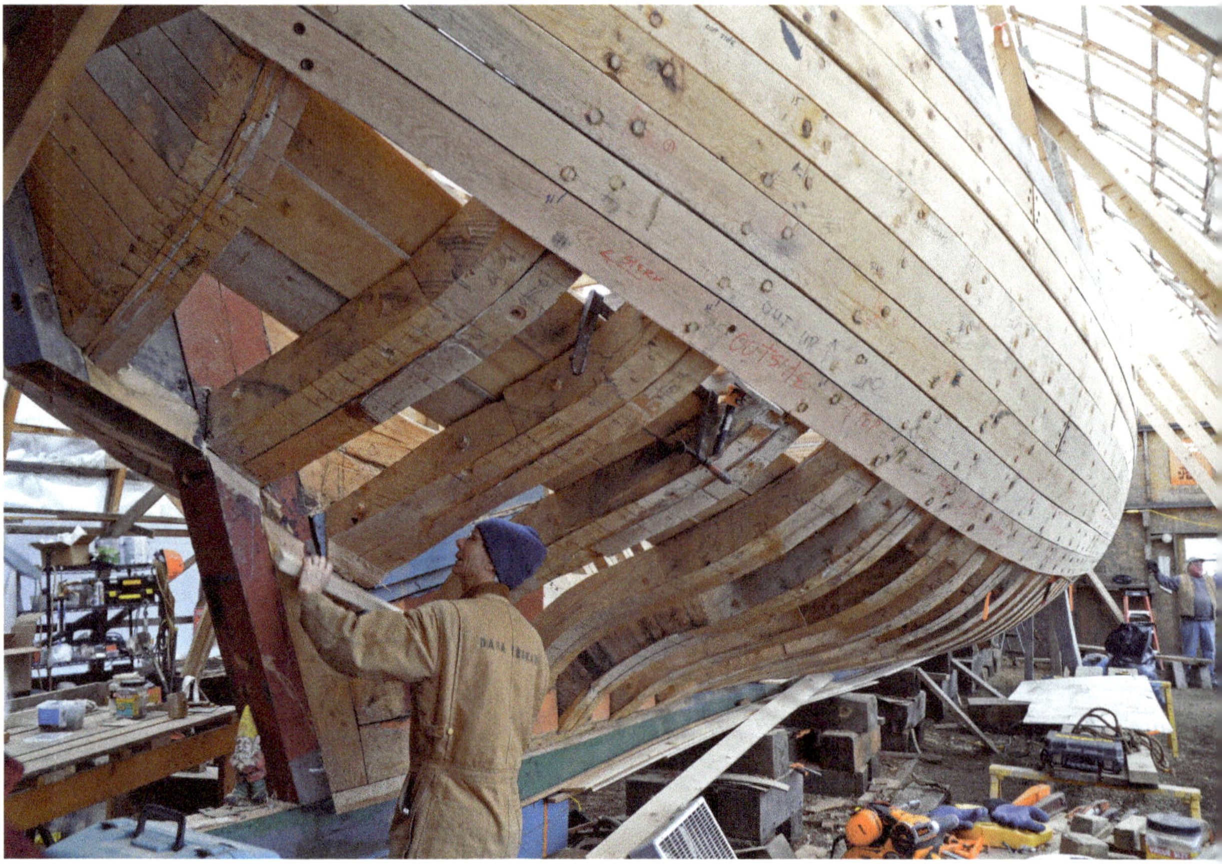

Dana Leonard works on the starboard side of the Virginia.

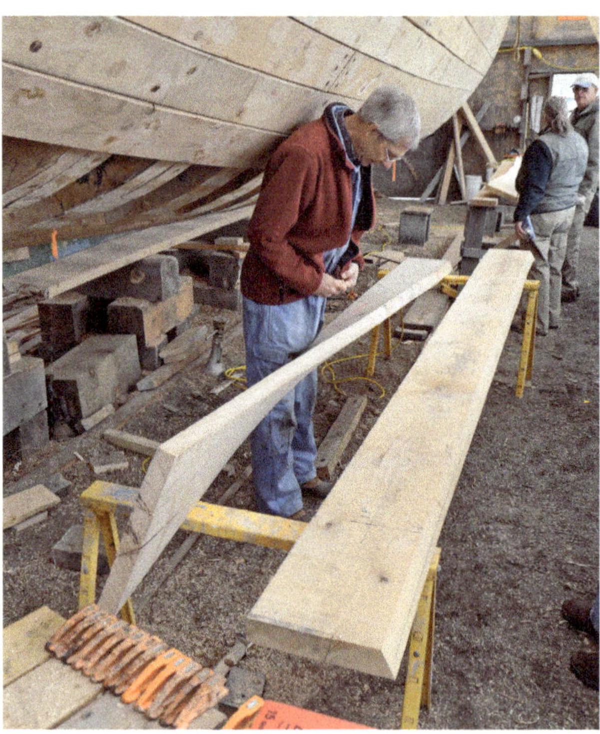

Dana checks out a starboard garboard plank.

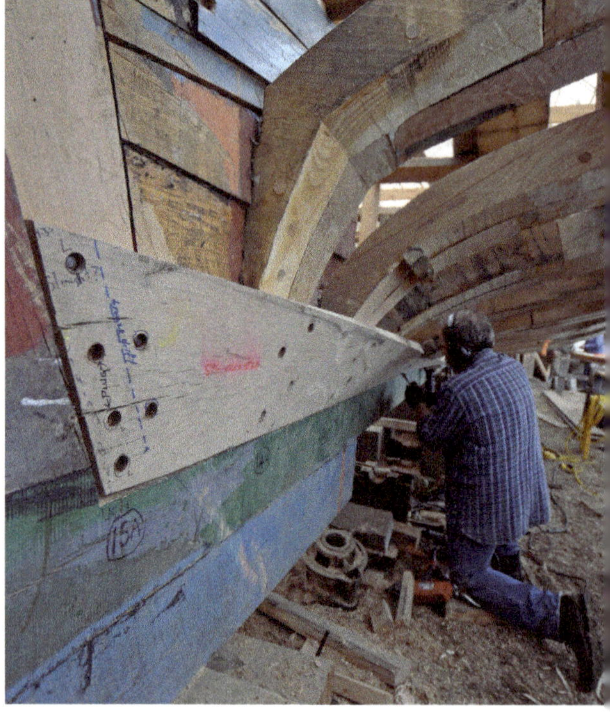

Some planks required more twisting than others.

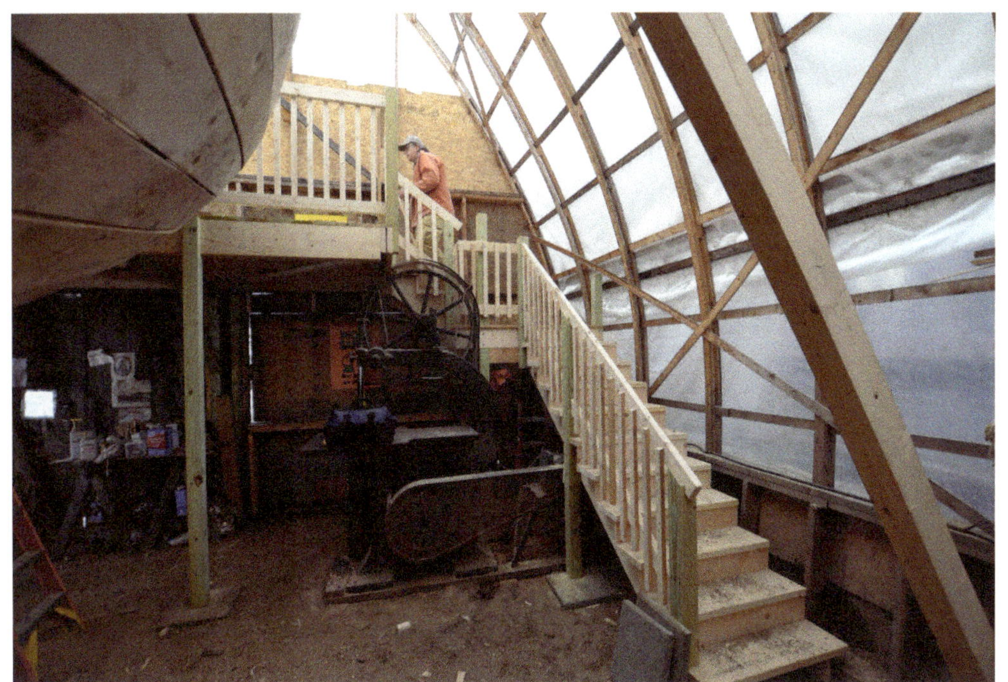

A new set of stairs and a work platform.

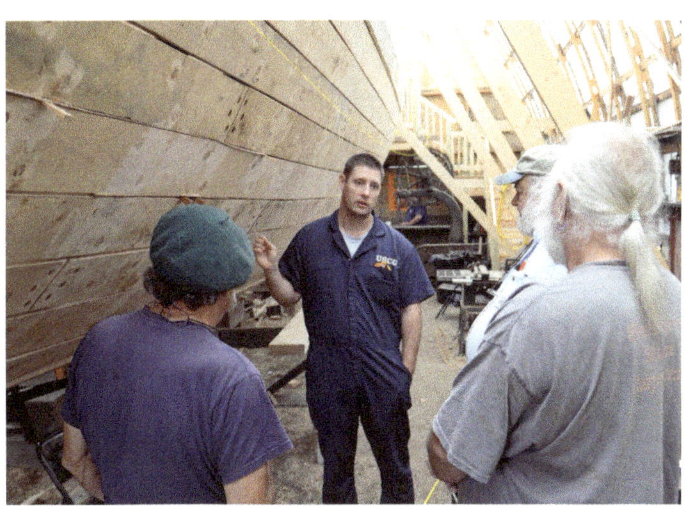

Coast Guard inspection.

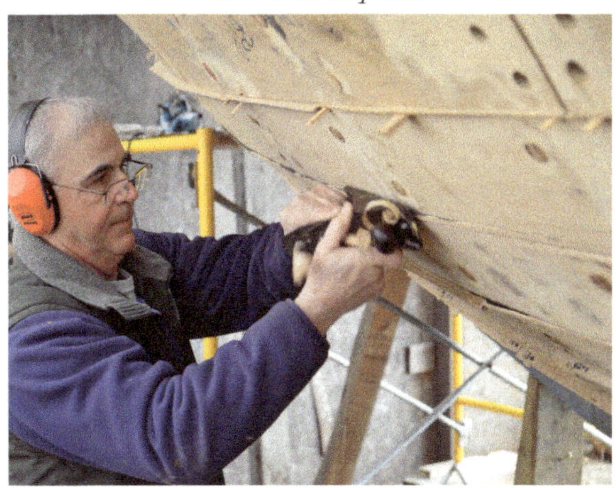

*Matt Murray uses a hand planer to smooth out
the joints of the hull.*

Rigging Blocks

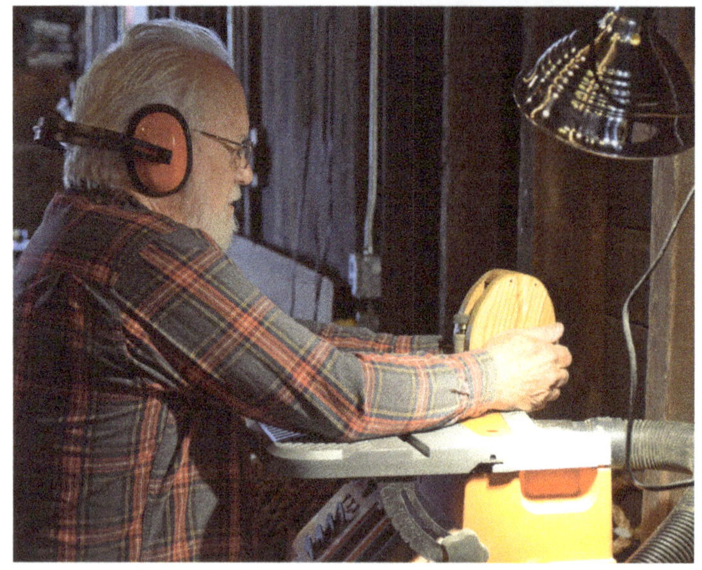

Rigger Robert Ireland hard at work on the rigging blocks.

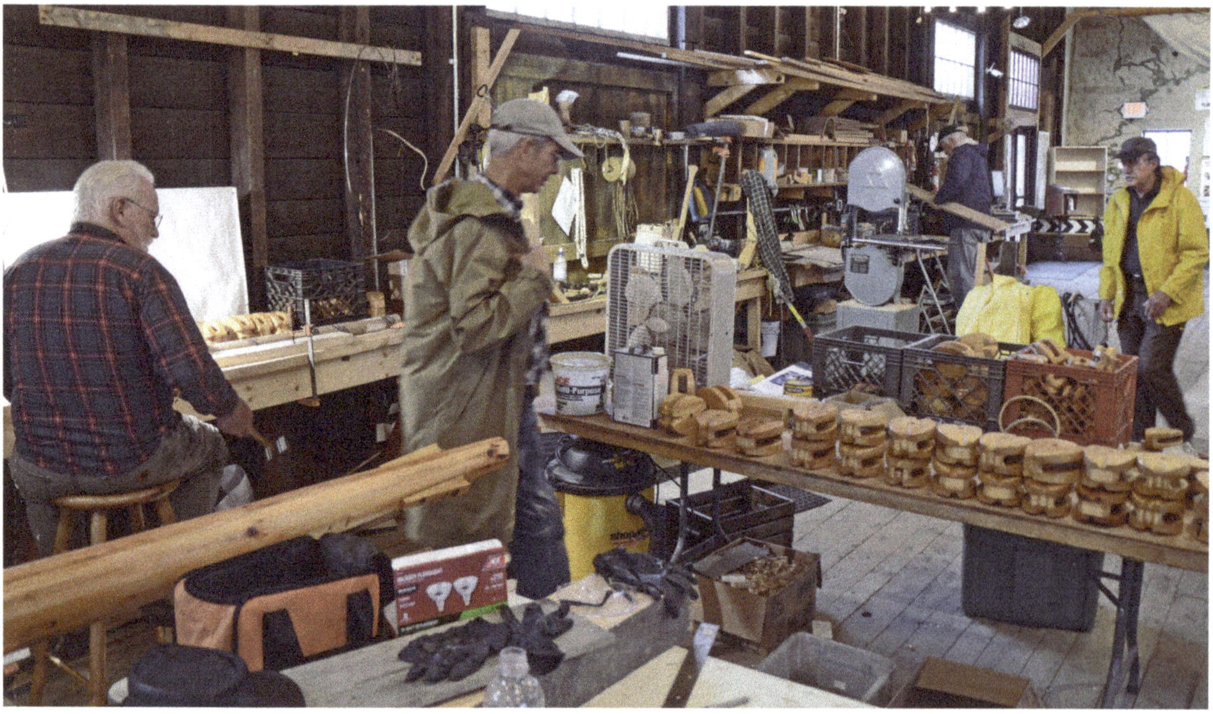

Dana Leonard checks out blocks created by the riggers.

Celebrating Another Year

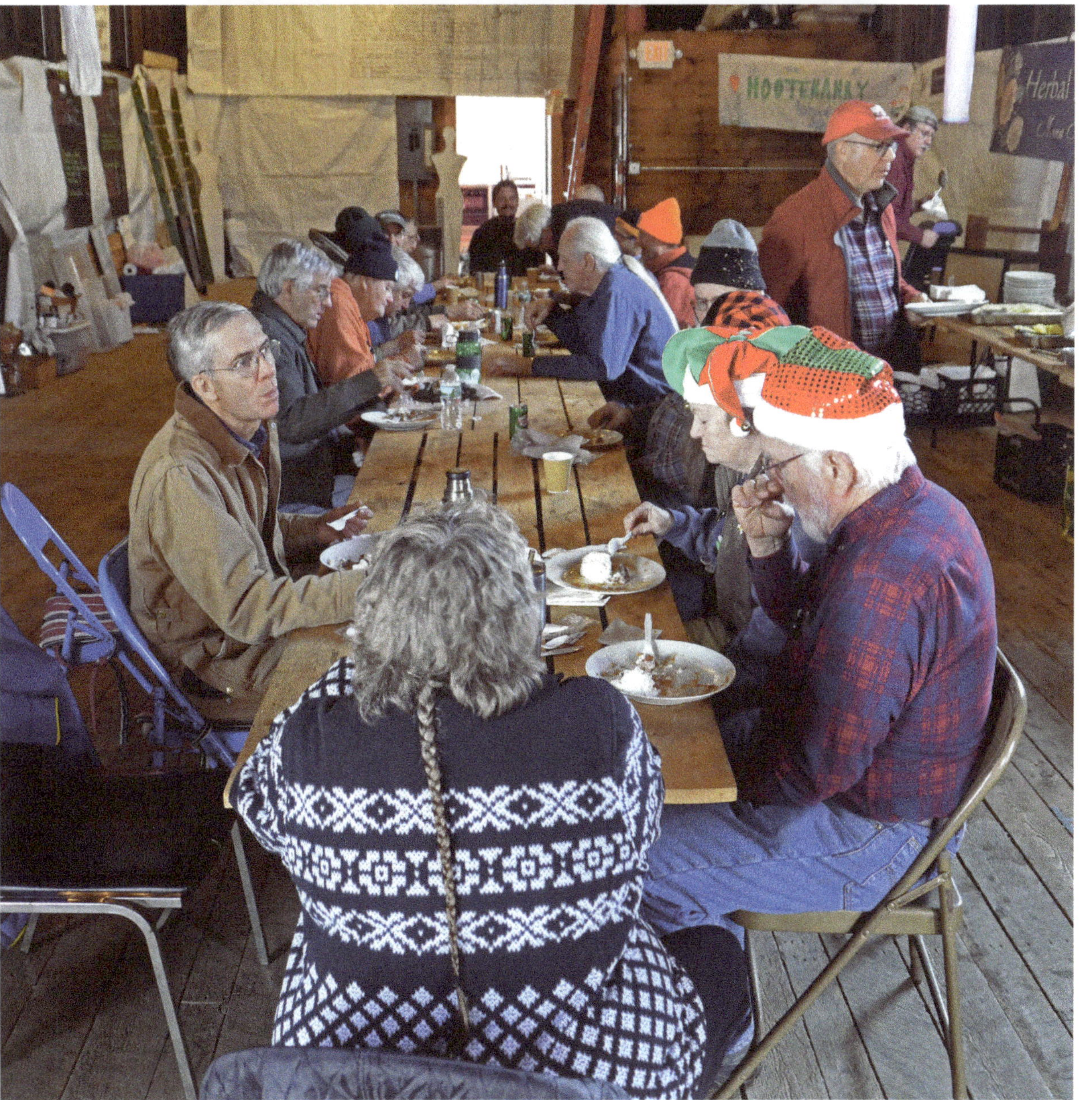

A banquet to celebrate another year ending.

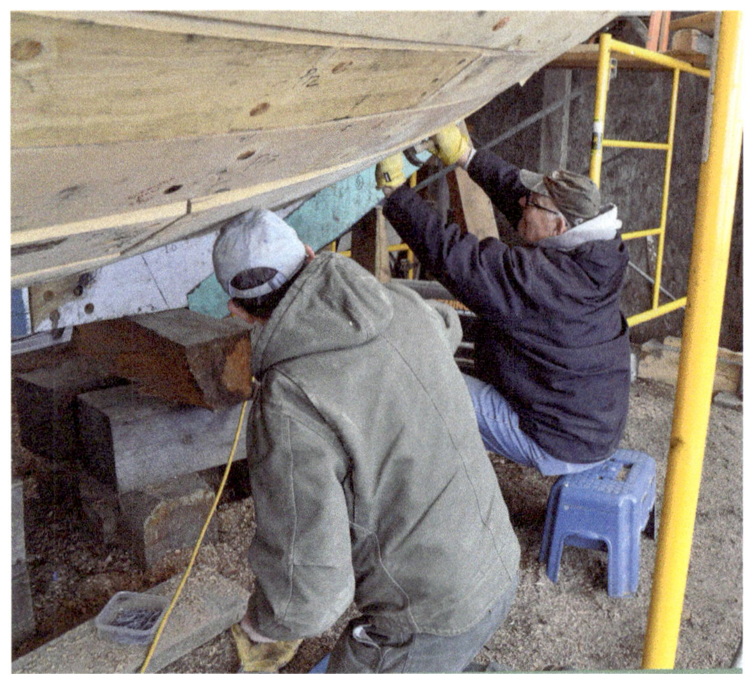

Dick Forrest and Paul Cunningham worked near the bow.

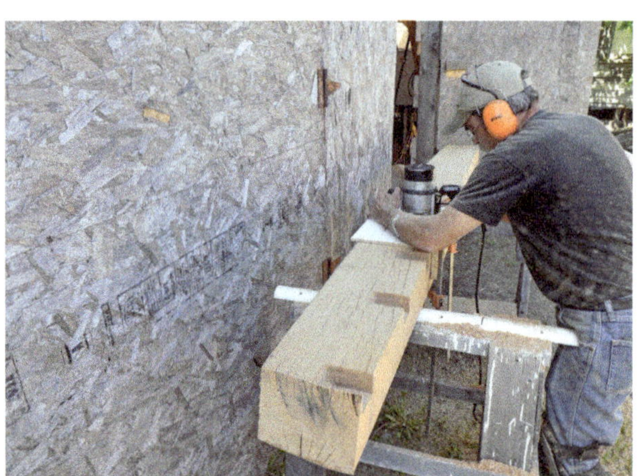

Charlie Pelletier working on the stern.

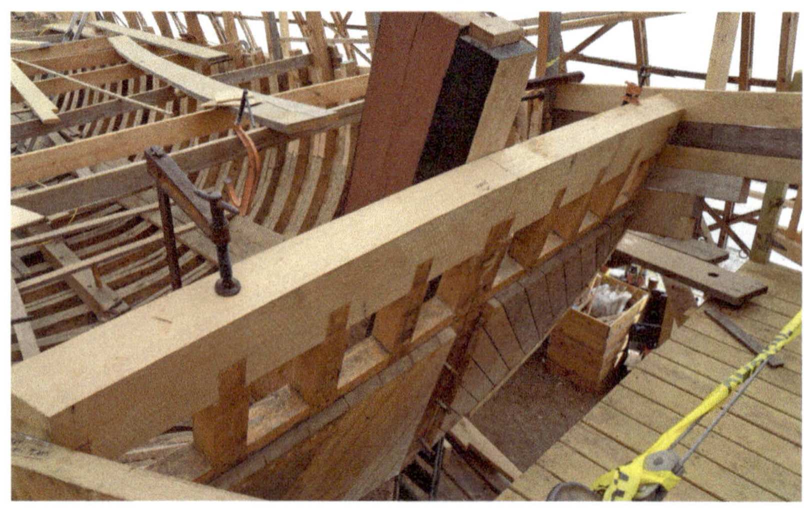

Endowment Fund

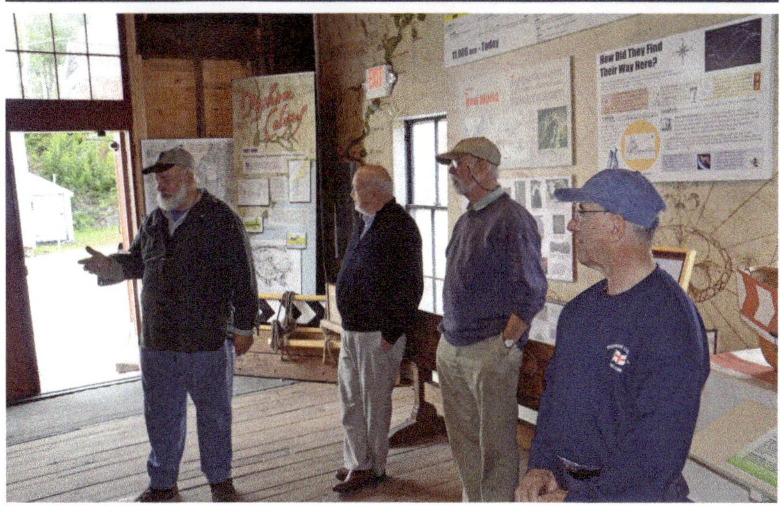

*Orman Hines (left) announces the donation to the endowment fund
by Bob (right) and Diane Weggel (not shown).*

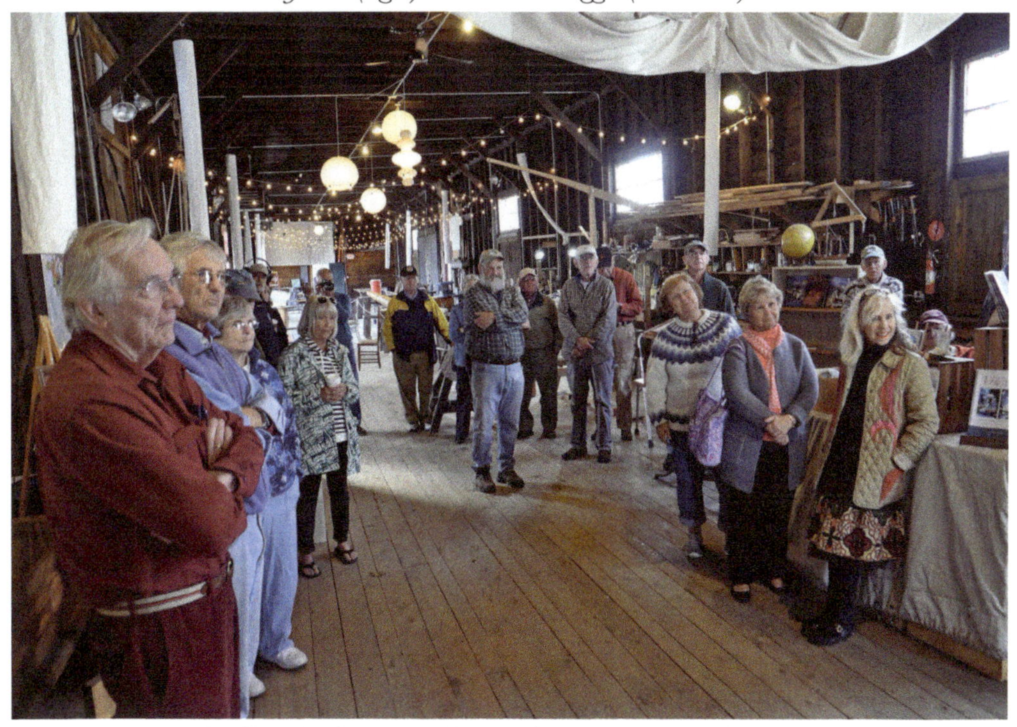

Staff and volunteers gather to celebrate a wonderful donation.

Installing the Deck

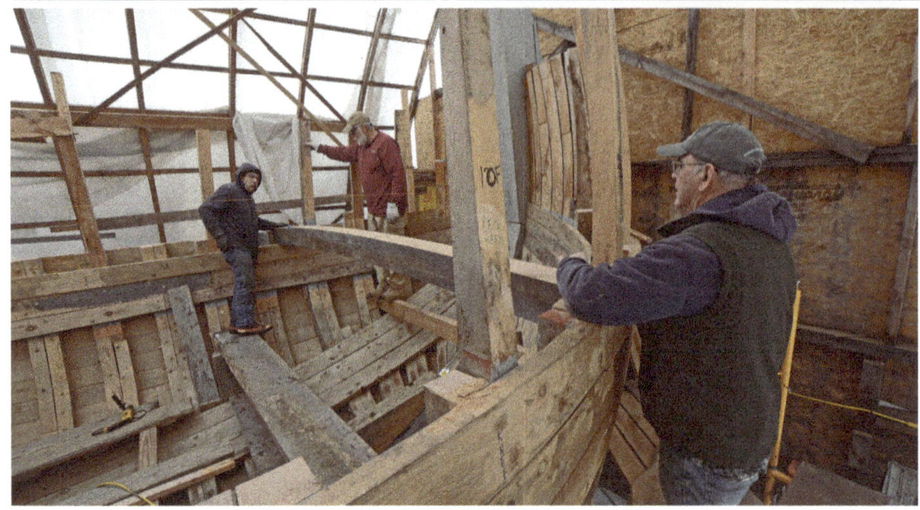

Charles Pelletier (left), Jim Amundsen (center), and Matt Murray (right) begin work on the deck beams.

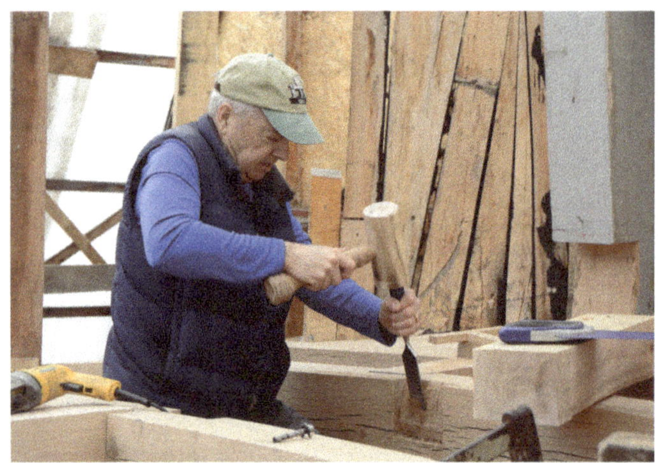

Joe Arsenault mortises a deck beam.

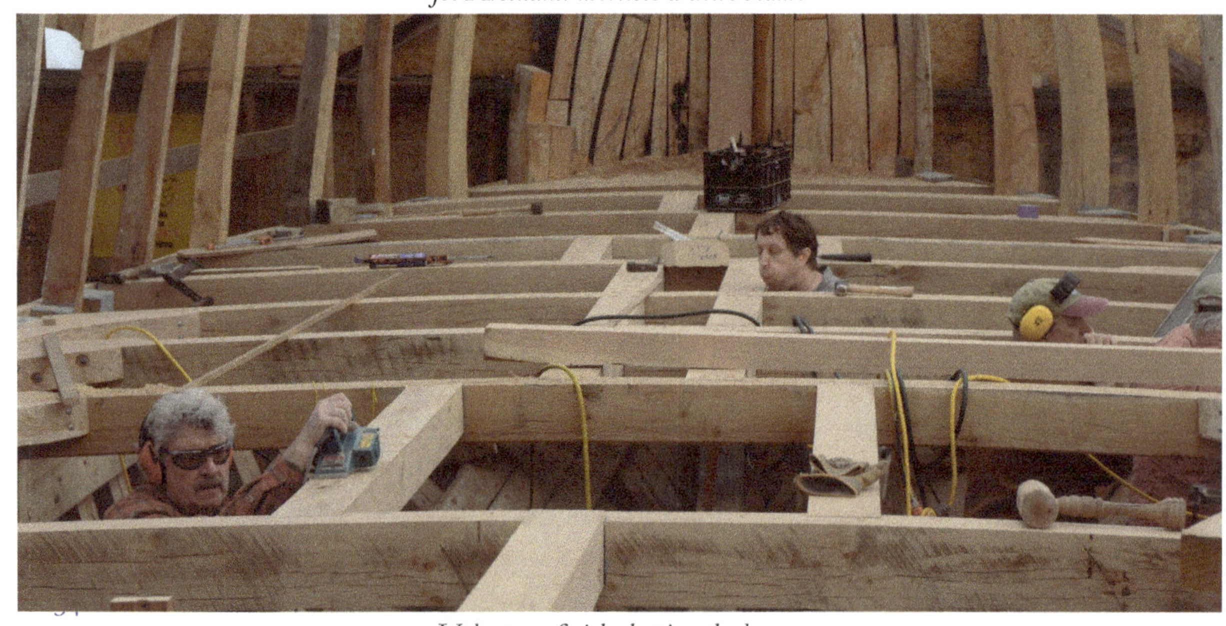

Volunteers finish shaping the beams

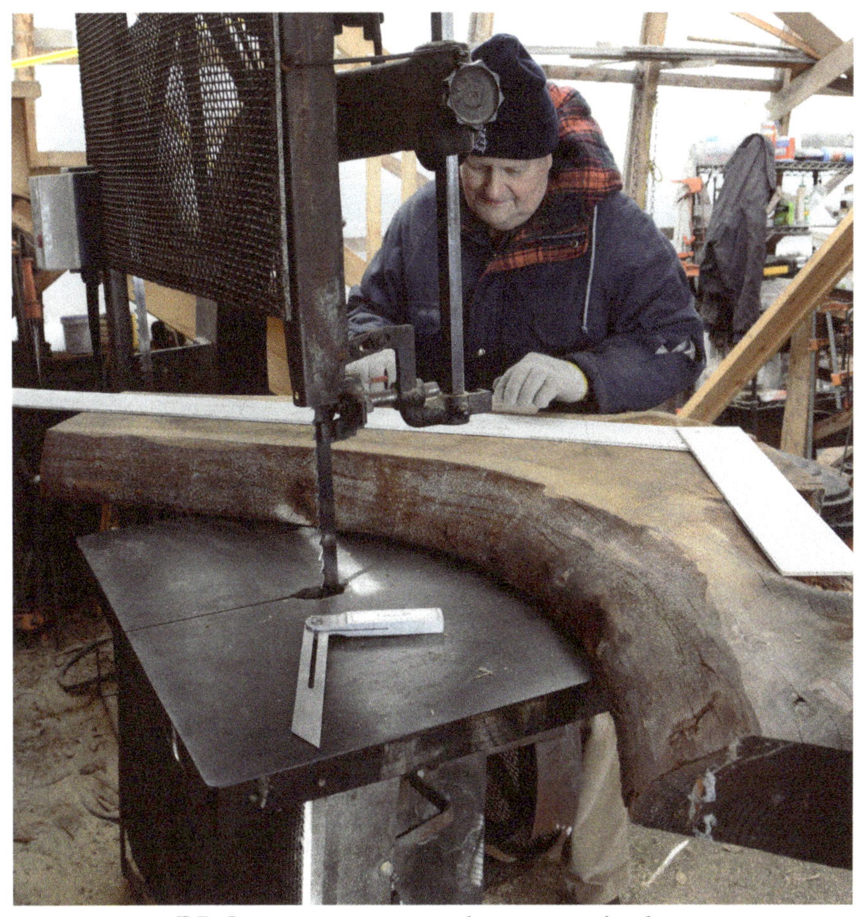

RB Omo uses a pattern to draw out another knee.

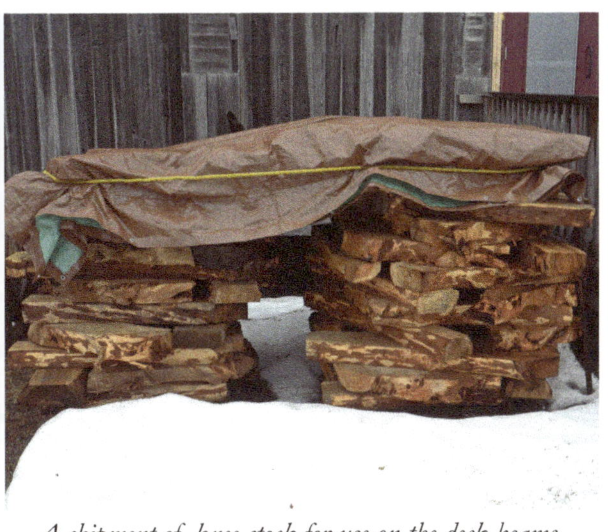

A shipment of knee stock for use on the deck beams.

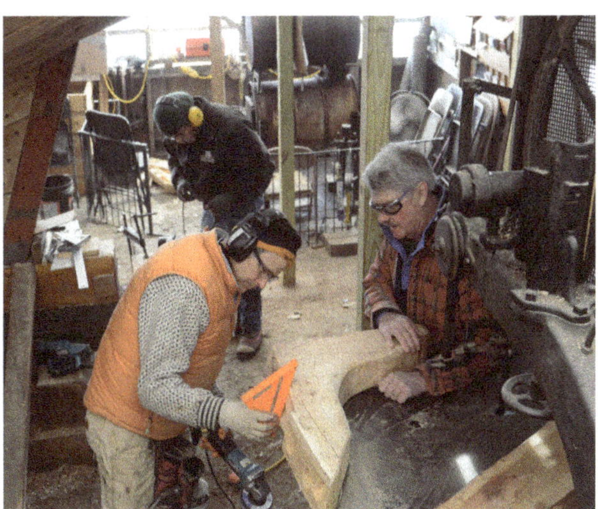

Tim Emerson and Paul King shape a deck knee.

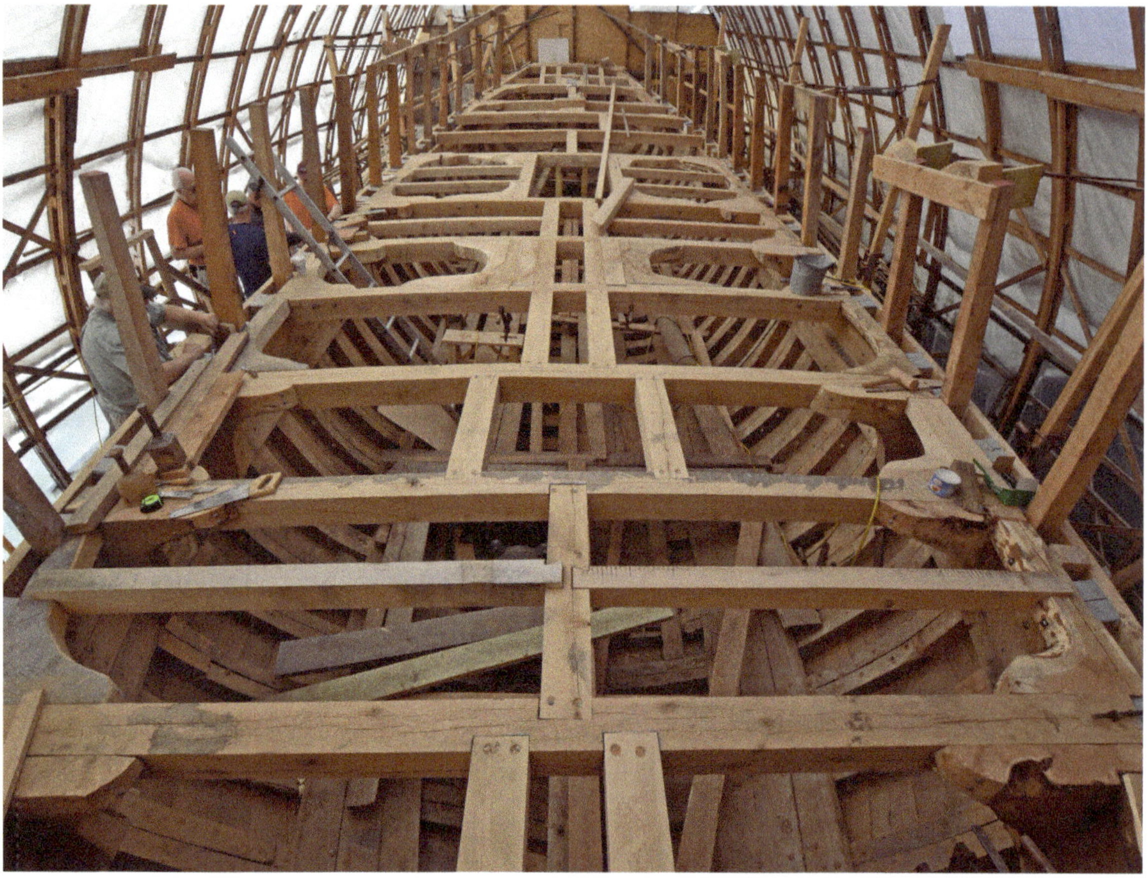

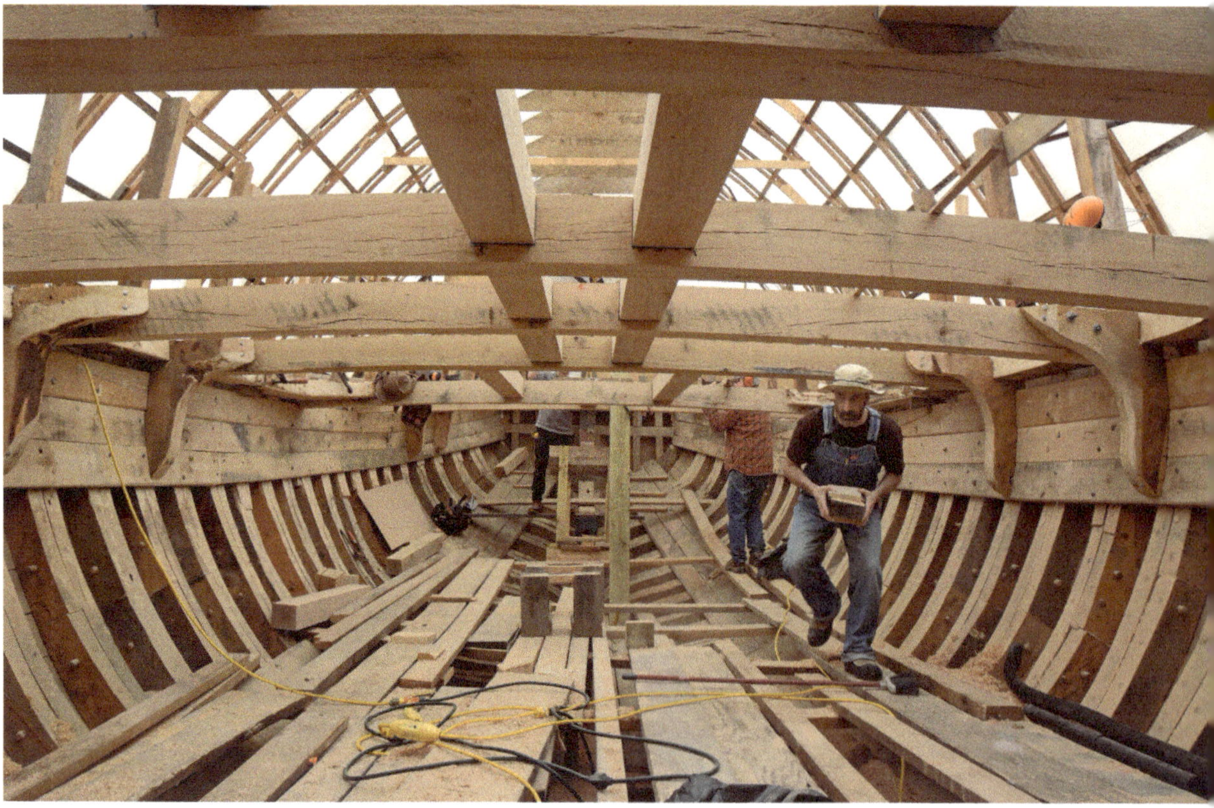

The deck supports from above and below.

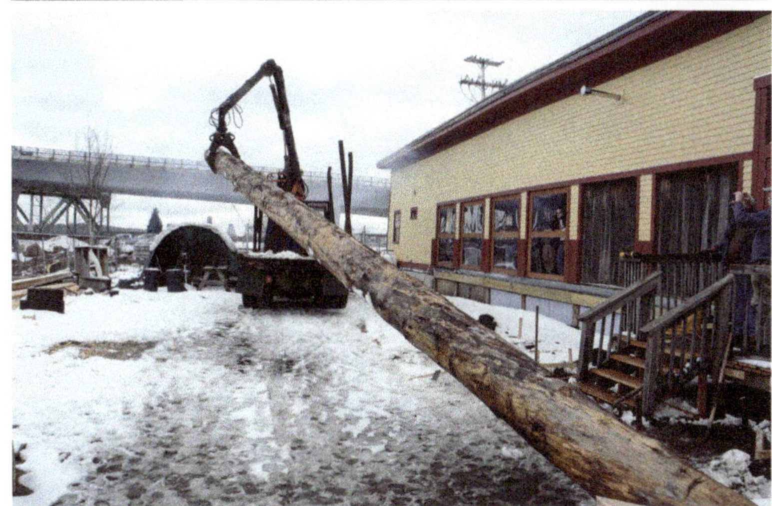

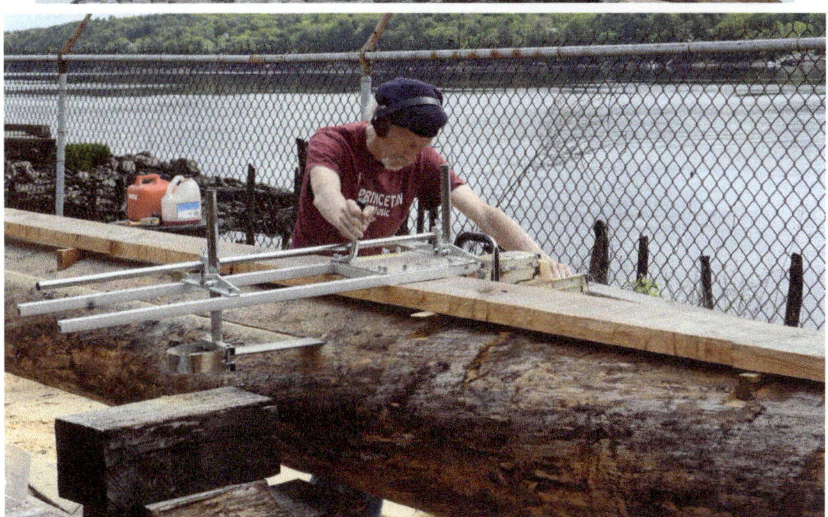

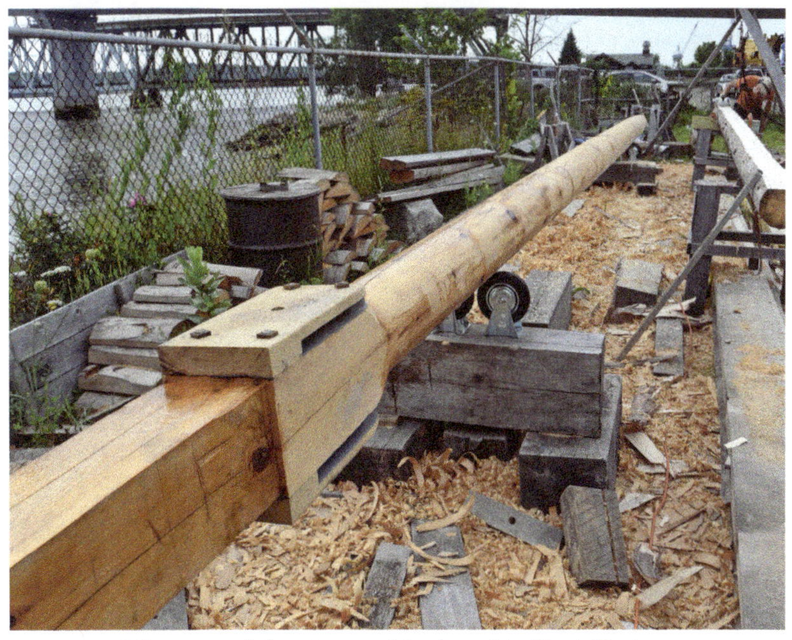

Mast material arrives and is shaped by Fred Gosbee.

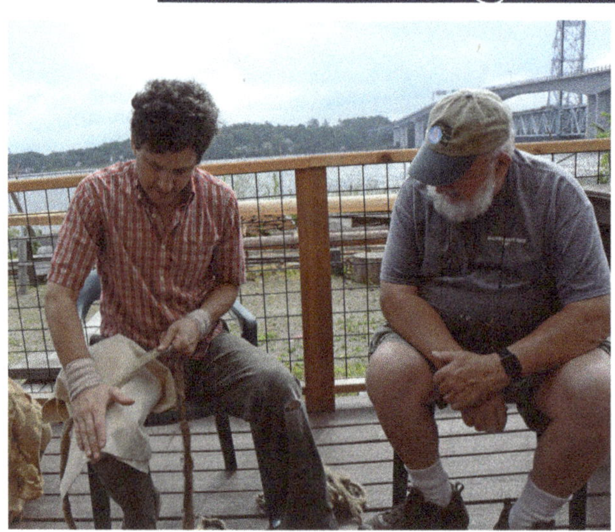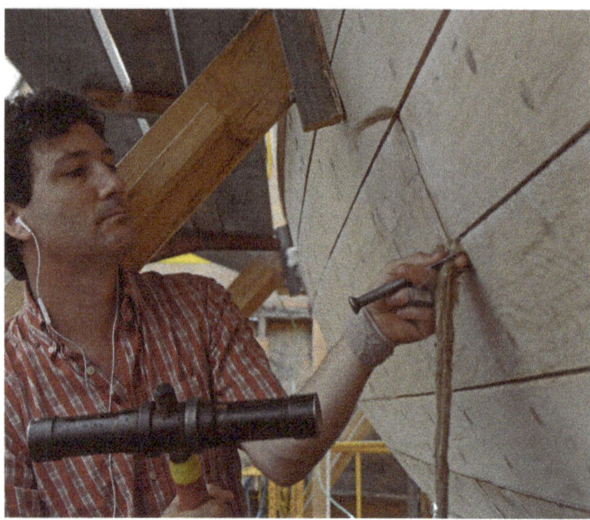

Andros Kypragoras, a professional caulker, arrives and begins work.

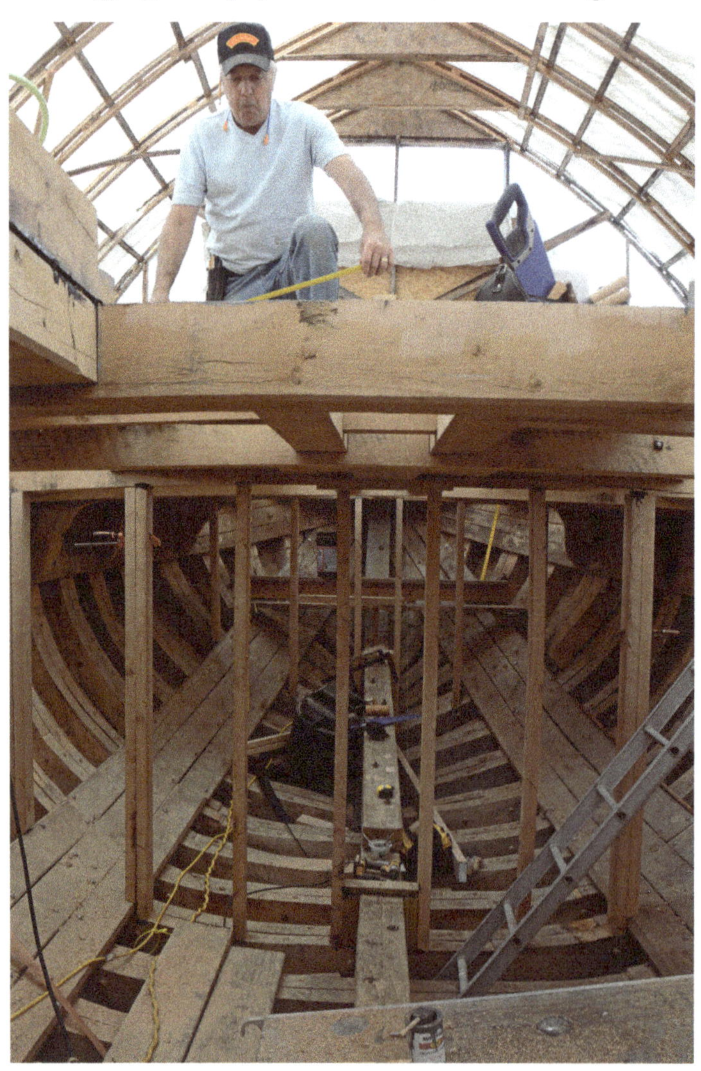

Joe Arsenault works on the deck. Below the watertight bulkhead is framed in.

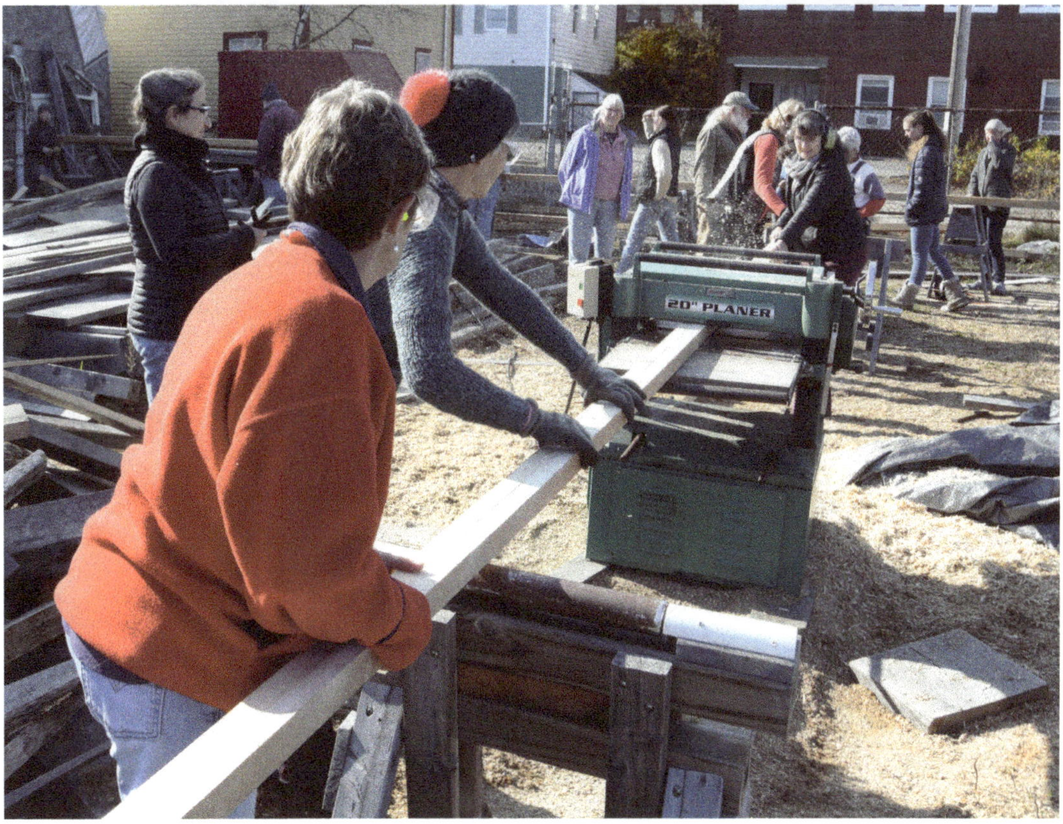

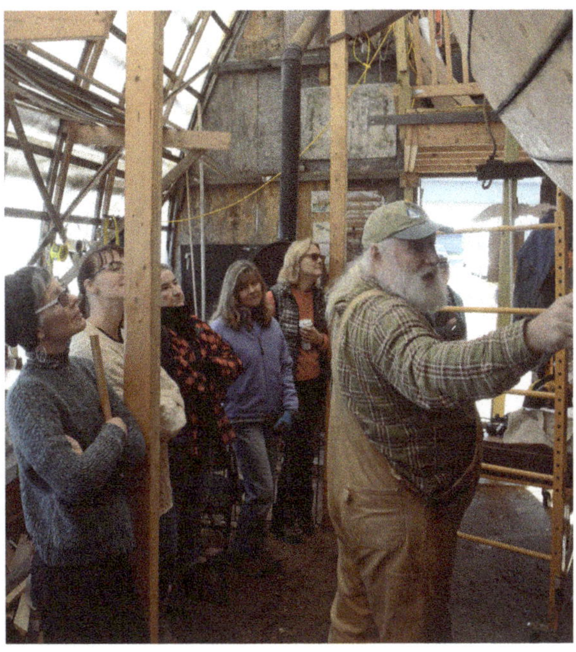

Each year beginning in 2015, a women's workday was scheduled in early November.

Women volunteers gather for instruction for the day's work.

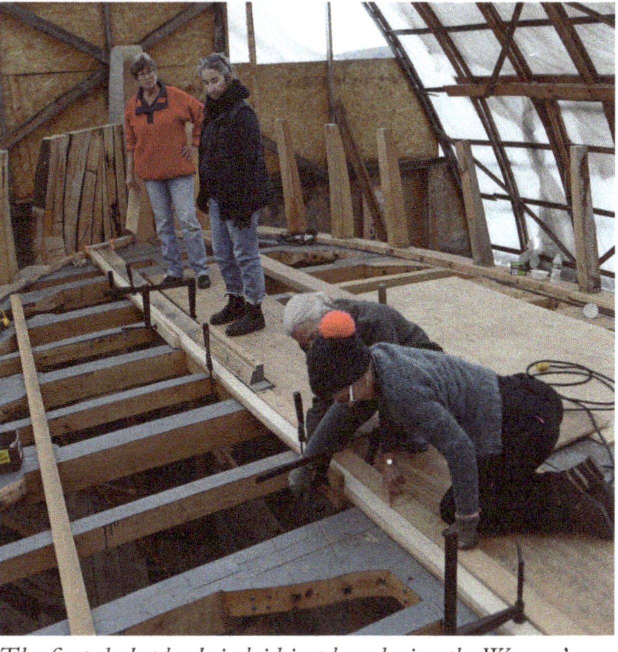

The first deck plank is laid in place during the Women's Work Day 2015.

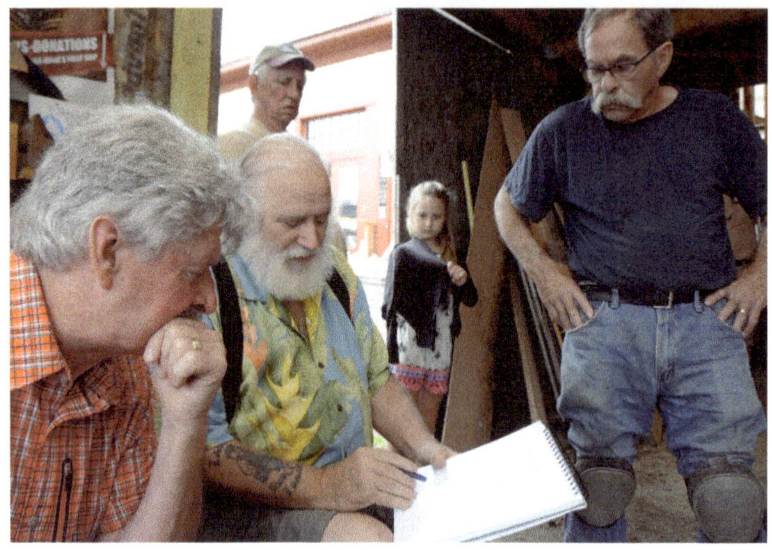

Rob Stevens (center) reviews the plans with Paul King (left) and Charlie Pelletier (right).

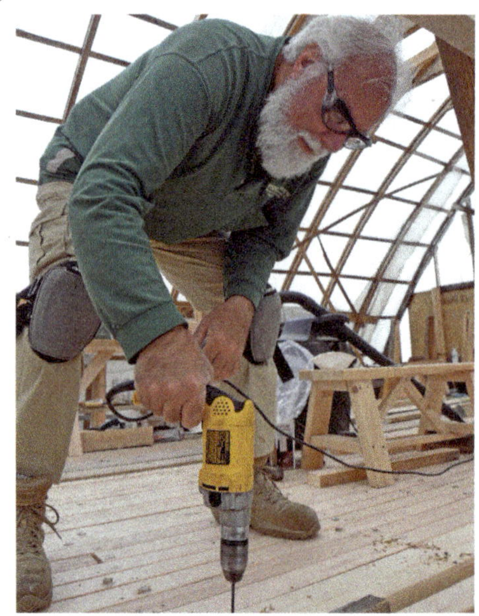

Jim Amundsen drills pilot holes for deck screws.

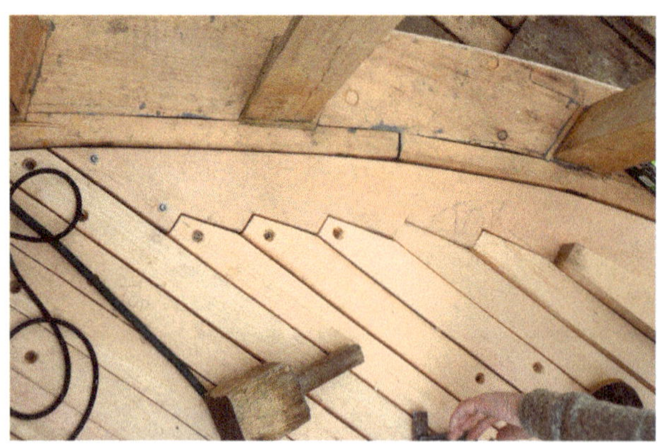

Pattern created when installing deck planks.

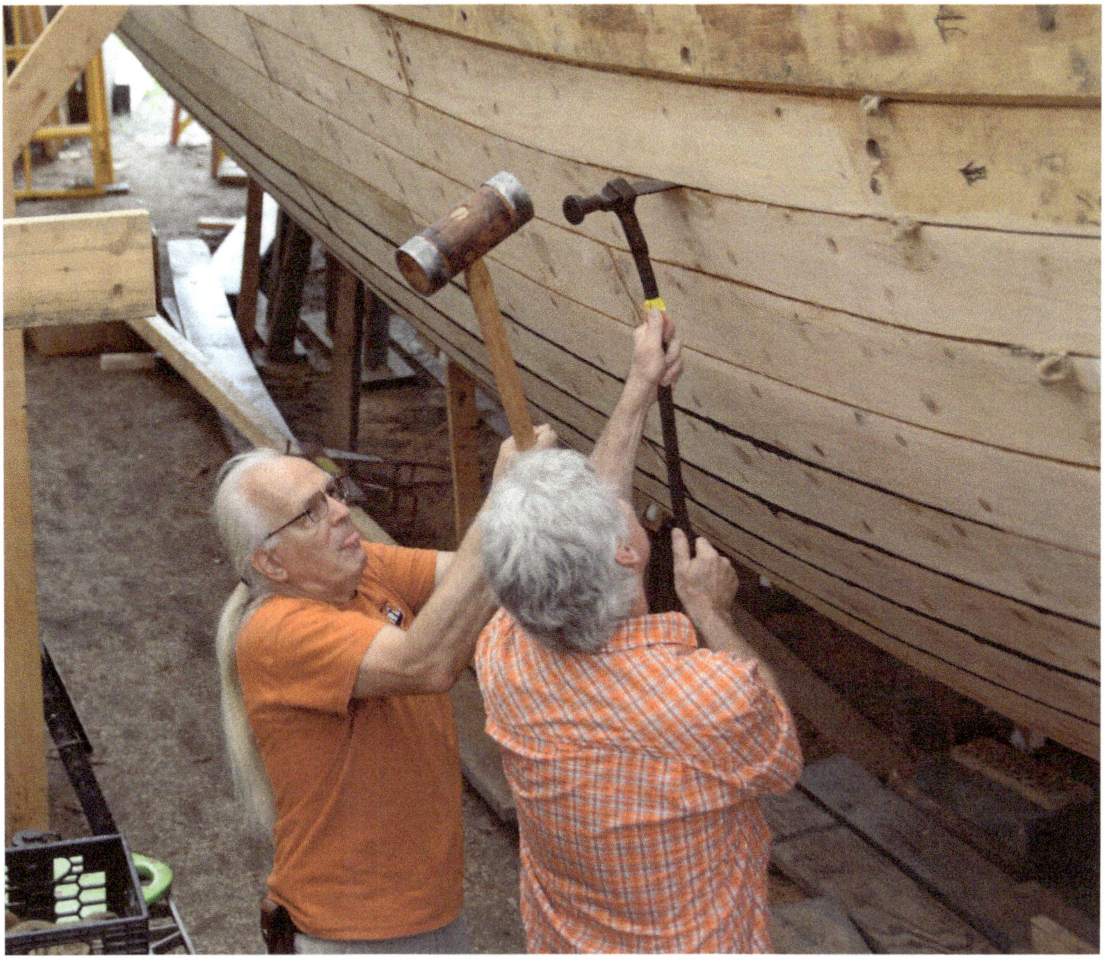

Steve Taylor (left) and Paul King compressing the caulking into the hull.

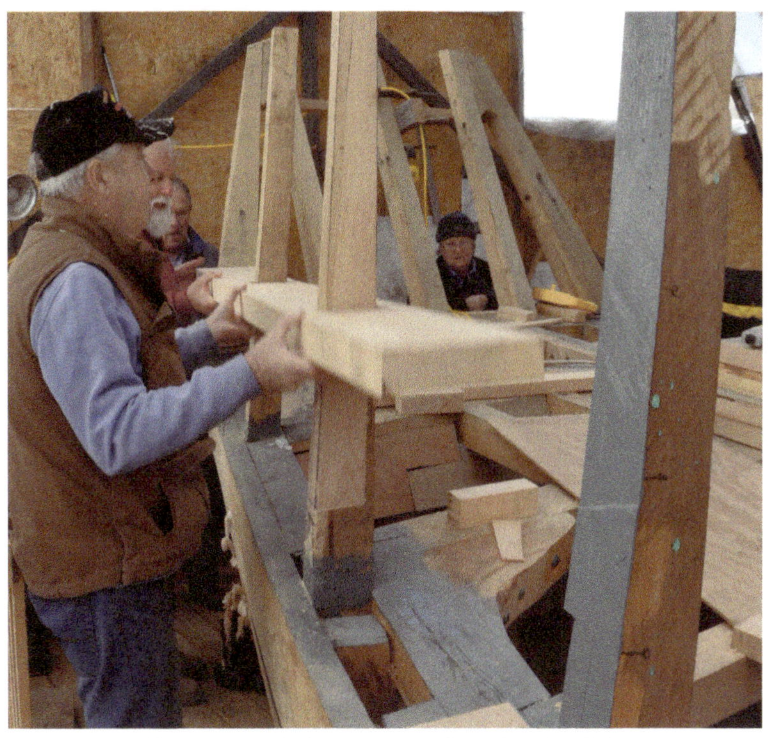

Joe Arsenault fits a covering board to the deck.

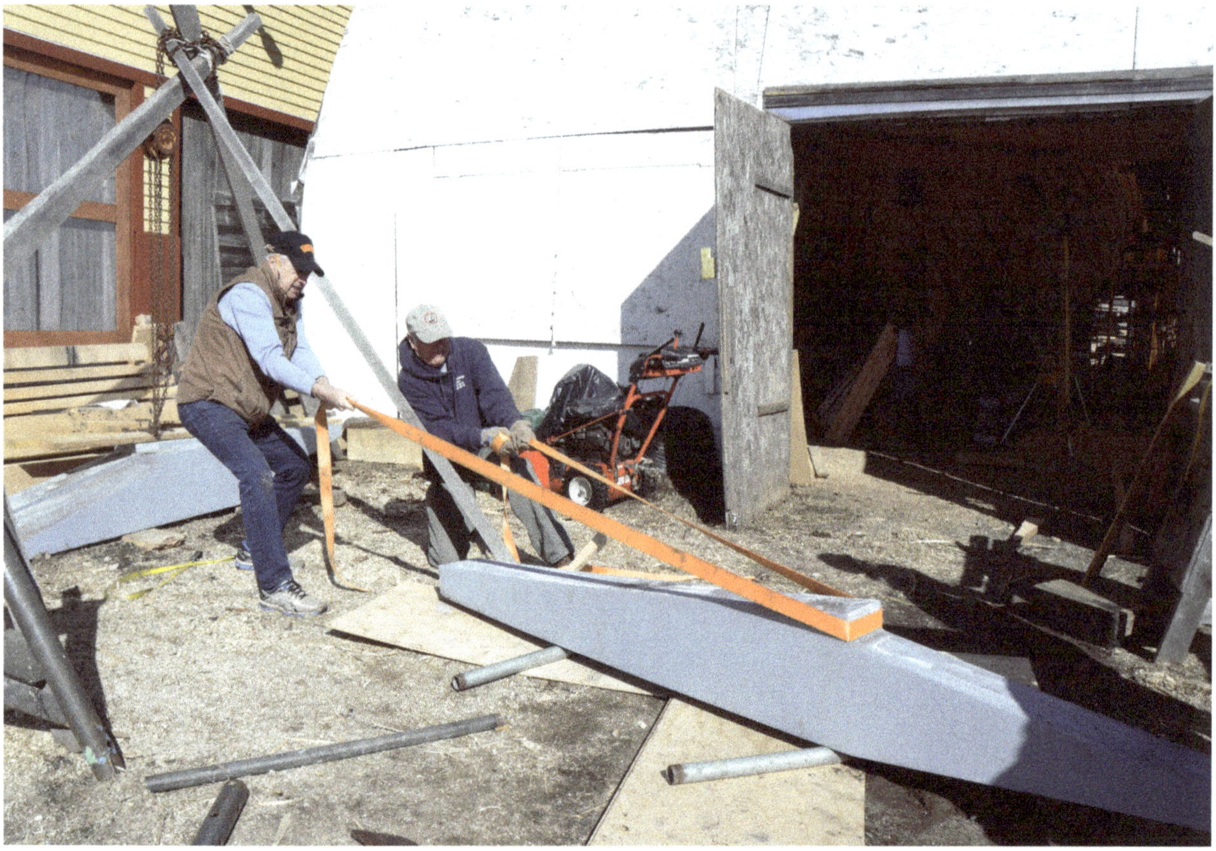

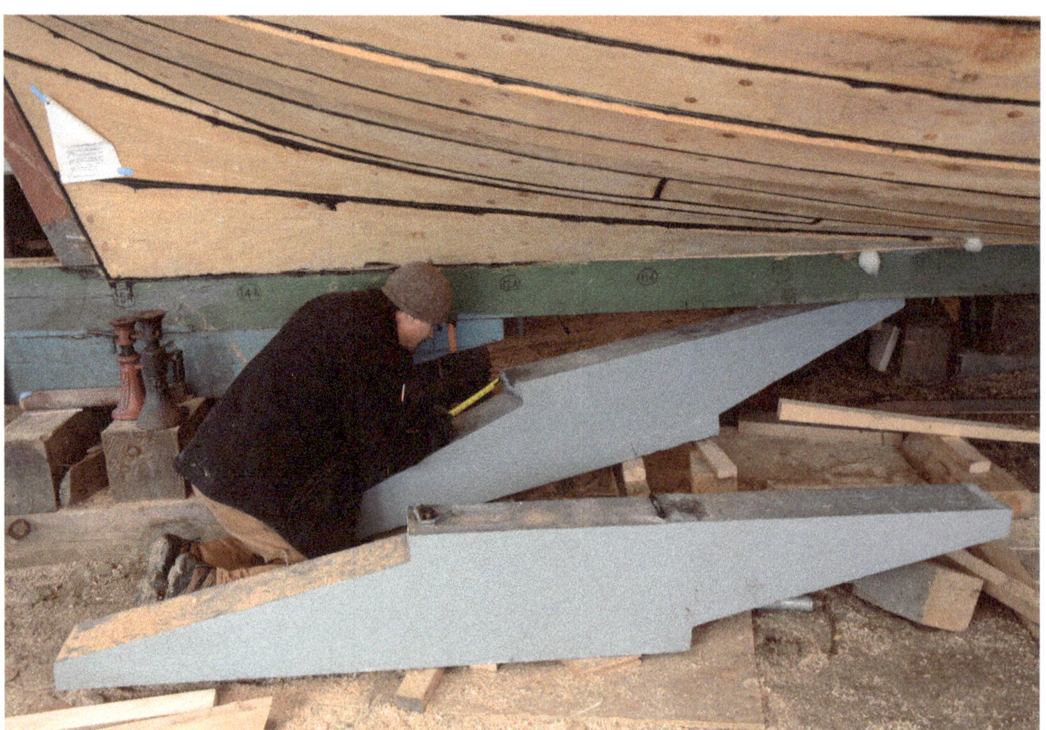

Pieces of lead ballast arrive. Each piece weighs 3,000 pounds and
must to be secured to the keel.

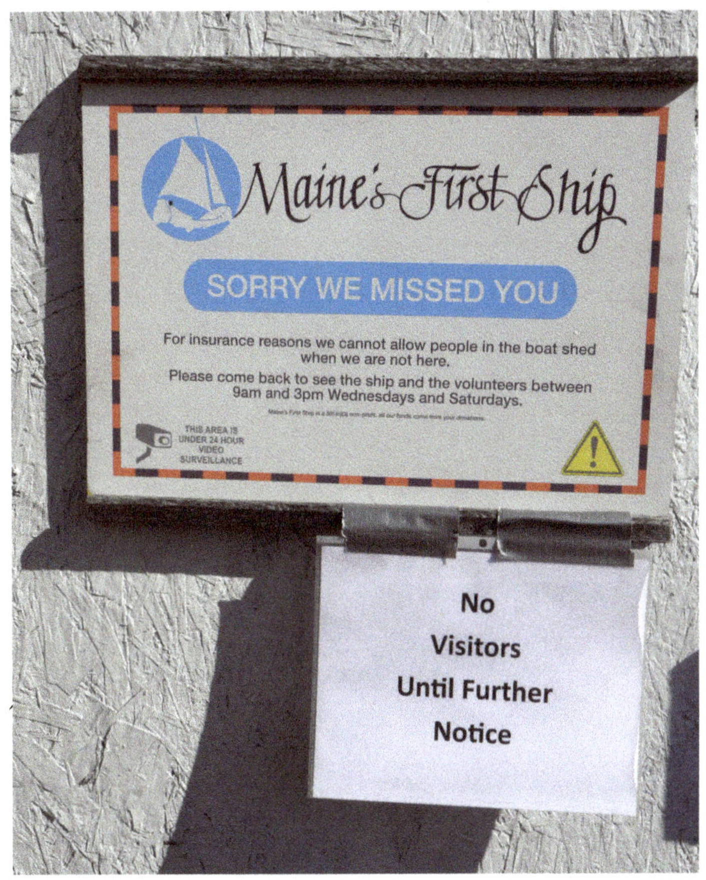

COVID stops work from April until June 2020.

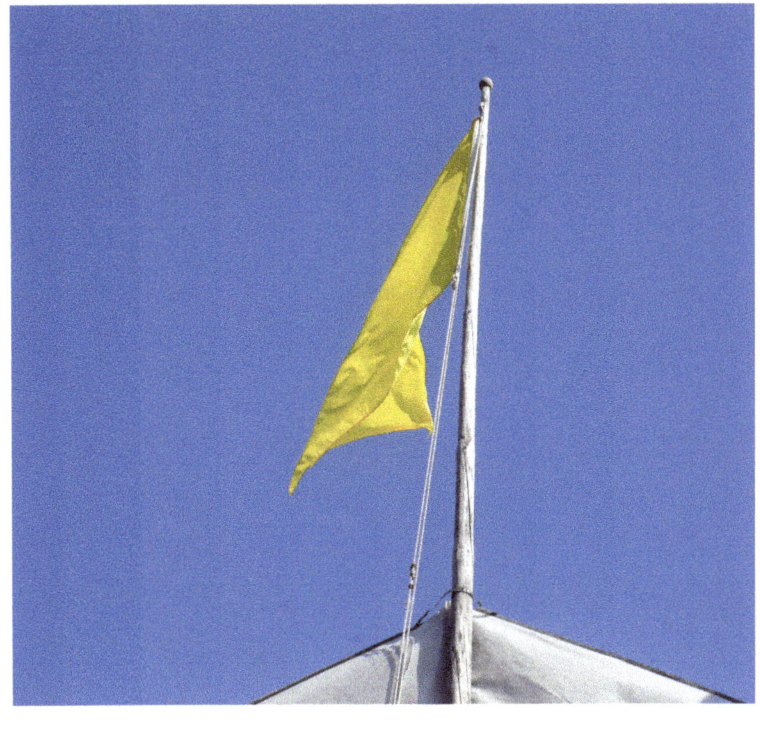

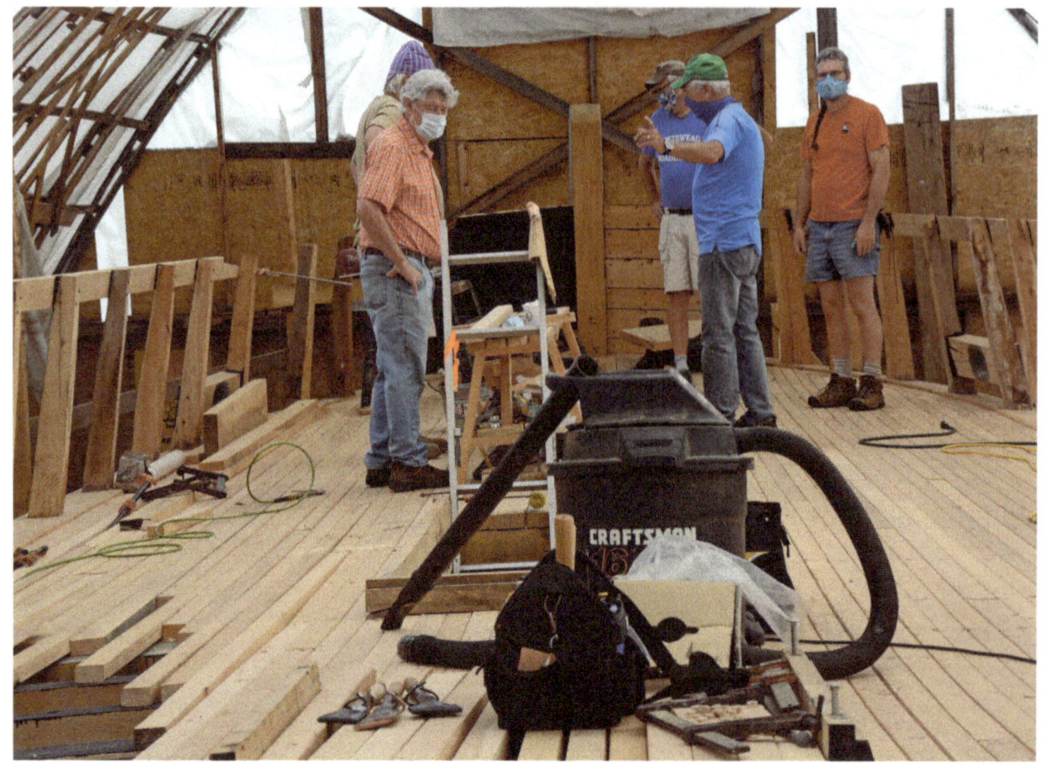

The deck is finished when work resumes.

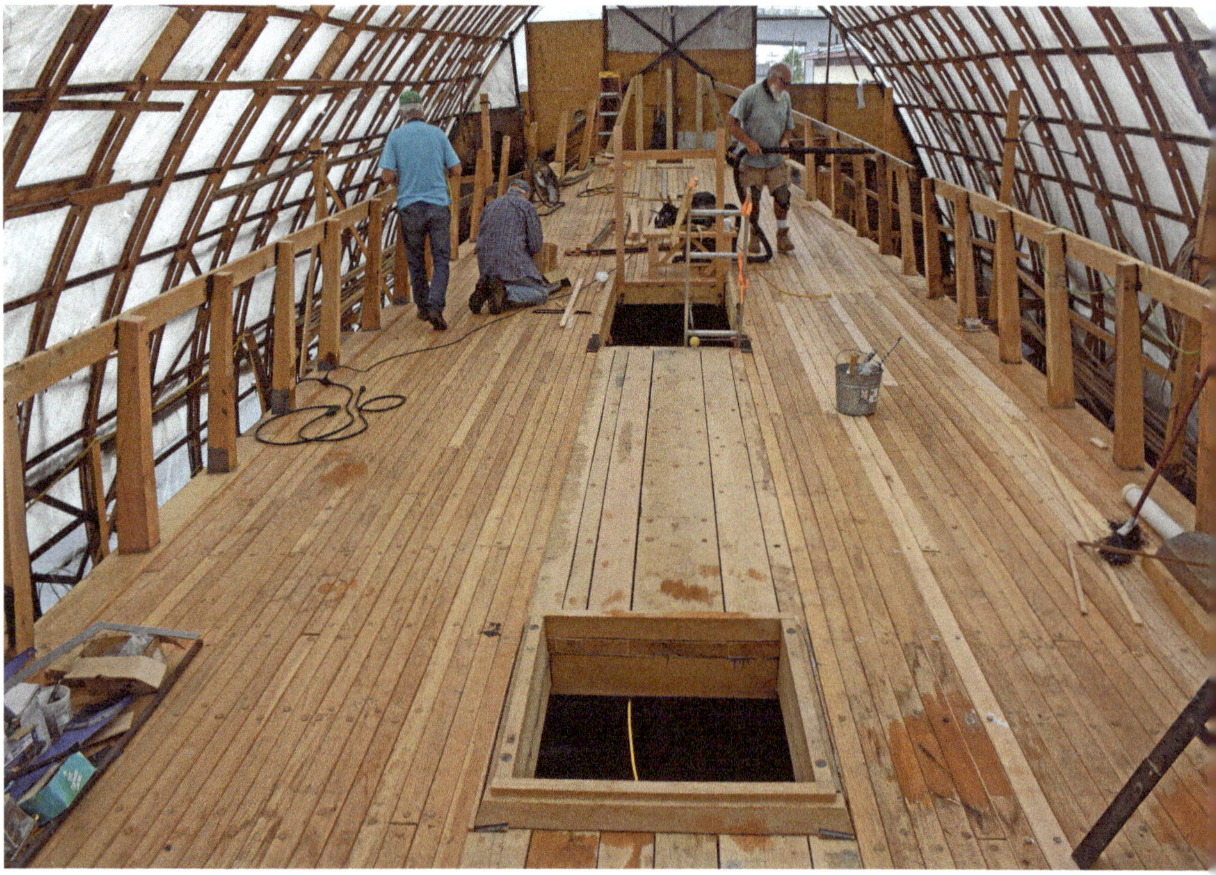

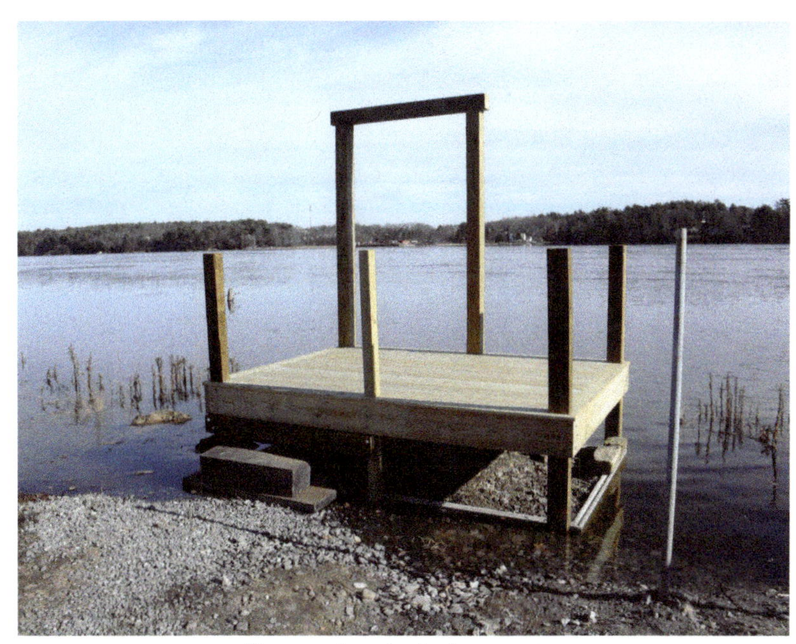

Preparations begin for our pier.

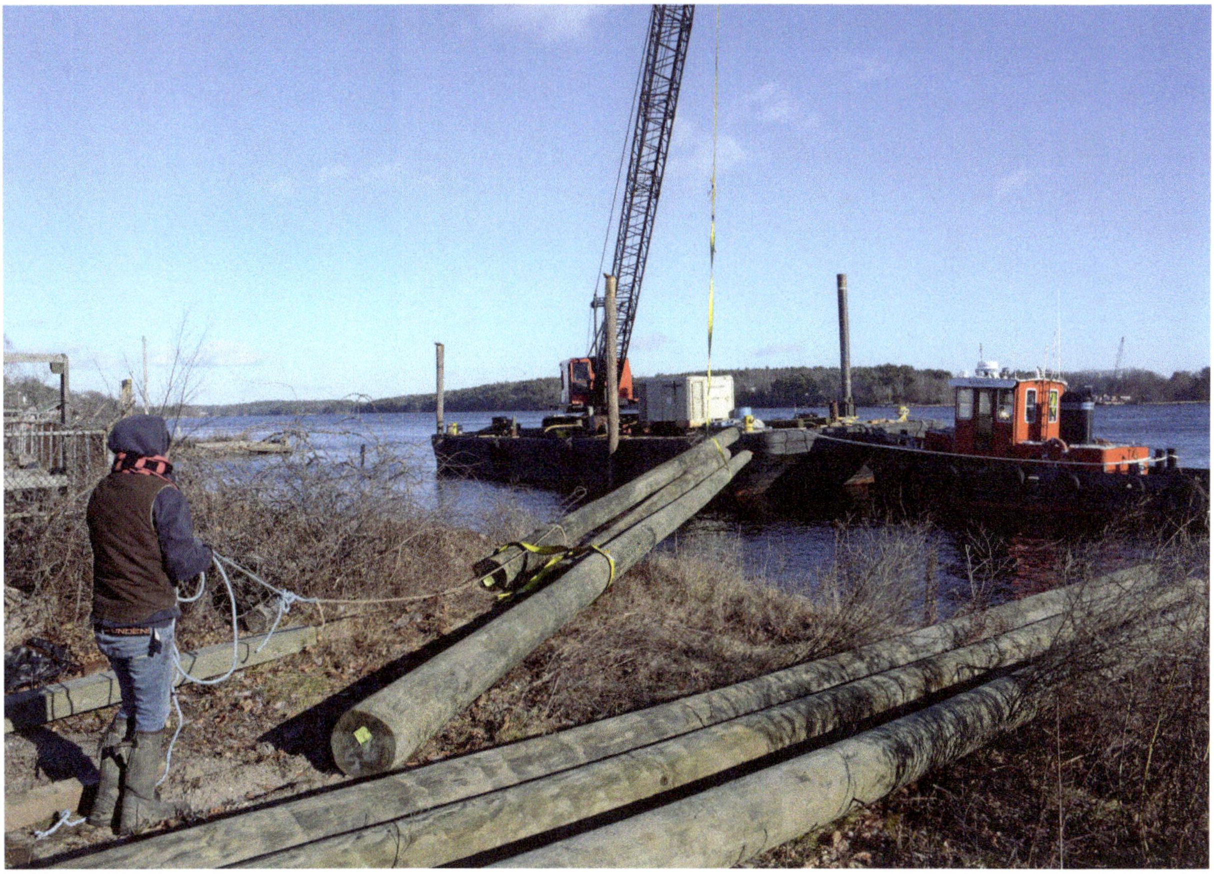

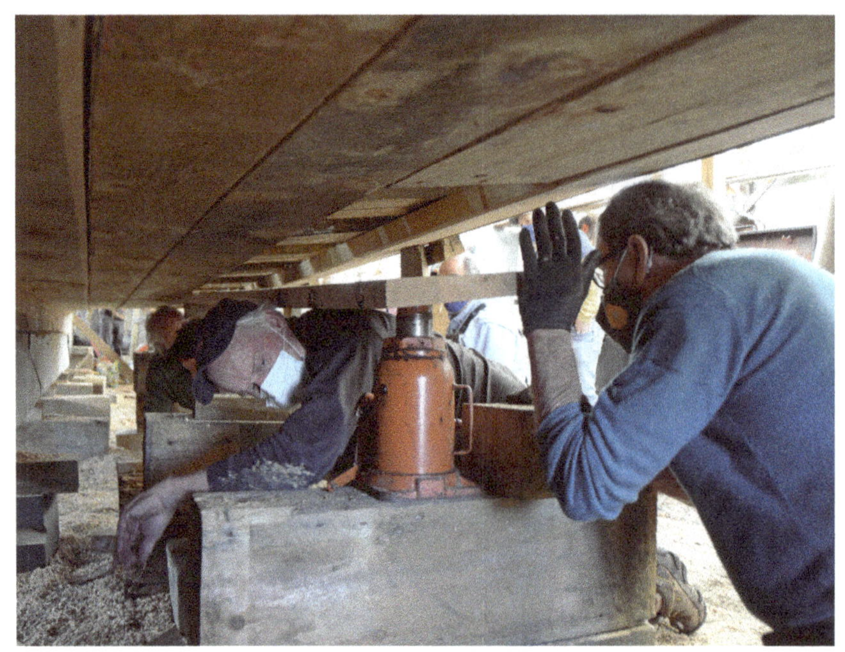

The shutter plank is installed!

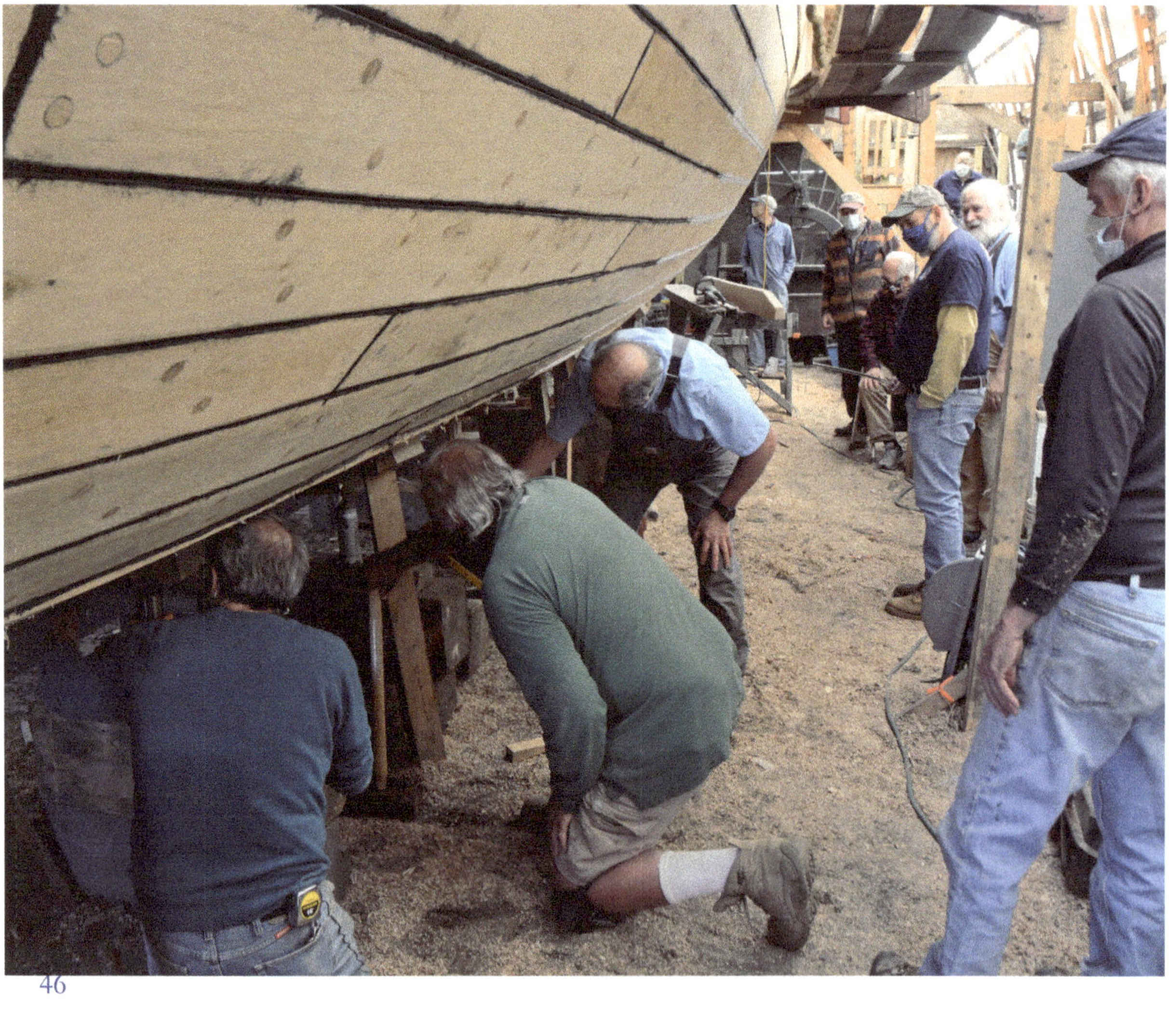

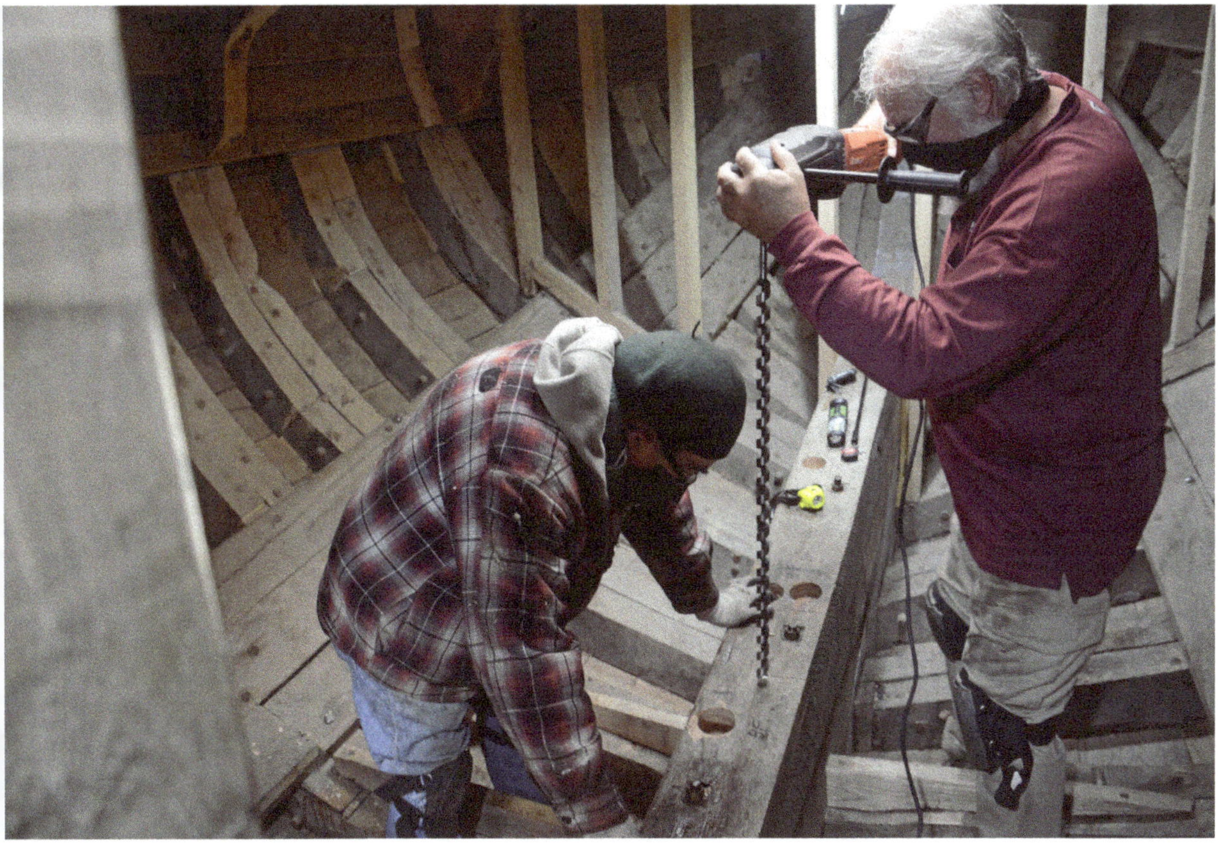

Charlie Pelletier and Jim Amundsen drill through the keel to secure the lead ballast.

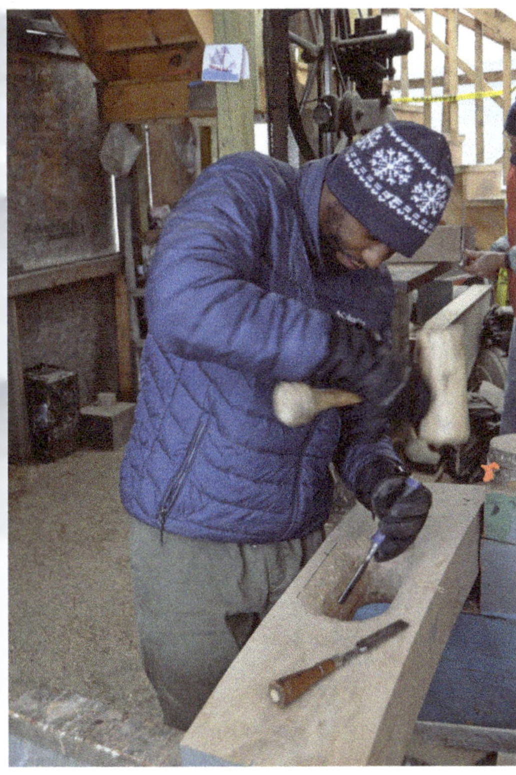

*A Navy volunteer chisels a mooring line hawesh-
ole into a piece of oak.*

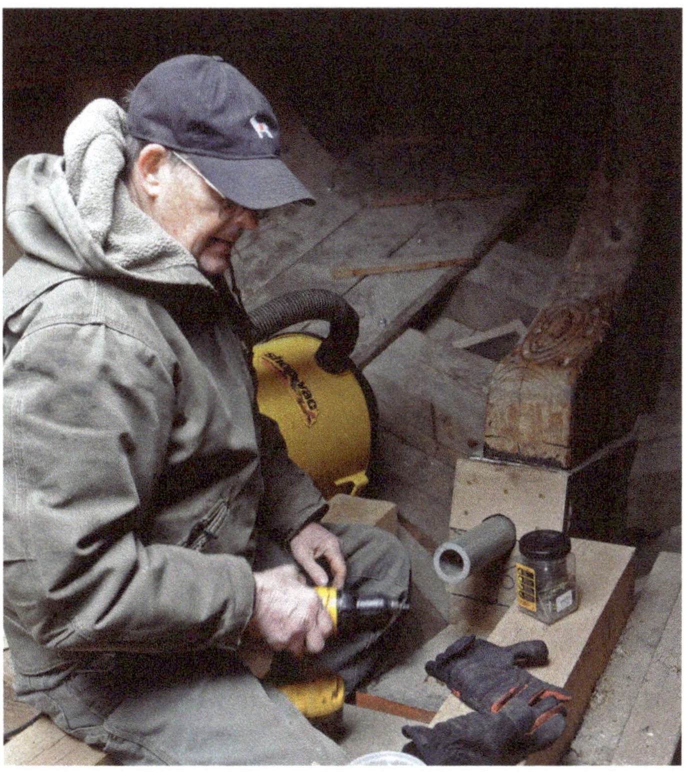

Dick Forrest works on the propellor shaft.

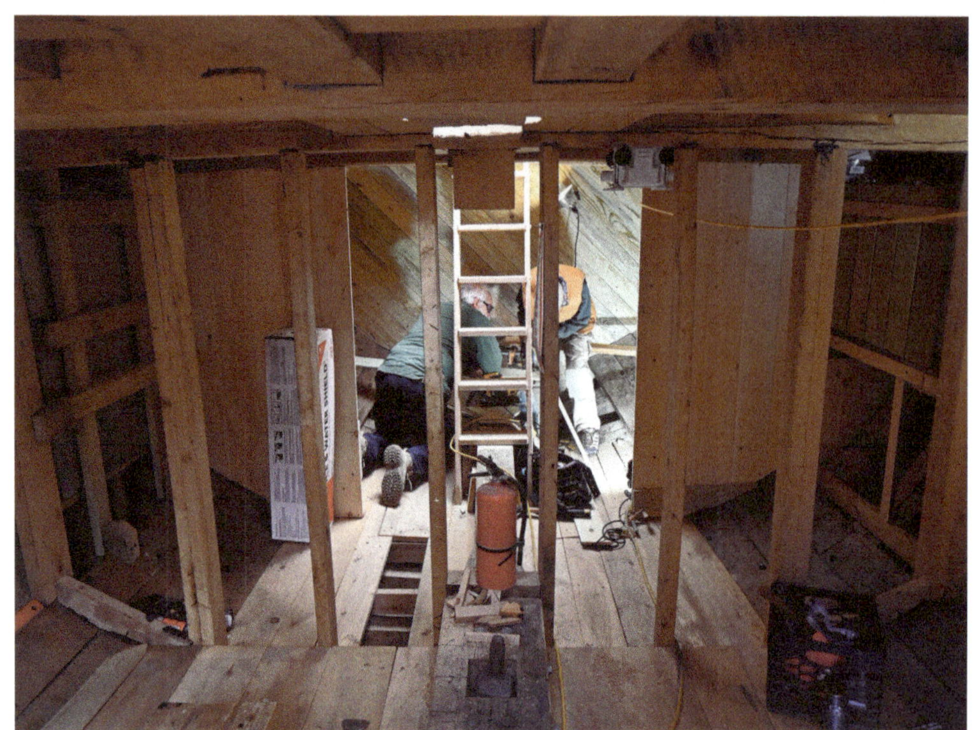

Volunteers work below deck on watertight bulkheads.

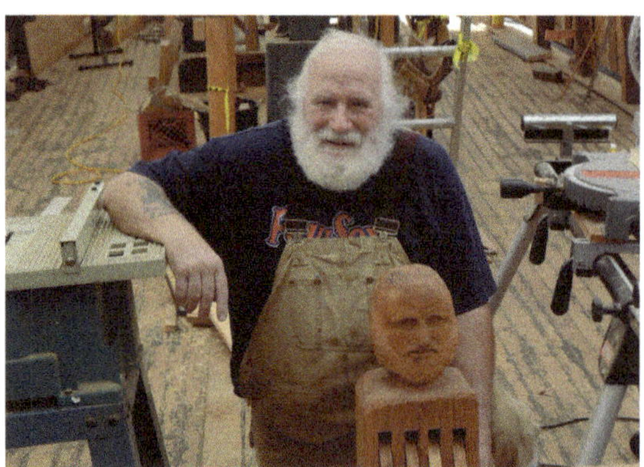

Rob Stevens and the Knighthead.

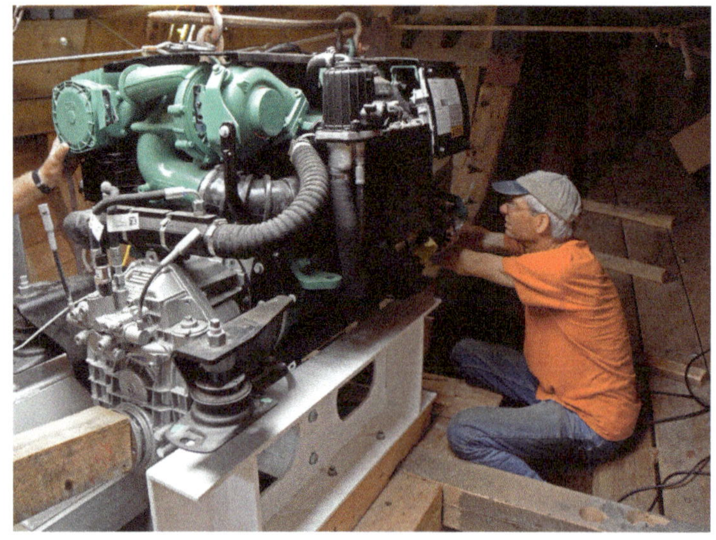

Dana Leonard installs the 175 hp Volvo Penta diesel engine.

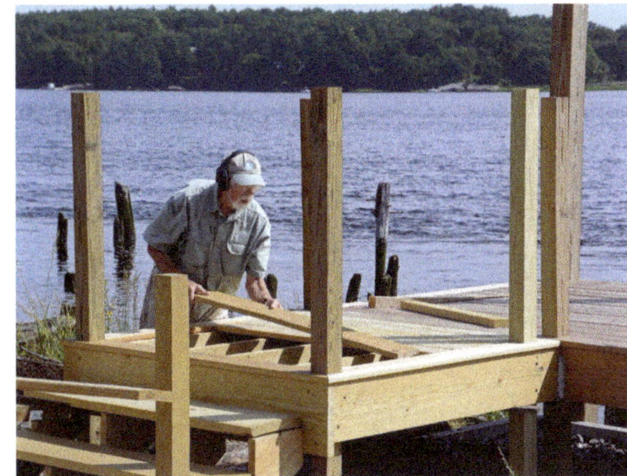

Dr. Dan Wood working on the pier.

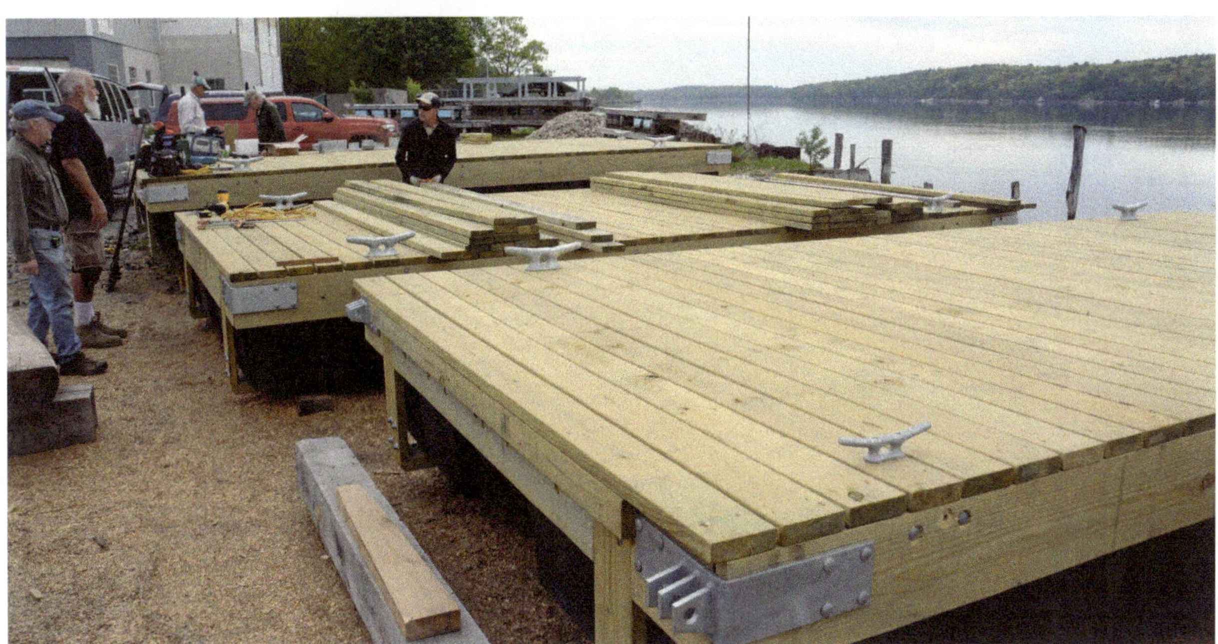

Above: Float construction completed.

Left: Fred Gosbee constructs the windlass.
Below: The windlass awaits installation.

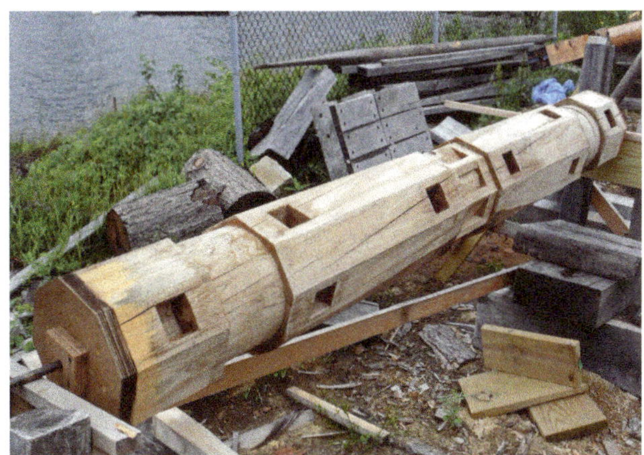

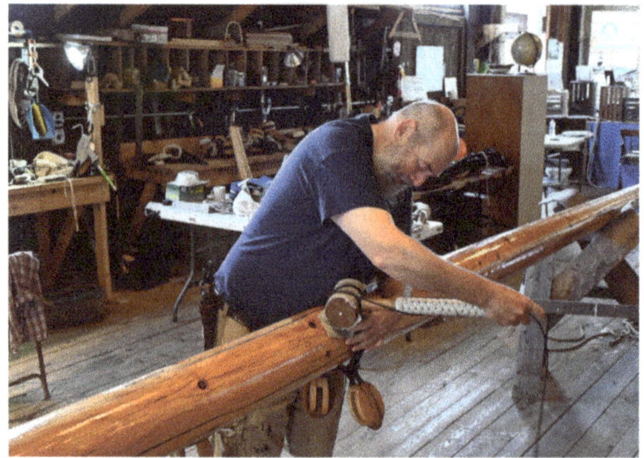

Head rigger Jim Nelson hard at work.

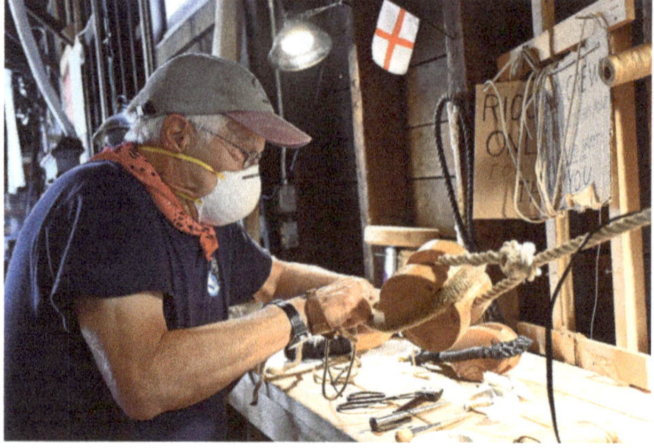

David Bellow, another rigger, working with a block.

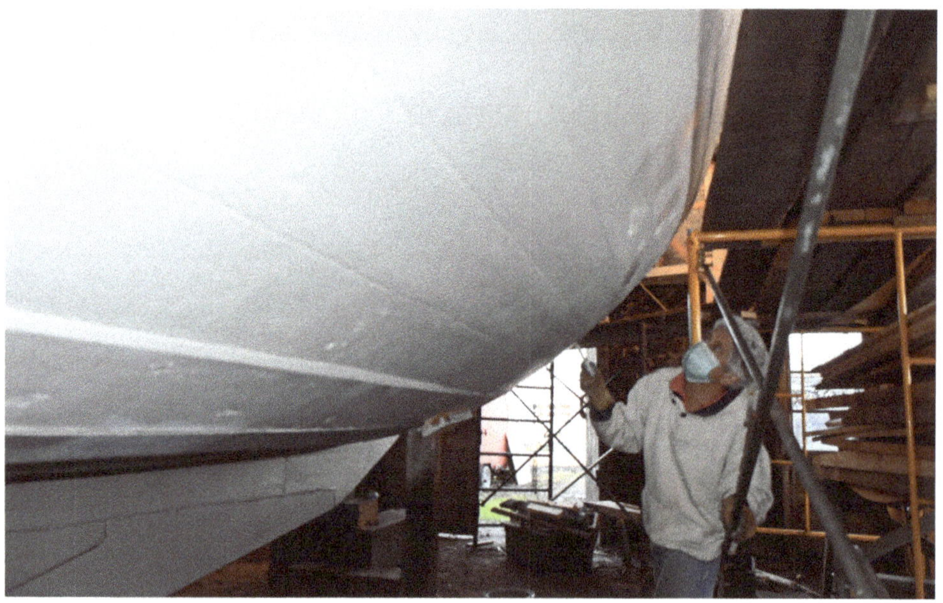

Elise Straus-Bowers painting the hull.

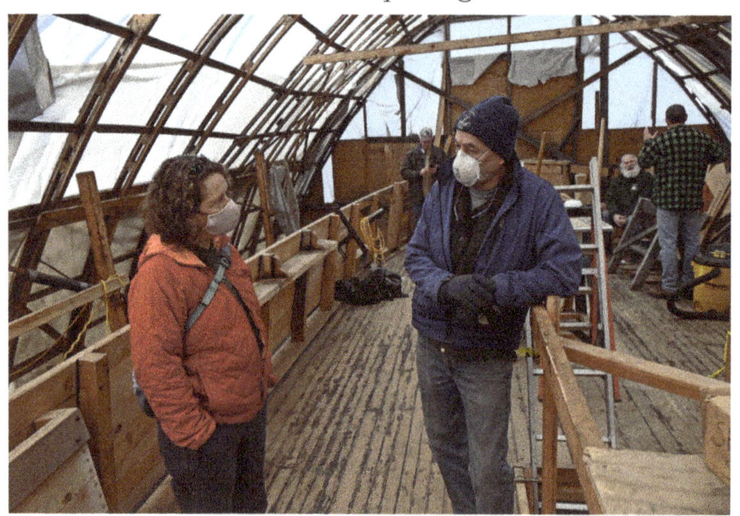

Roger Barry meets the new Executive Director, Kirstie Truluck.

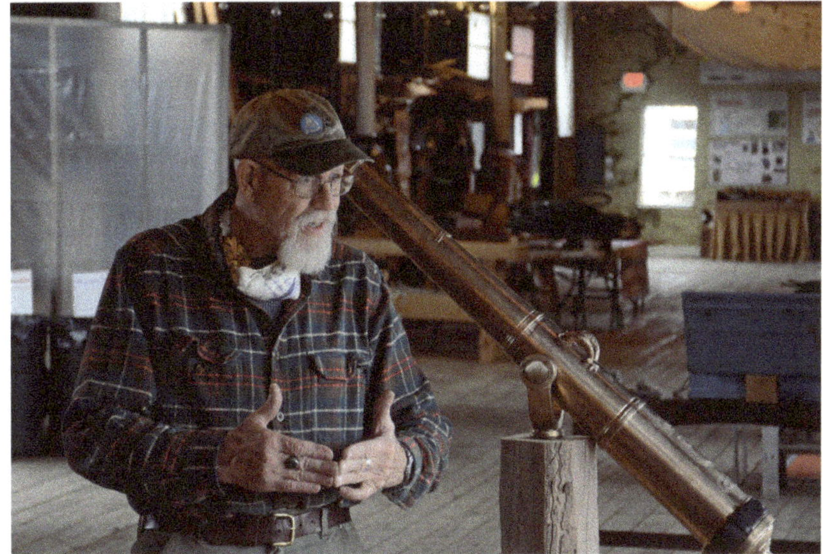

A class on the operation of our two new cannons by Tom Tomlinson.

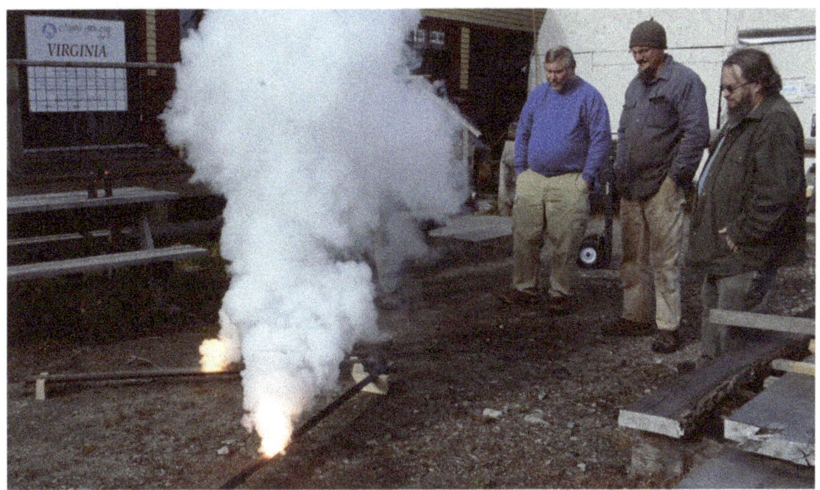

Volunteers watching the speed of two different powders burning.

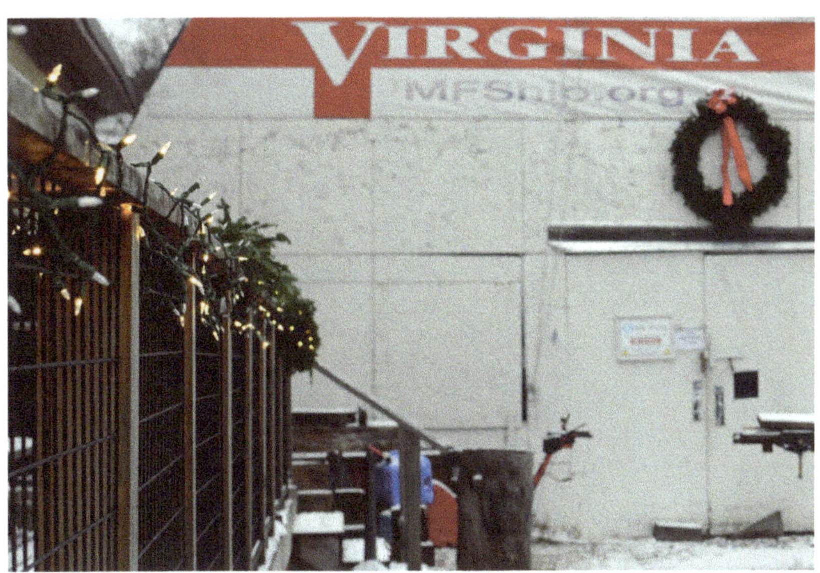

Another year ends.

"Weathah"

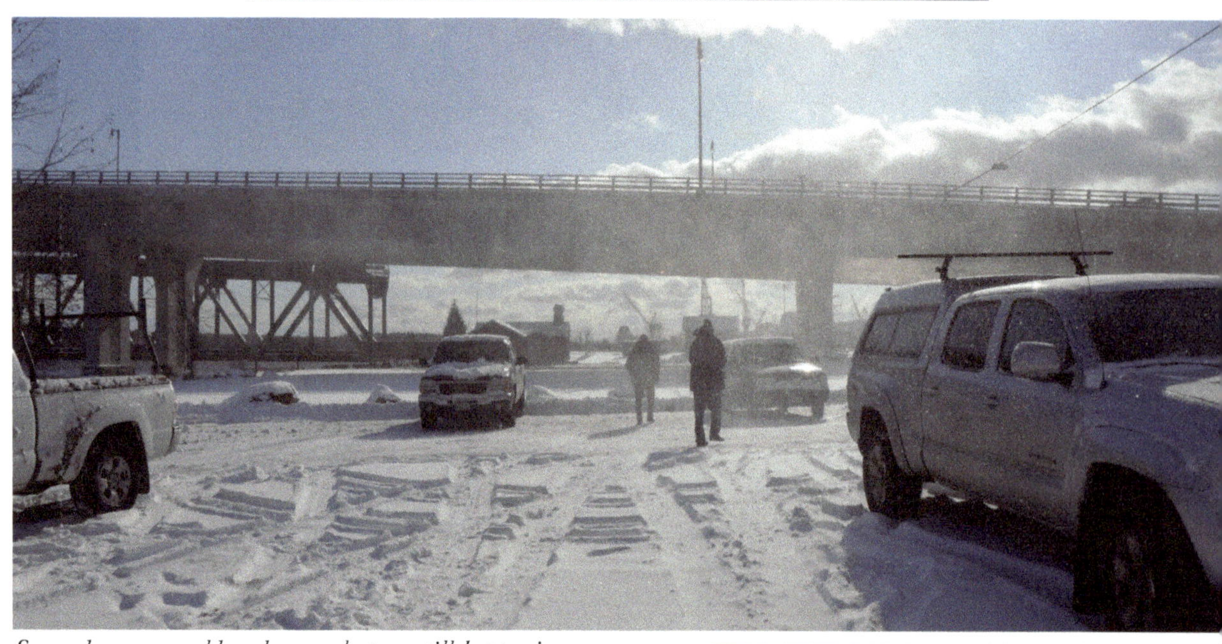

Some days were cold and snowy but we still kept going.

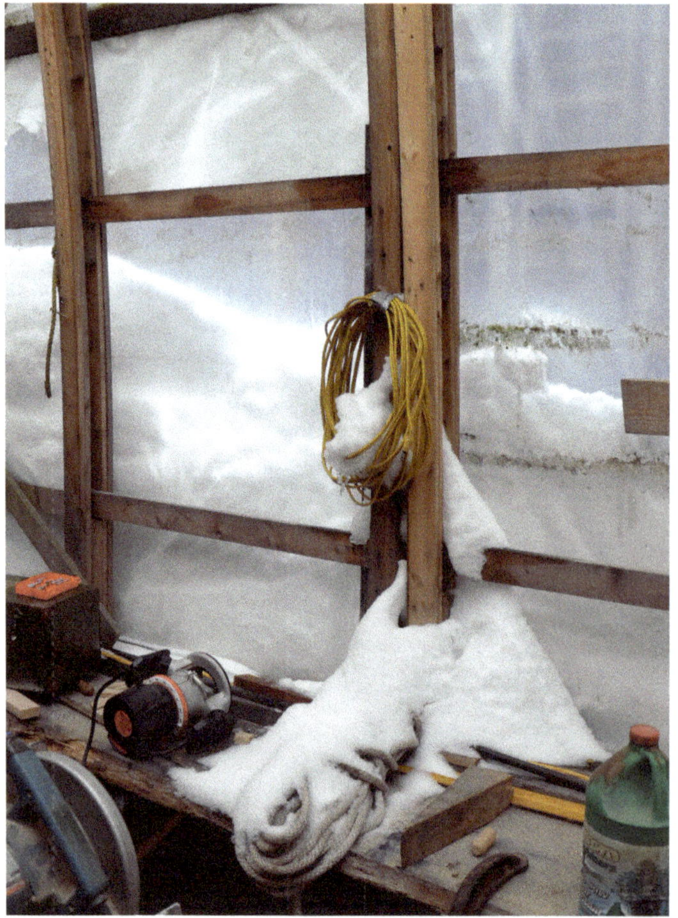

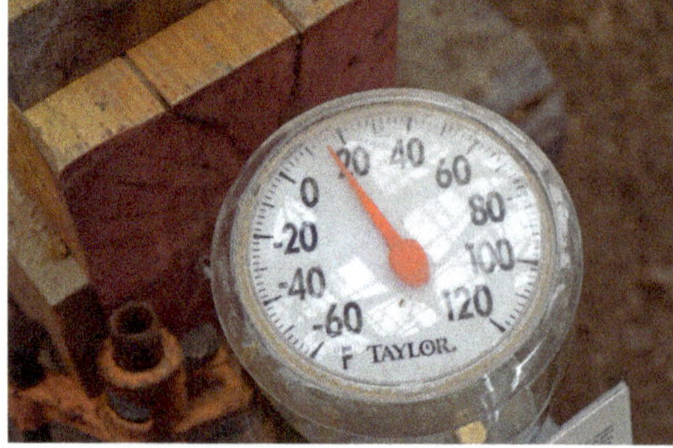

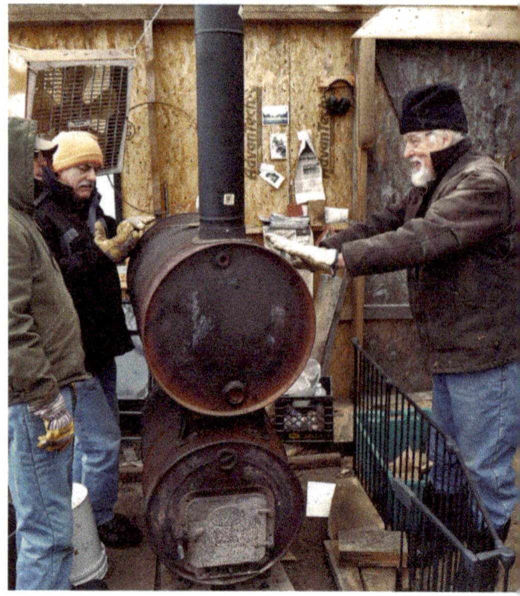

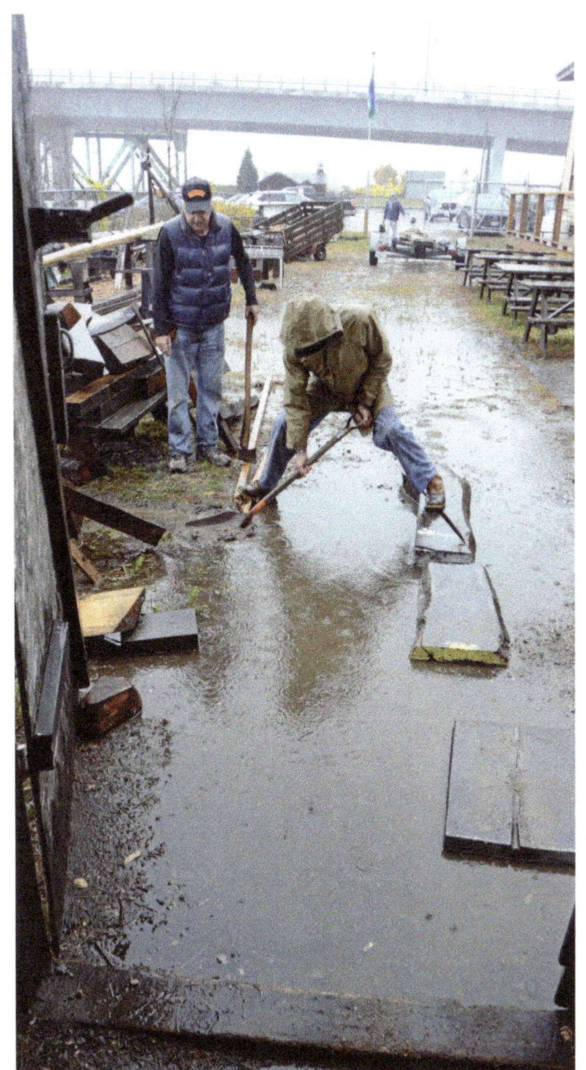

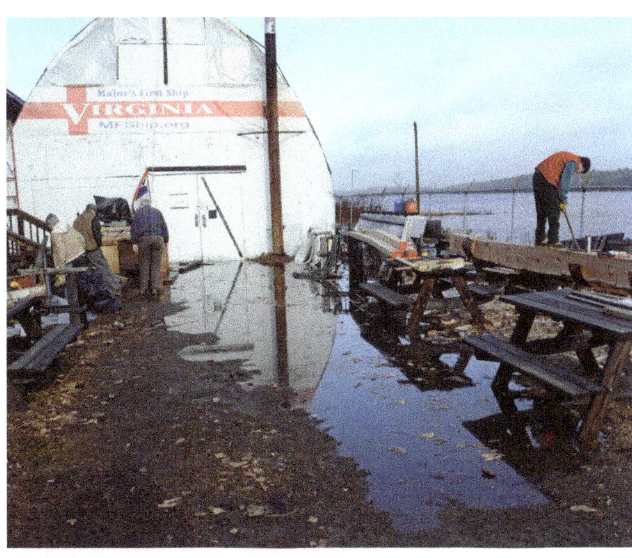

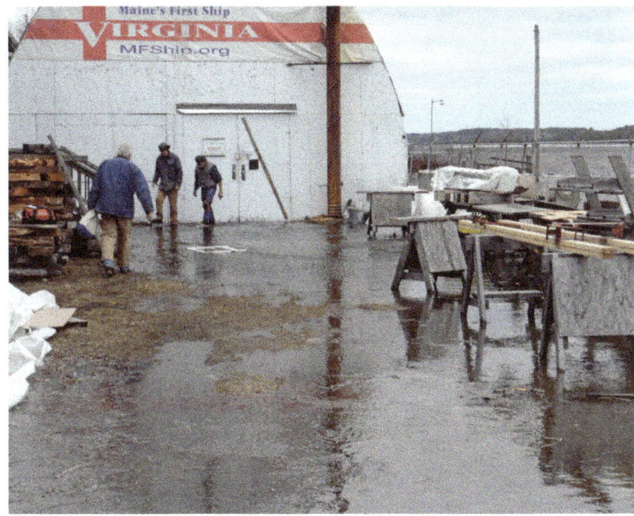

Other times, we dealt with floods and heat, and still we continued building.

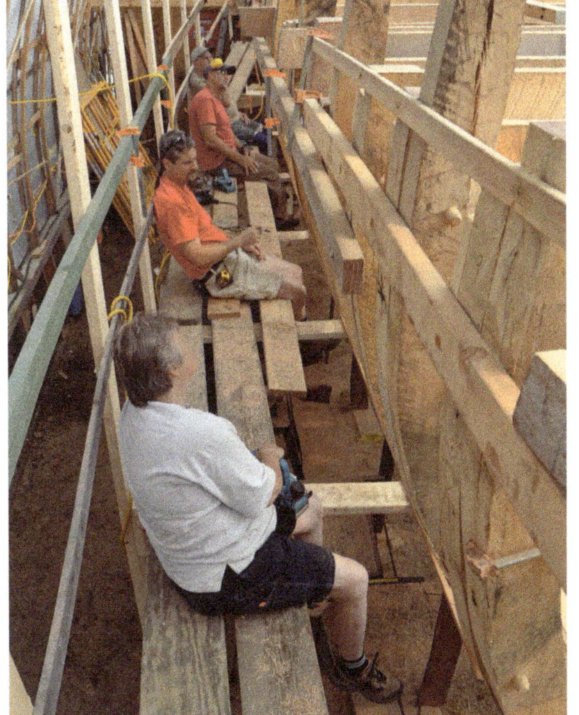

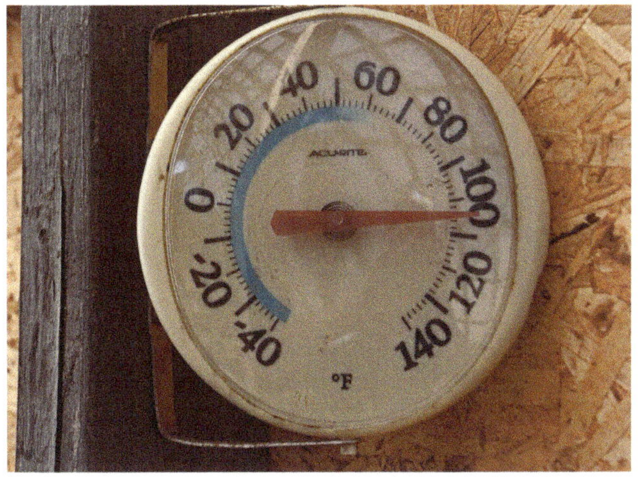

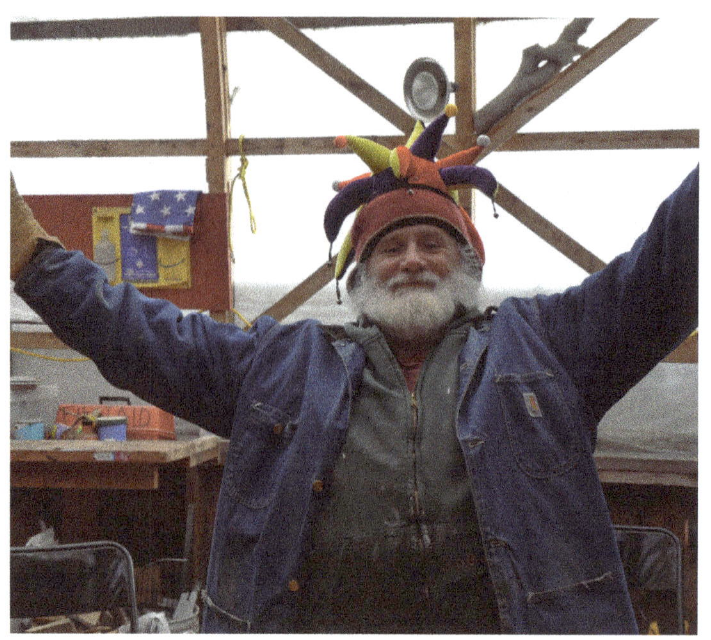

The Lighter Side

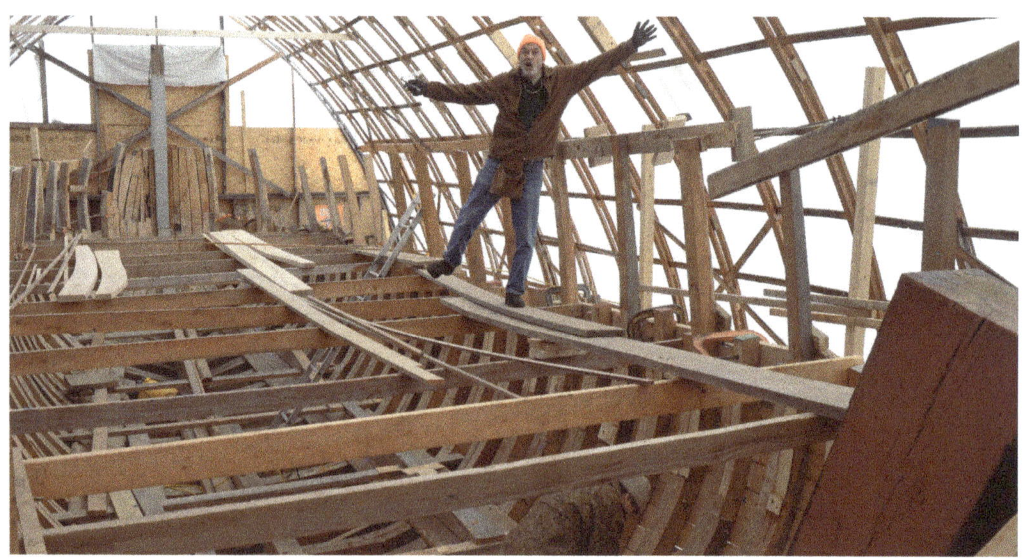

Rob Stevens (top), Roger Barry (above), and Dick Forrest with Roger (below).

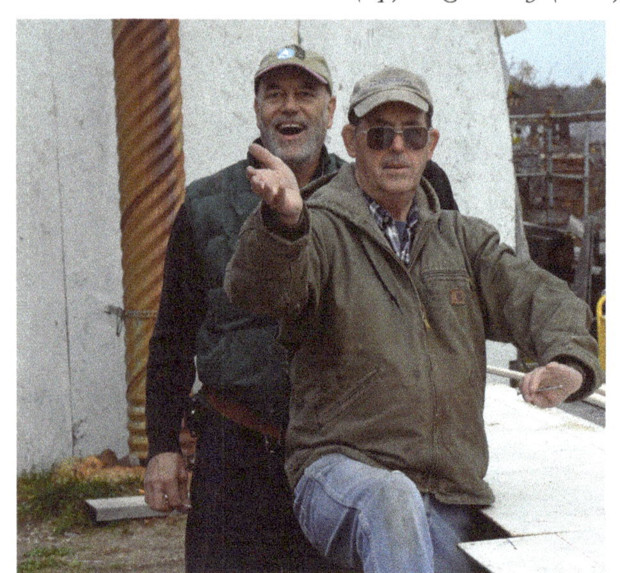

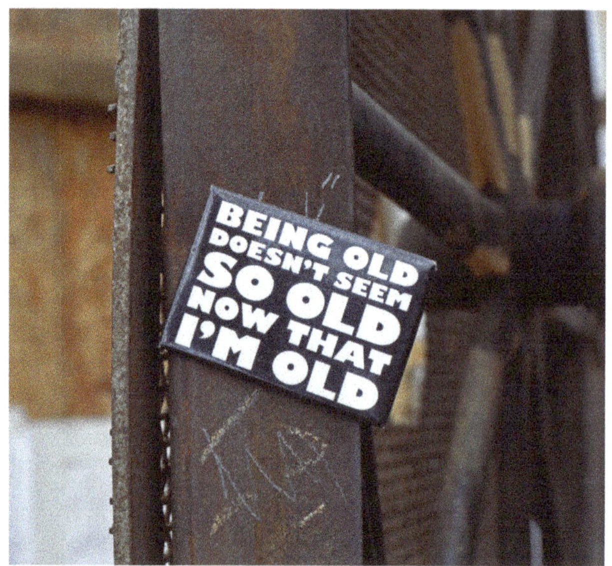

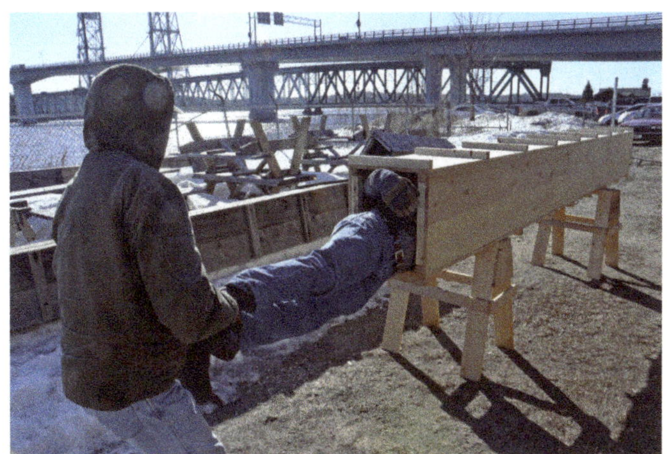

Shenanigans at the steamer.

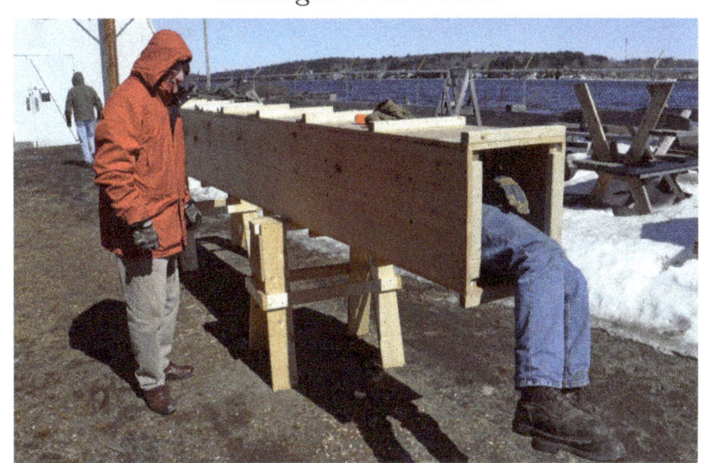

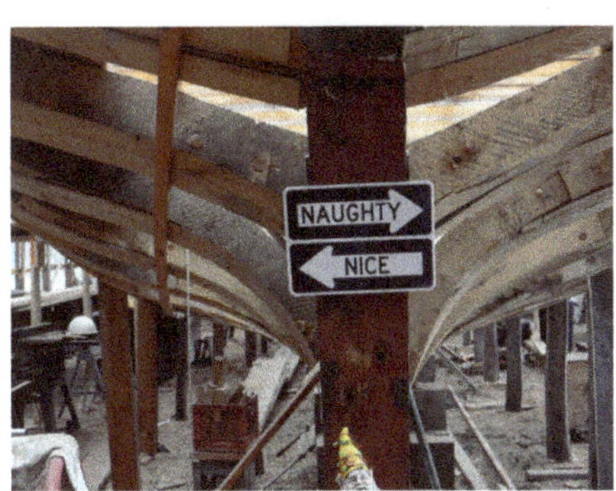

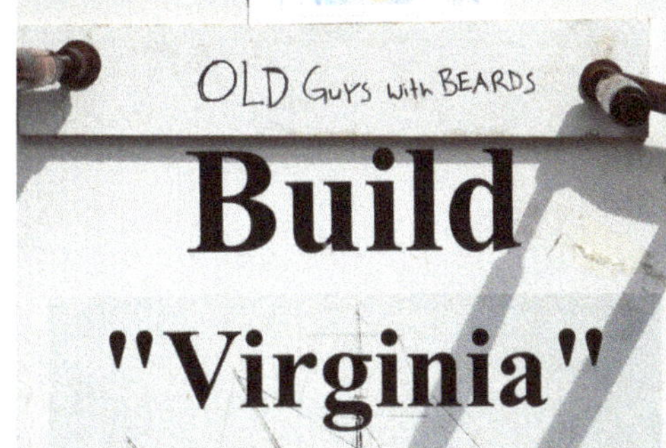

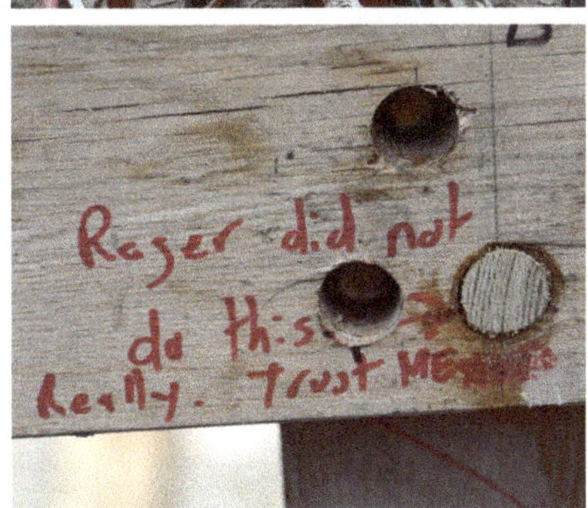

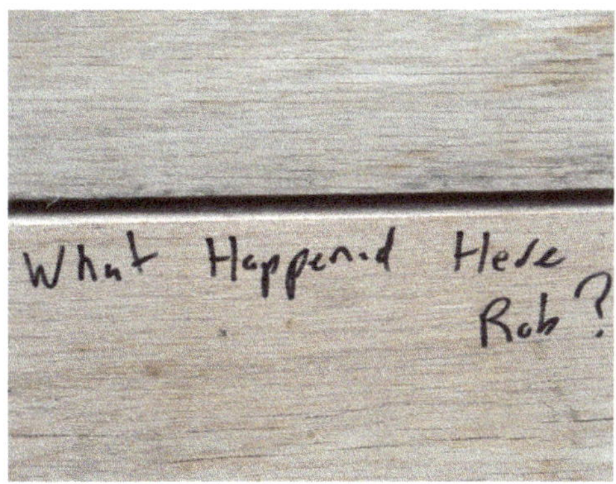

Here's your sign!

Mascots

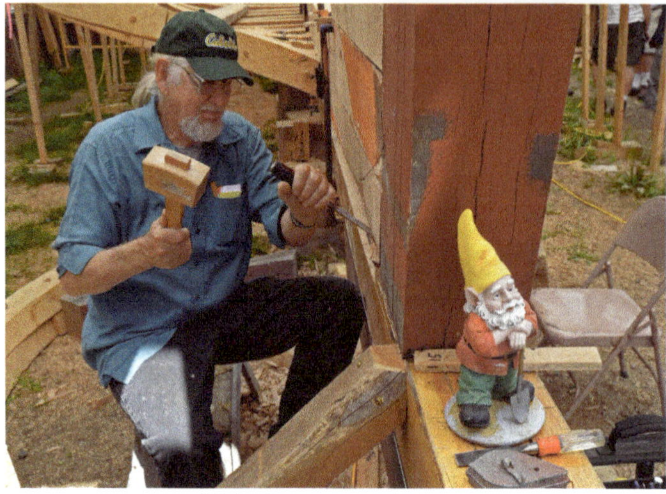

Help from unusual places.

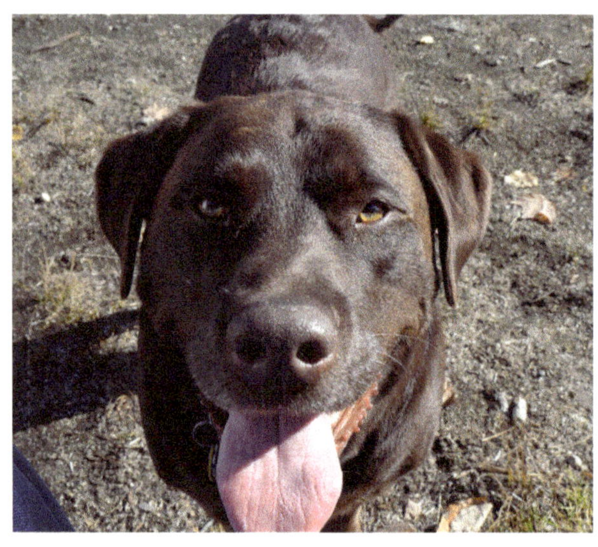

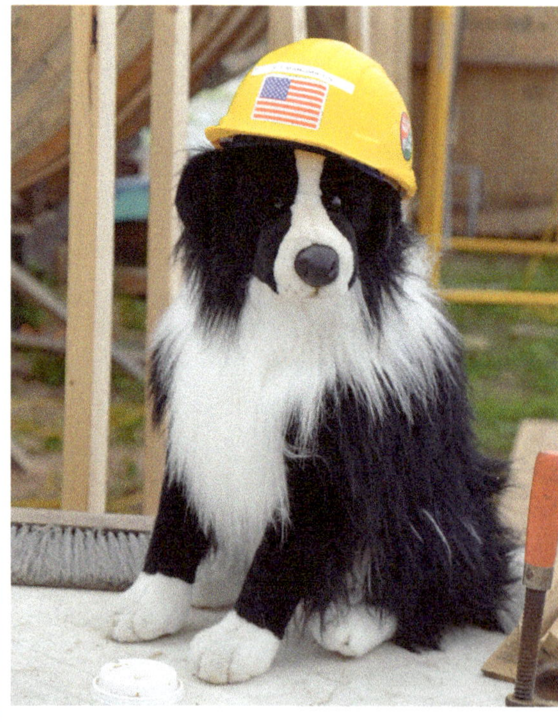

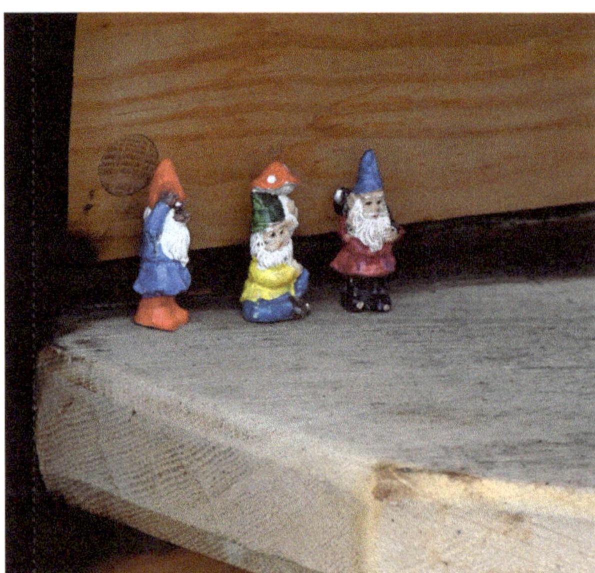

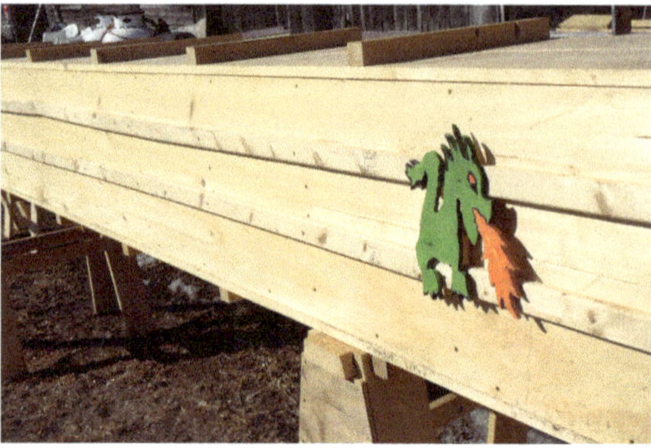

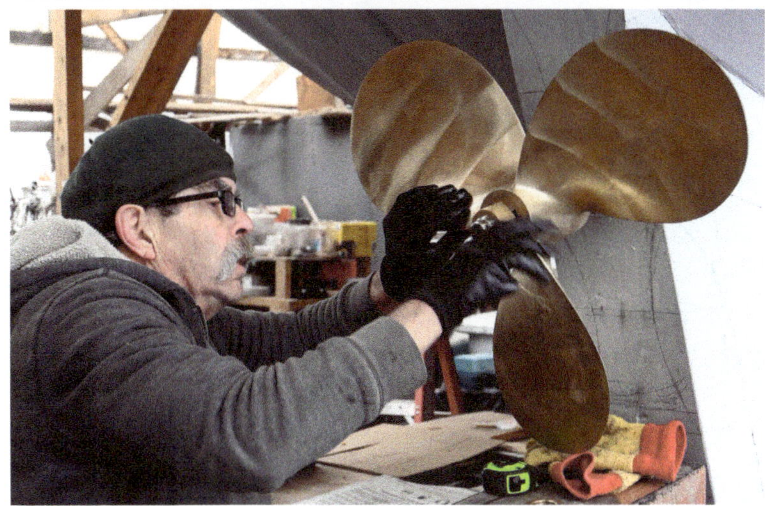

Charlie Pelletier attaches the propellor as we head down the home stretch.

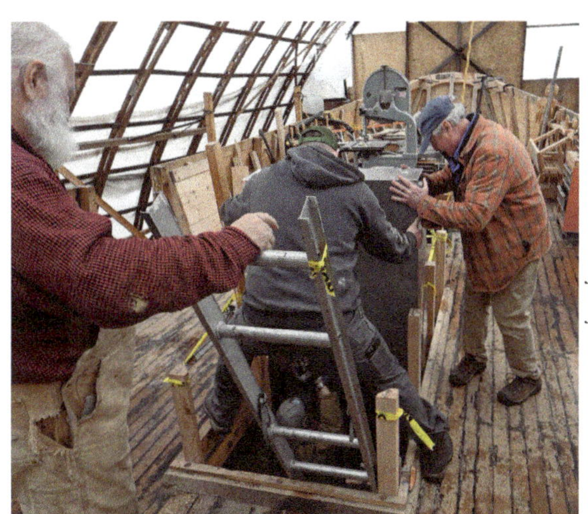

Paul King and other volunteers lower the fuel tank into position for installation.

Jim Admundsen and Charlie Pelletier assemble the companionway ladder that Charlie built at home.

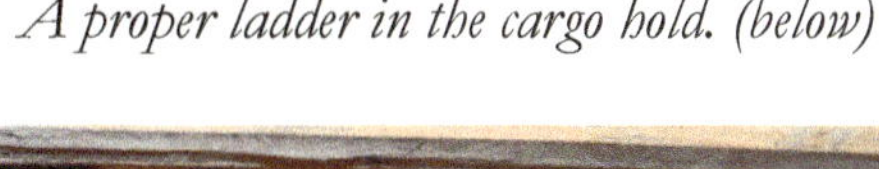

A proper ladder in the cargo hold. (below)

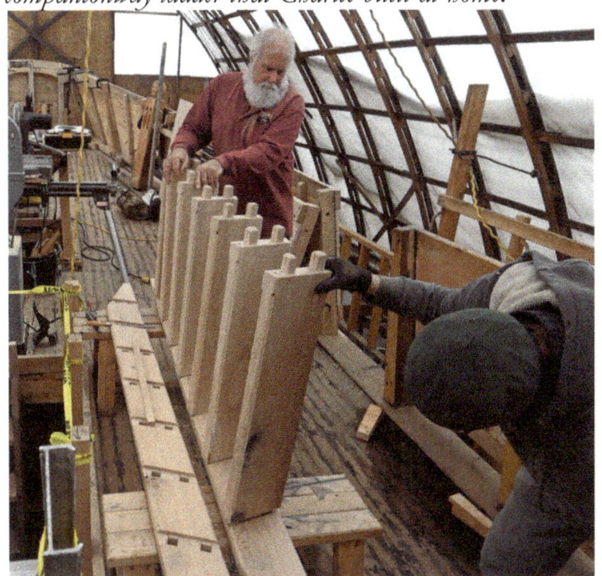

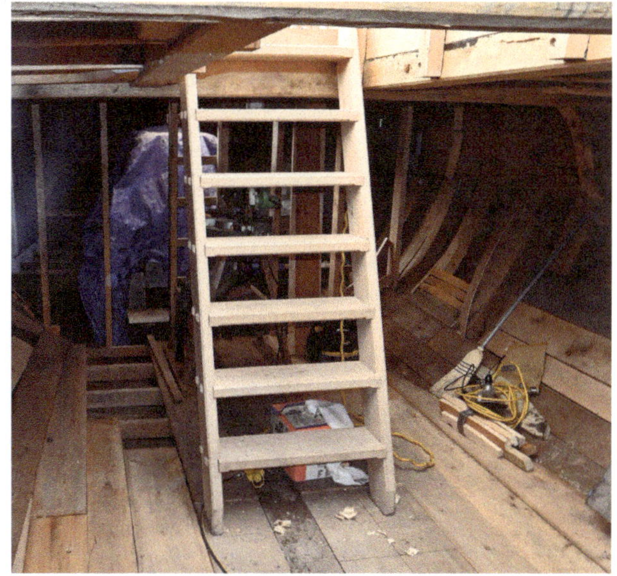

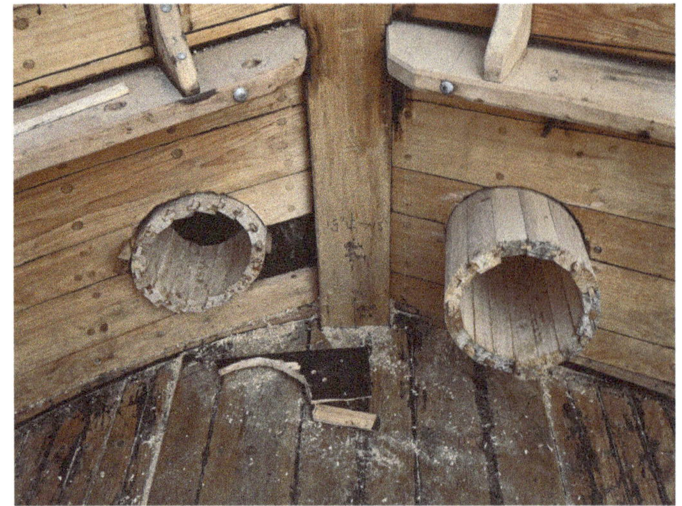

Roughed in hawesholes.

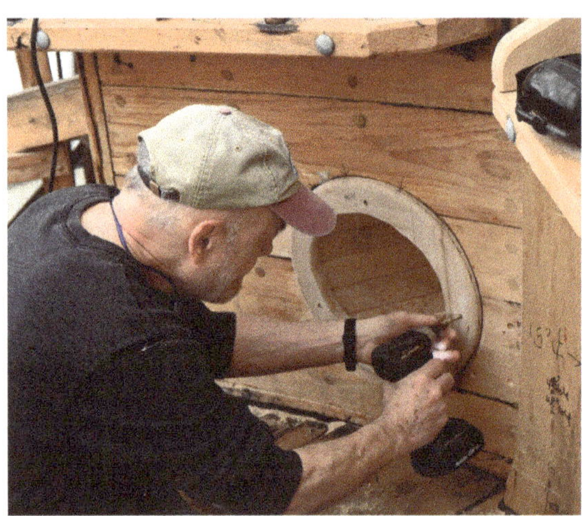

Roger Barry installs a faceplate onto the haweshole.

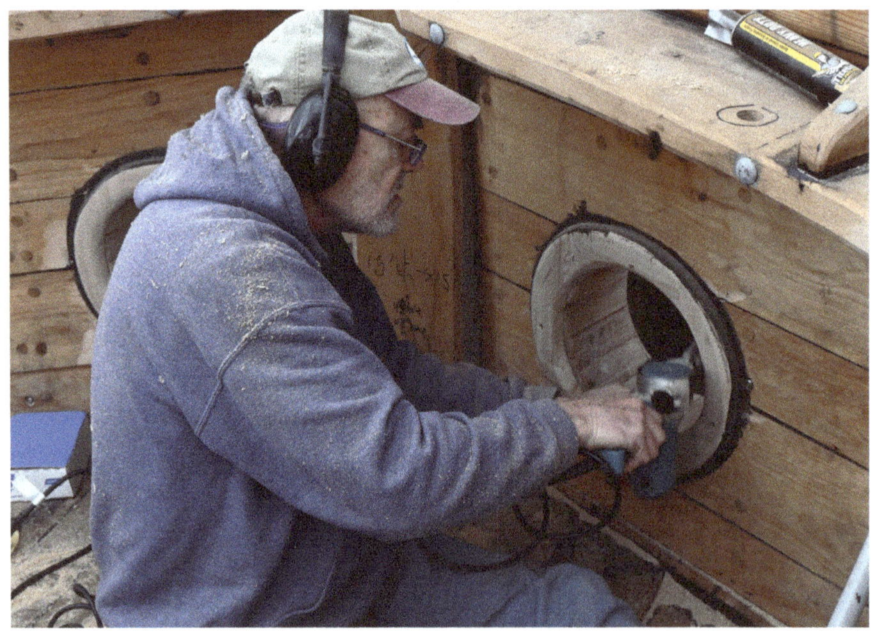

Roger finishes with a final sanding.

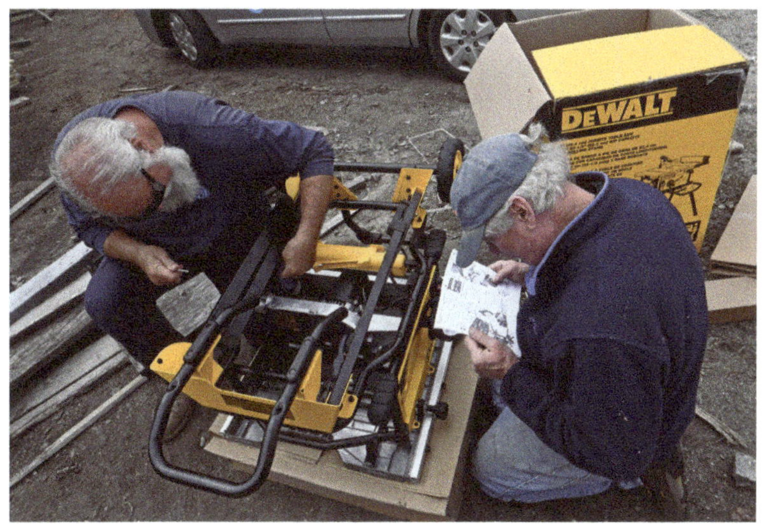

Jim Amundsen and Paul King assemble our new table saw.

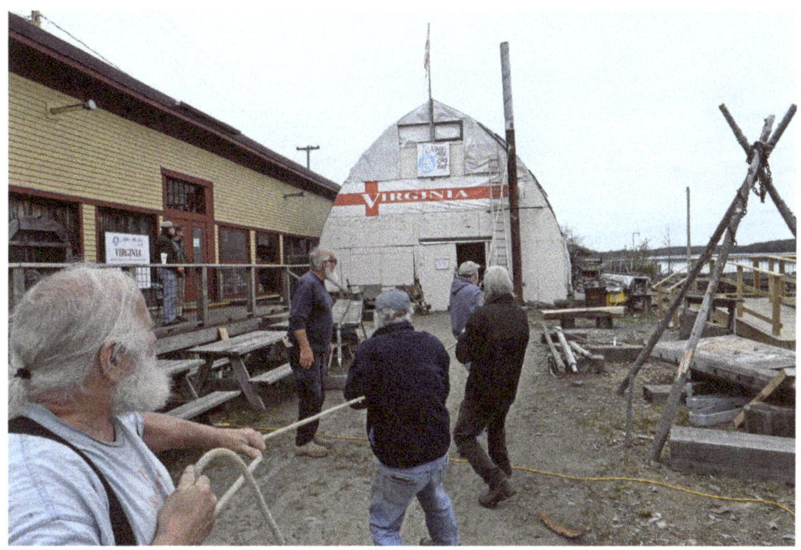

Pulling down the wood stove chimney pipe as launch day nears.

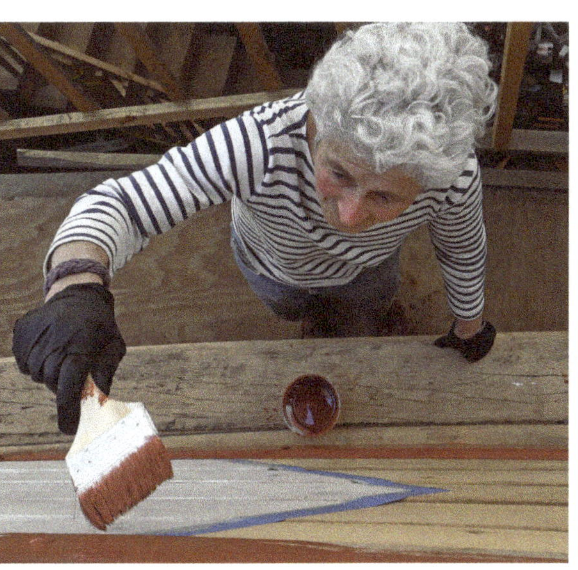

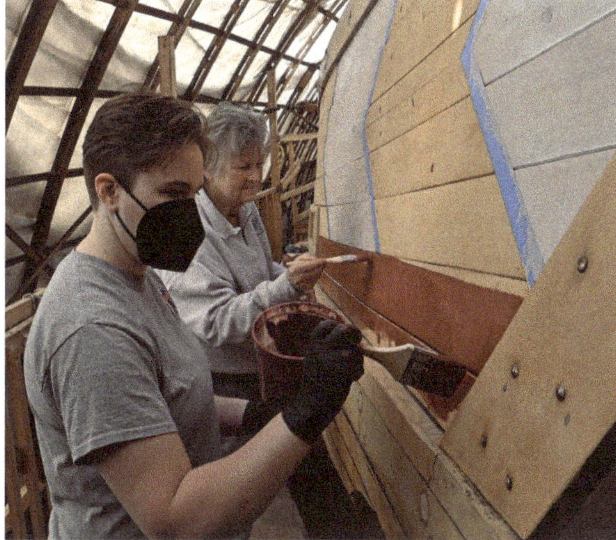

Elise Strauss-Bowers (left), Rowan Blaiklock (right) and Gail Smith (back) paint the hull.

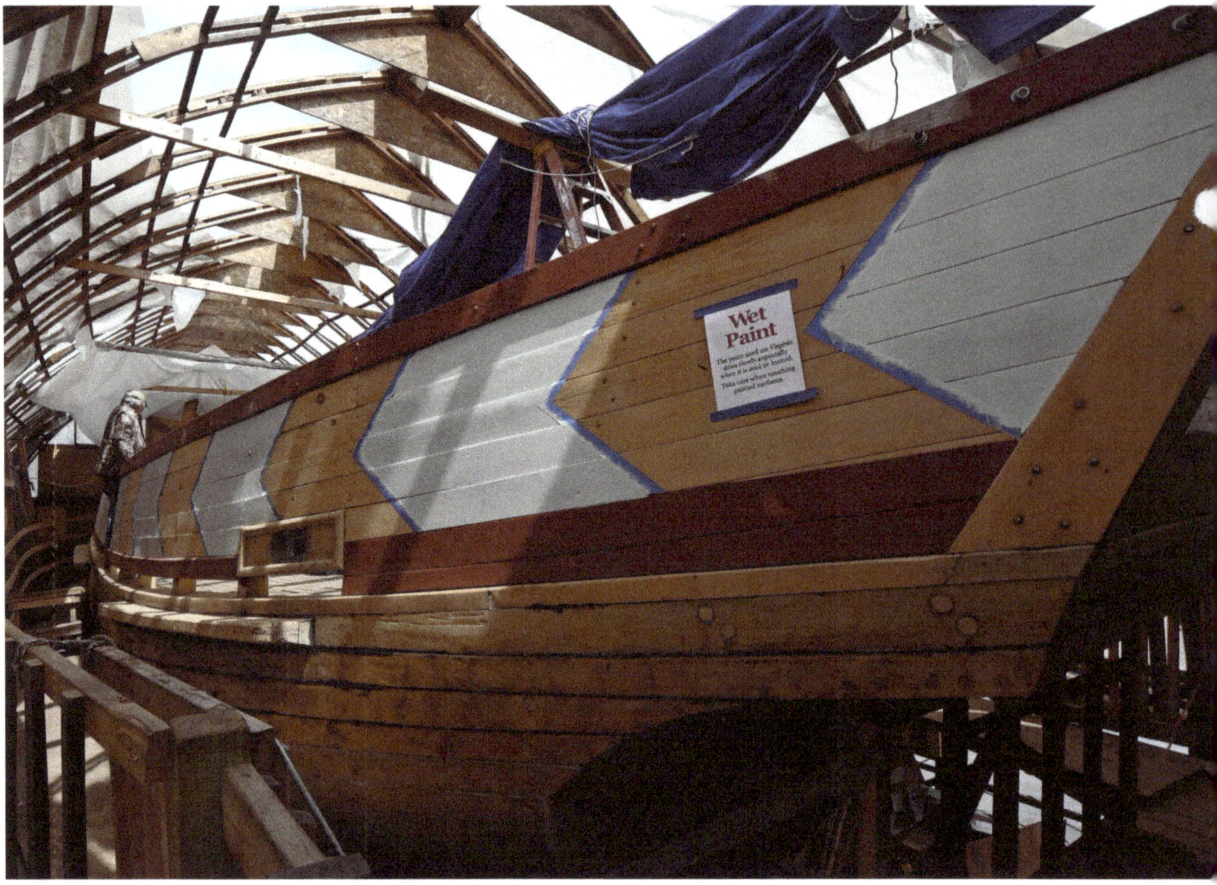

Wet paint. (above) The enclosure comes down and the Virginia bathes in the sunlight.(below)

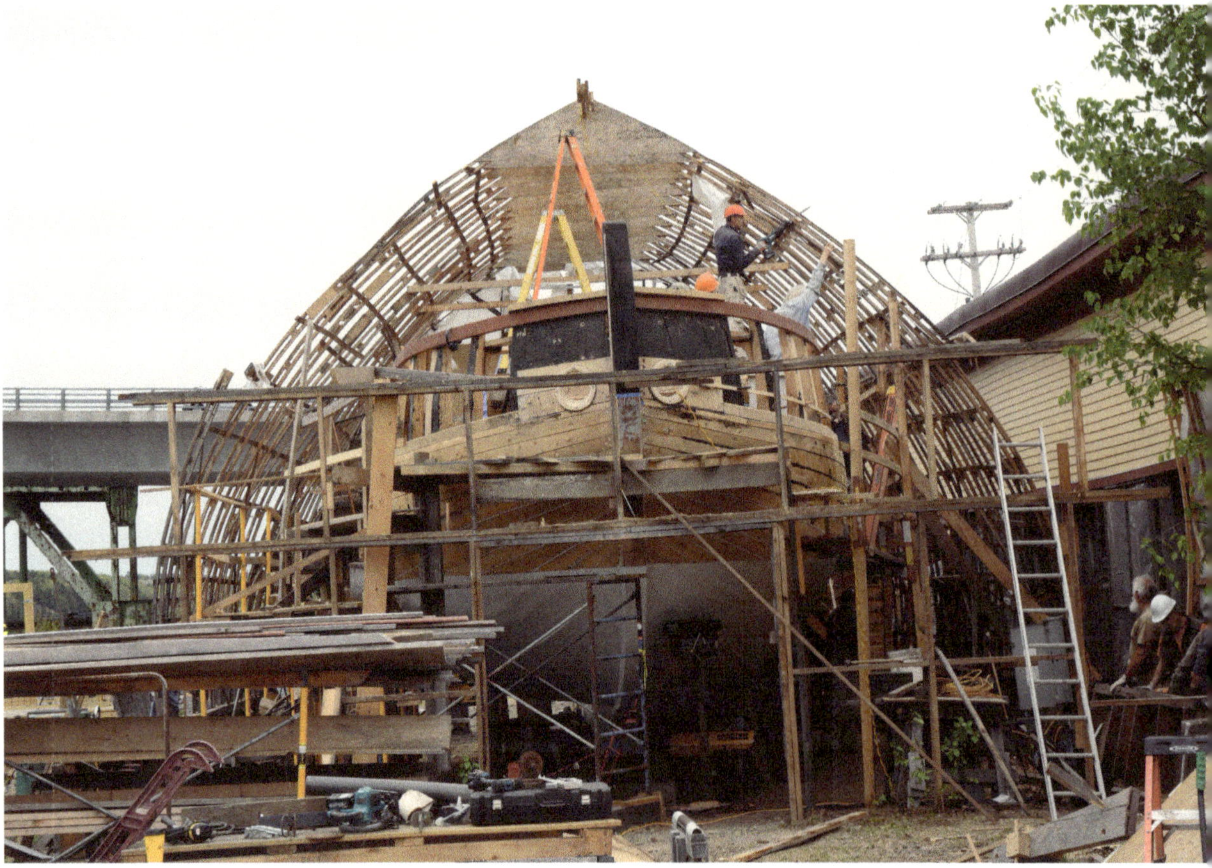

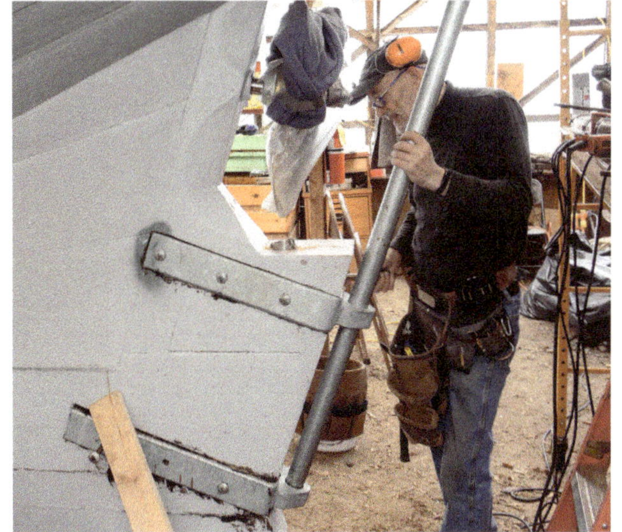

Roger Barry checks the rudder bracketts for proper alignment.

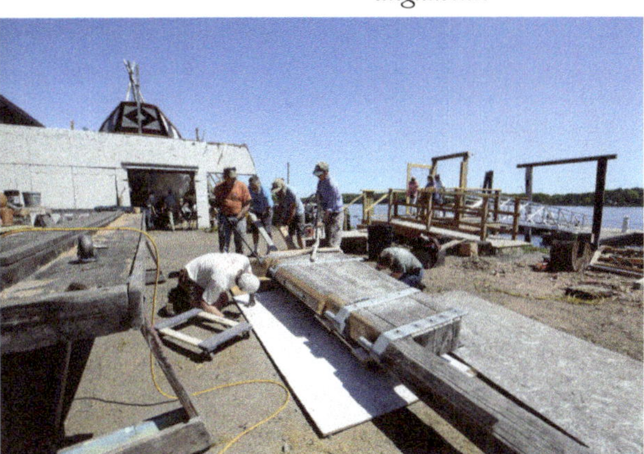

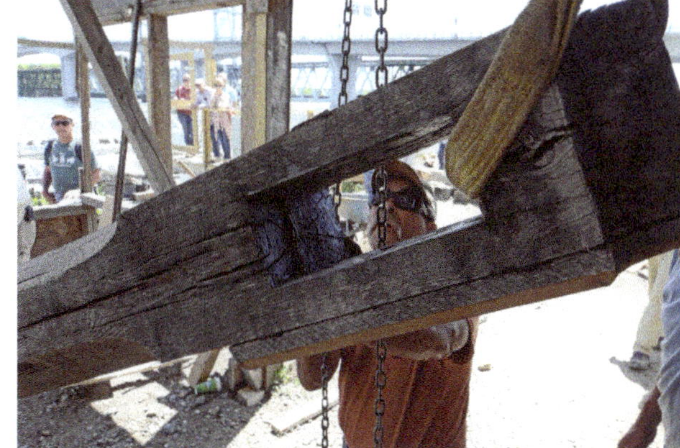

Mounting the rudder took an unexpected turn when it was discovered it is too long for the space under the ship. Solution: dig a hole to open the space.

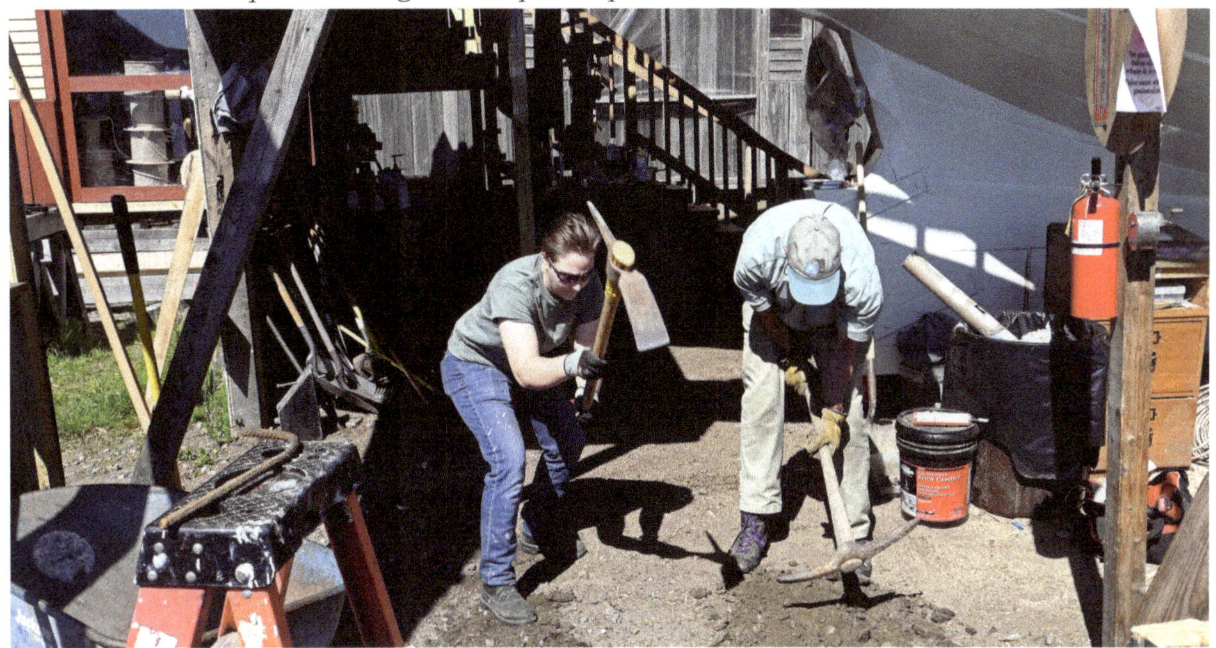

Rowan Blaiklock and another volunteer dig a hole to help mount the rudder.

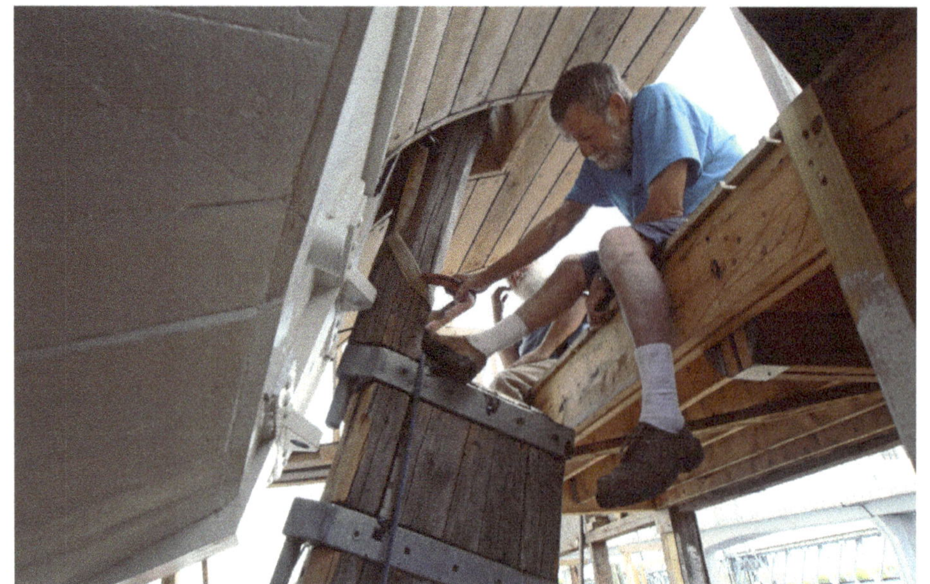

*Finally, the rudder is put in position (above) and those involved
take a break for a photo (below).*

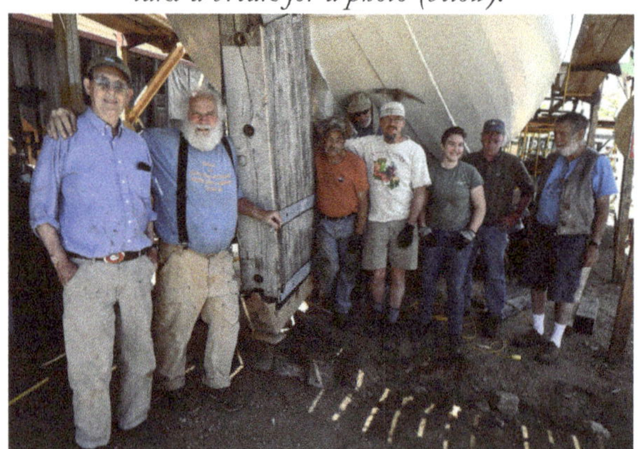

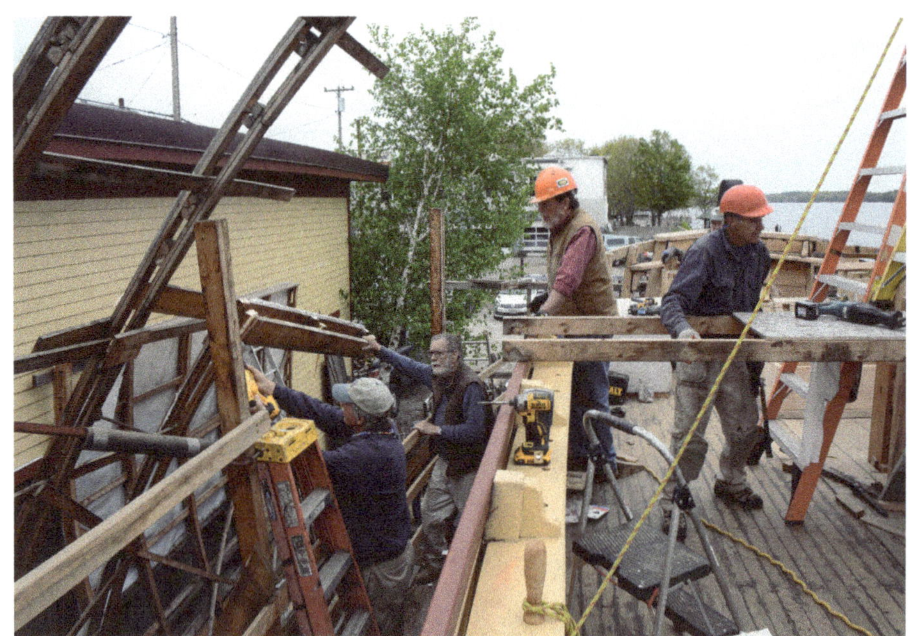

Volunteers removing the structure that has housed the ship since 2011.

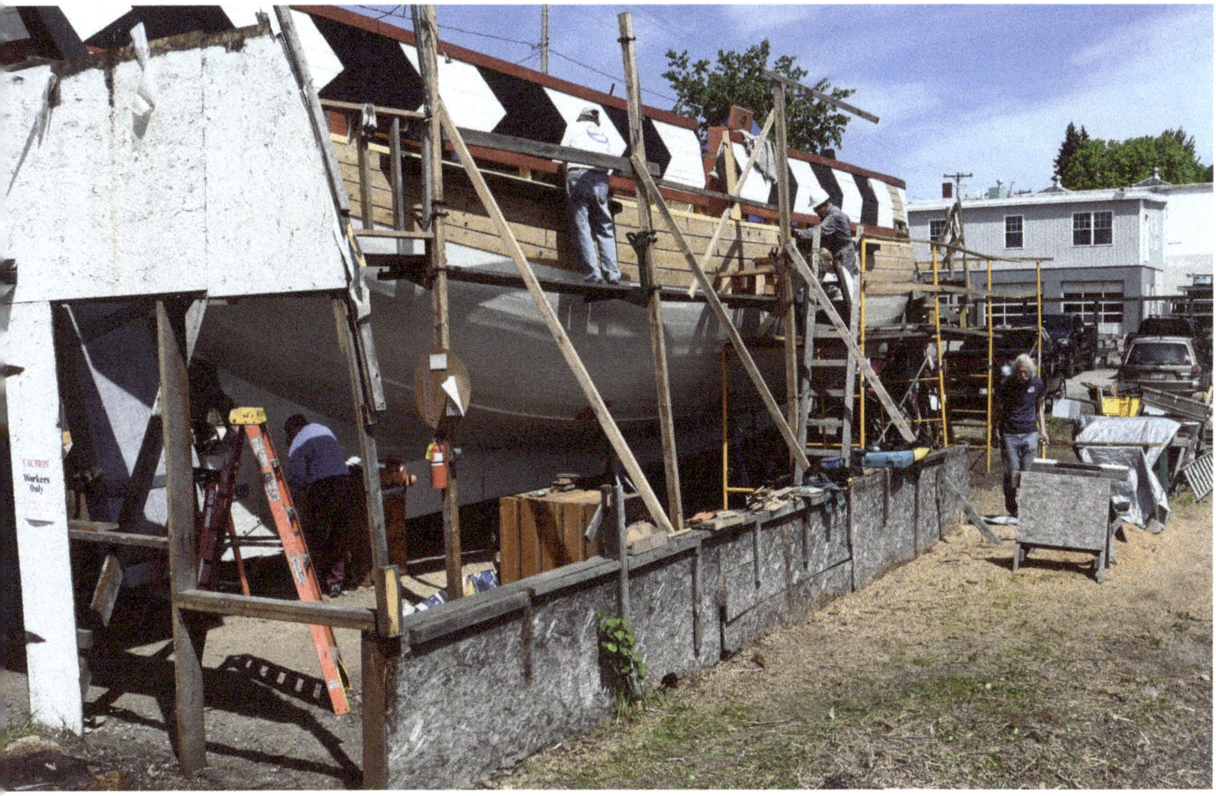

Volunteers continue removing the shelter.

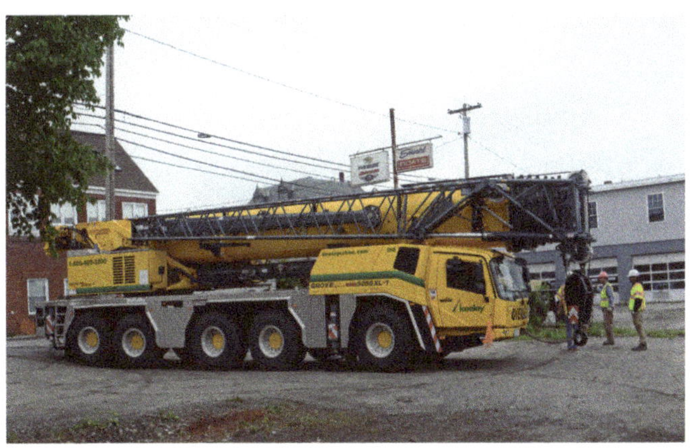

*A crane from Keeley Crane Company arrives and
prepares for the launching.*

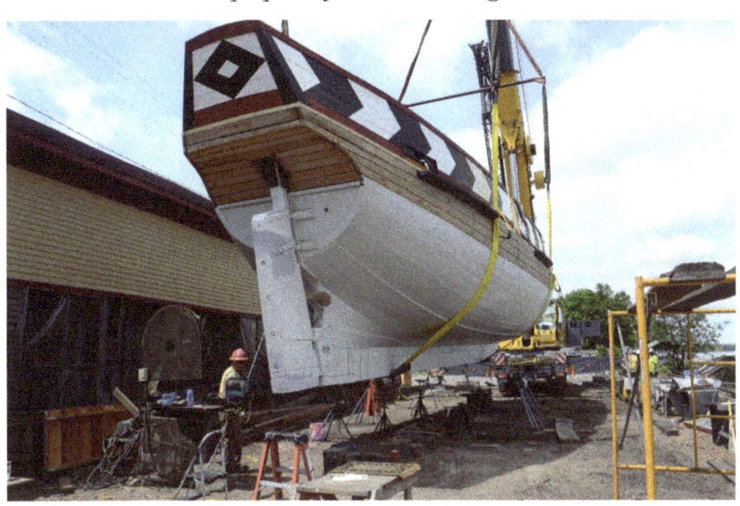

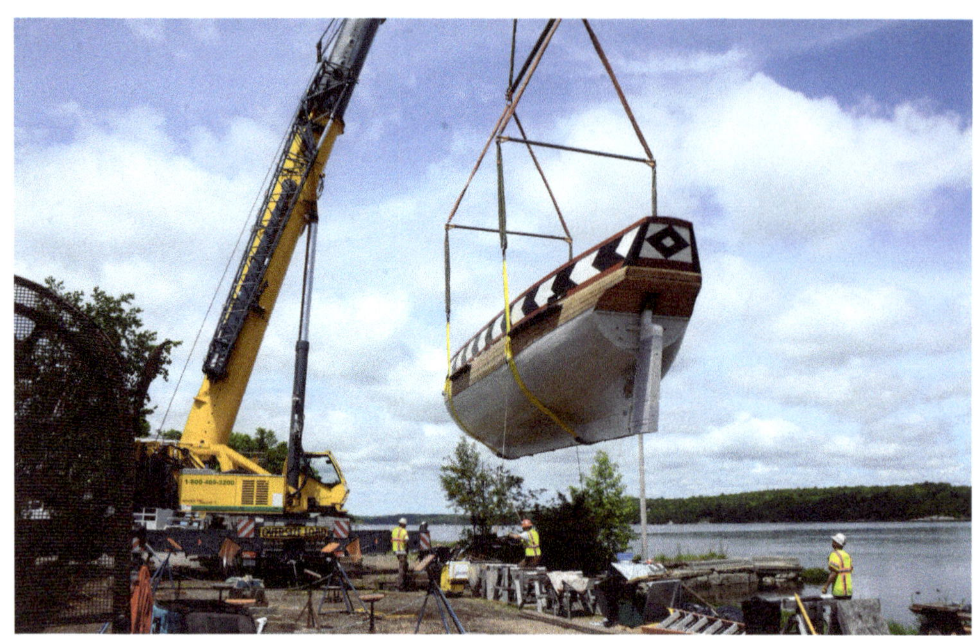

The crane lifts the 72,500-pound Viginia into launch position.

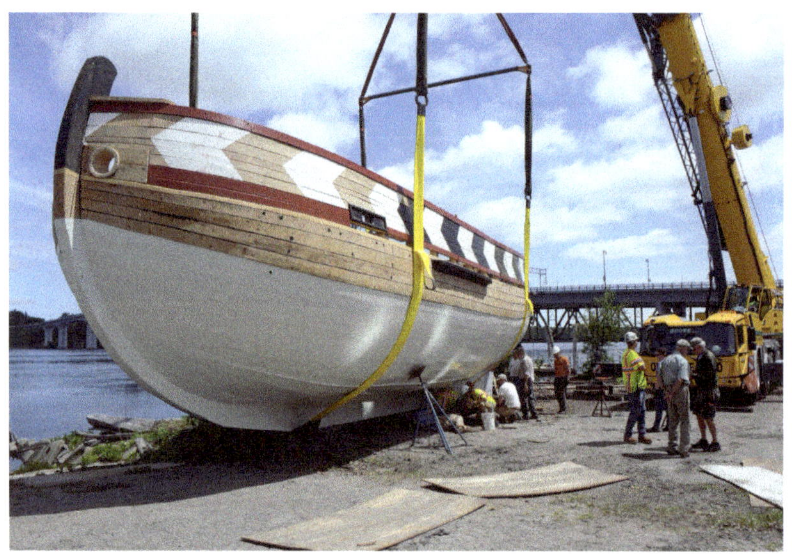

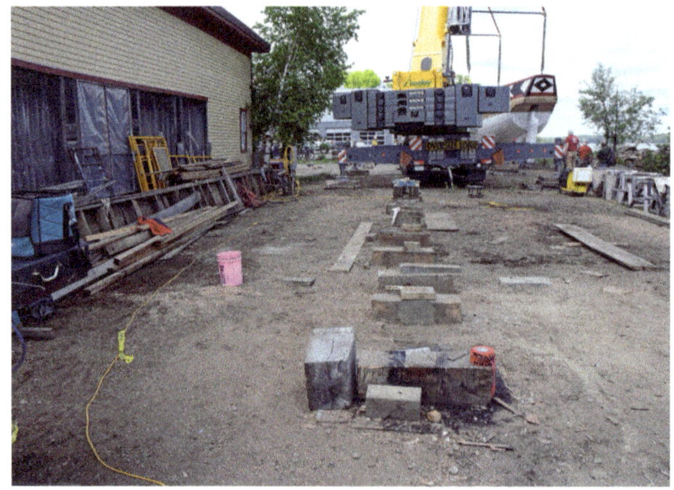

Blocks of wood are the only reminders of where the Viginia was built behind the freight shed.

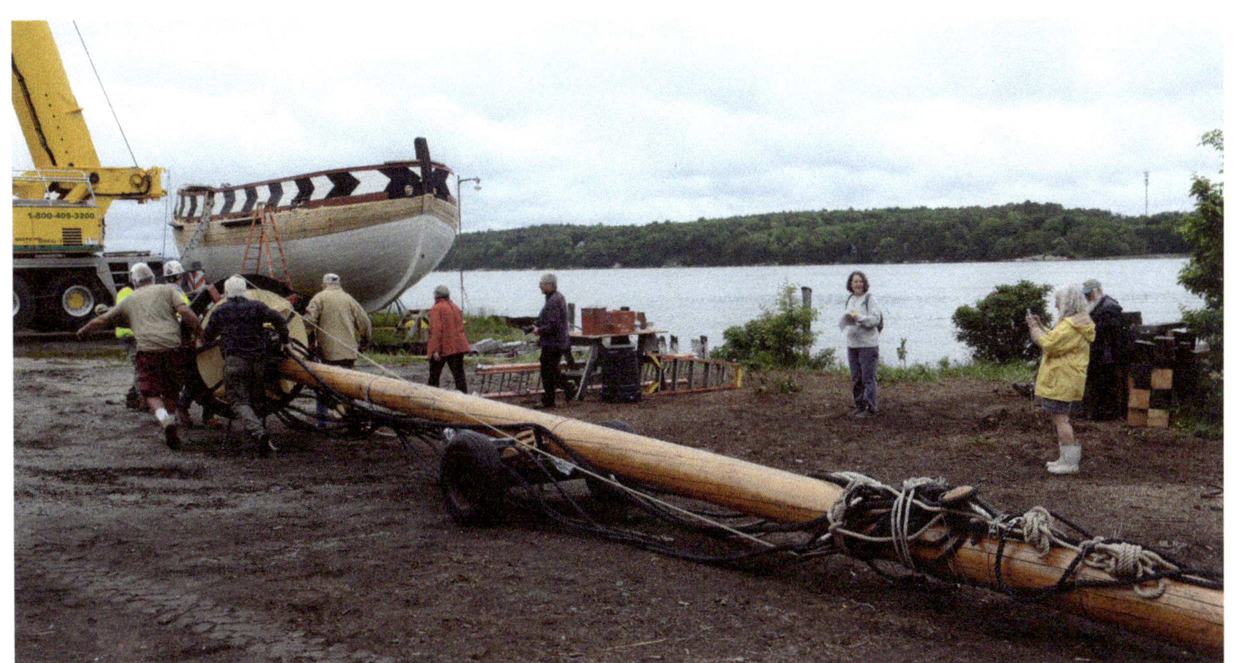

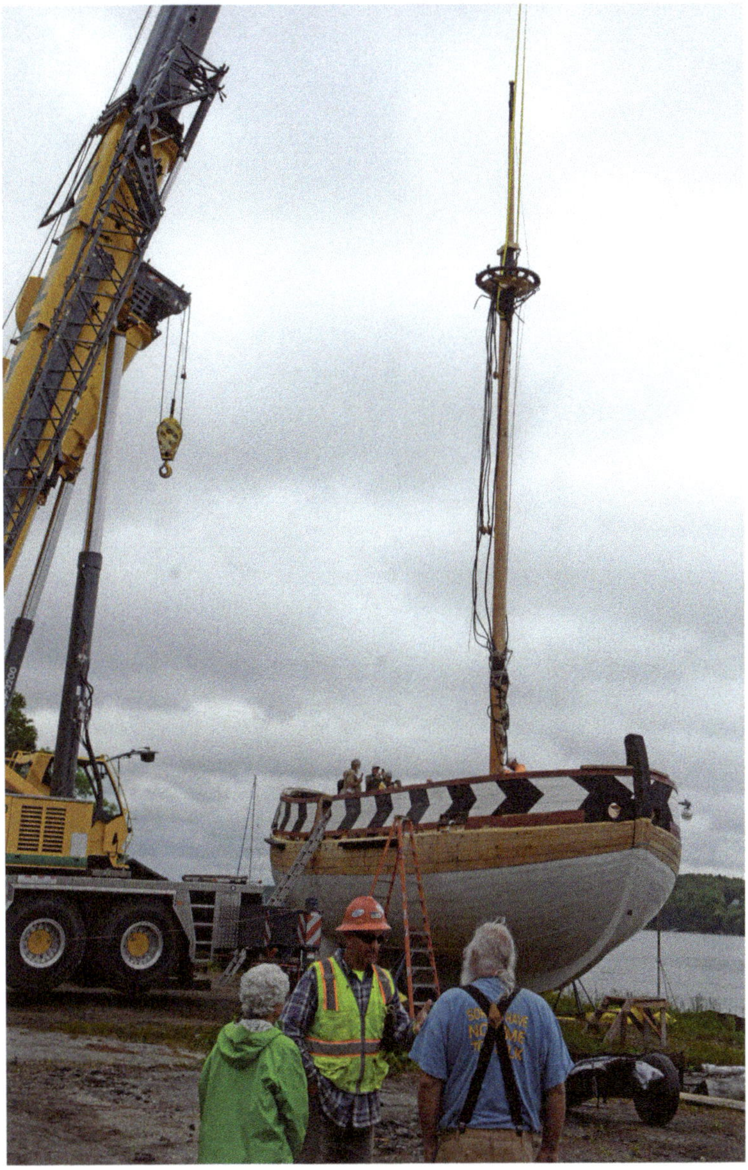

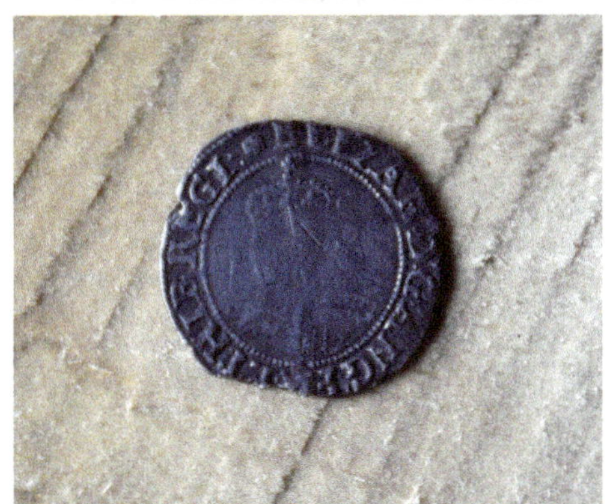

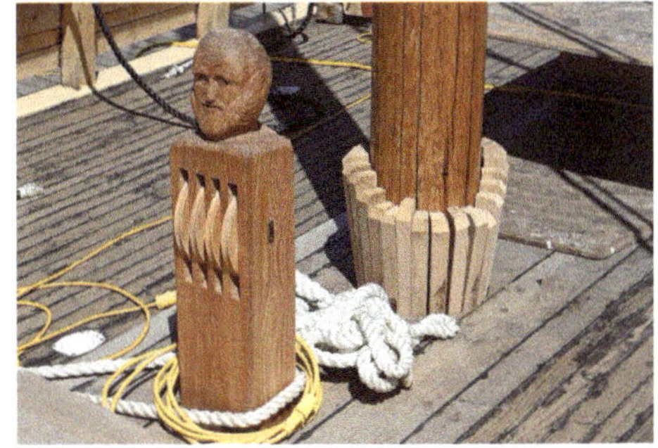

The Main Mast is lifted onto the ship. A coin from the early 1600s is placed under the mast and then the mast is wedged into position.

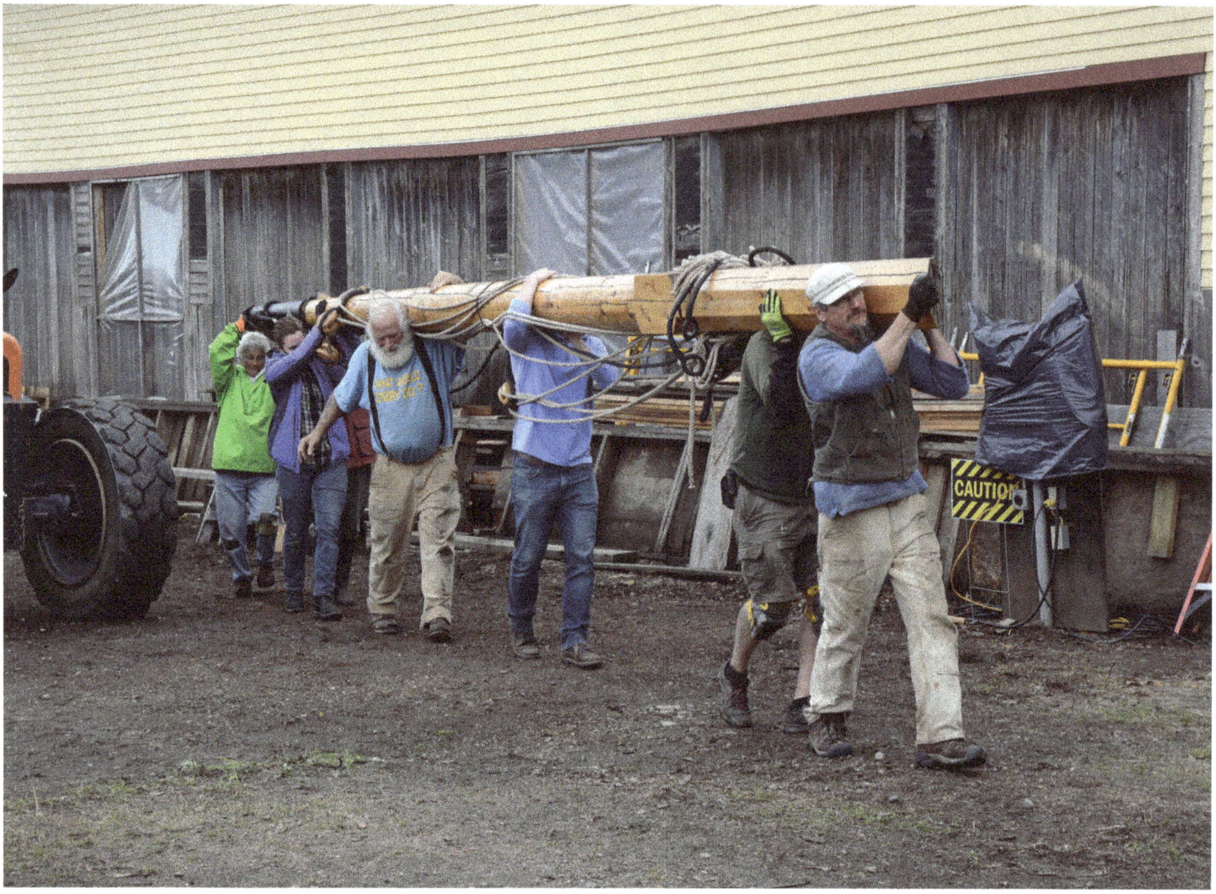

Volunteers carry the bowsprit to the crane. The crane then hoists it to the ship.

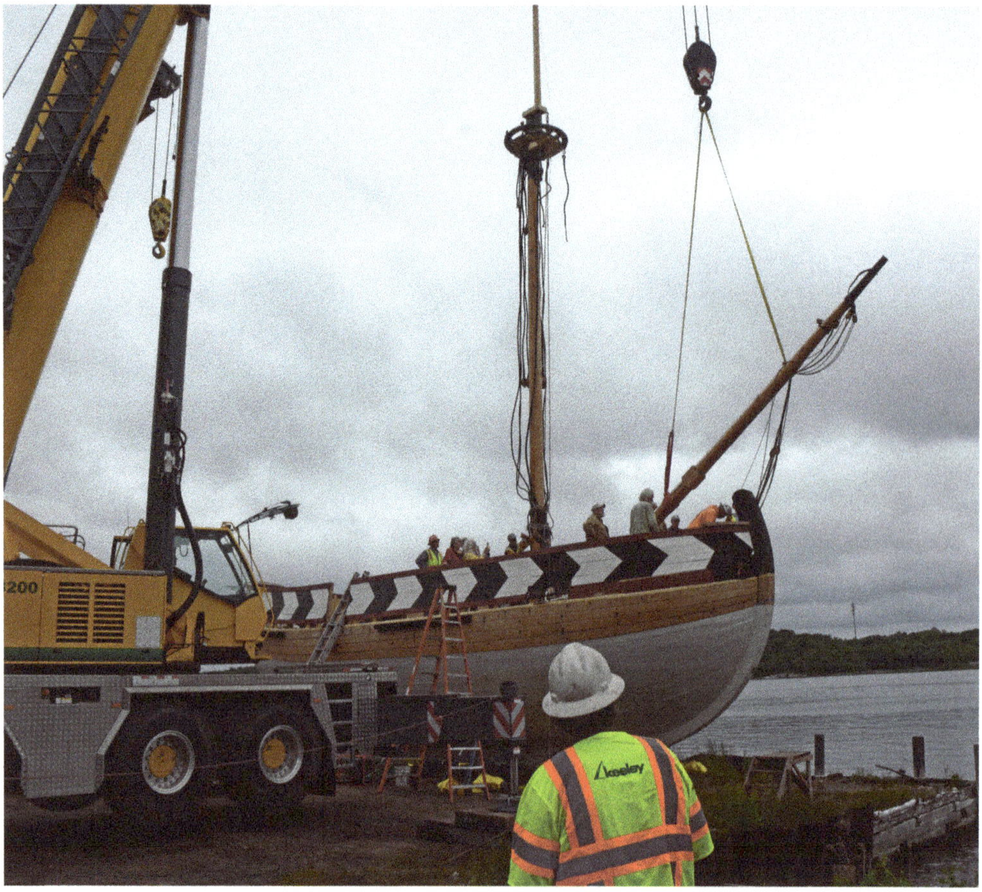

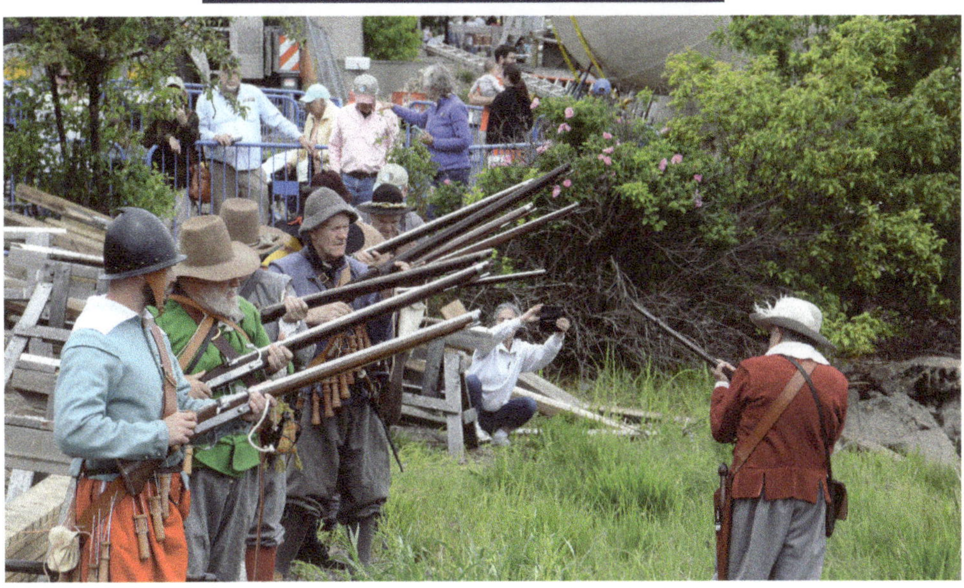

Reenactors demonstrate their flintlock skills.

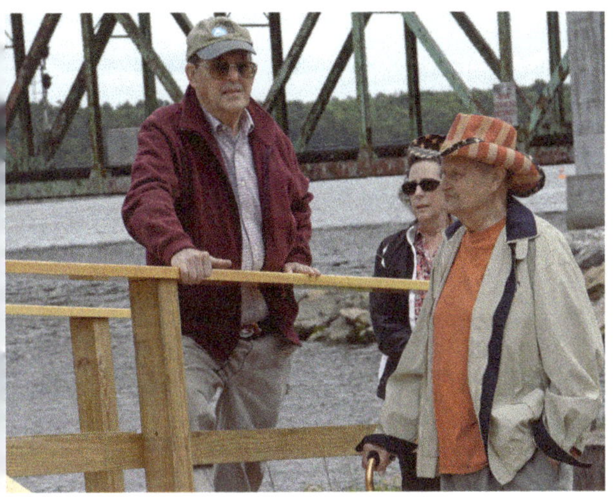

Dick Forrest and RB Omo watch the launch.

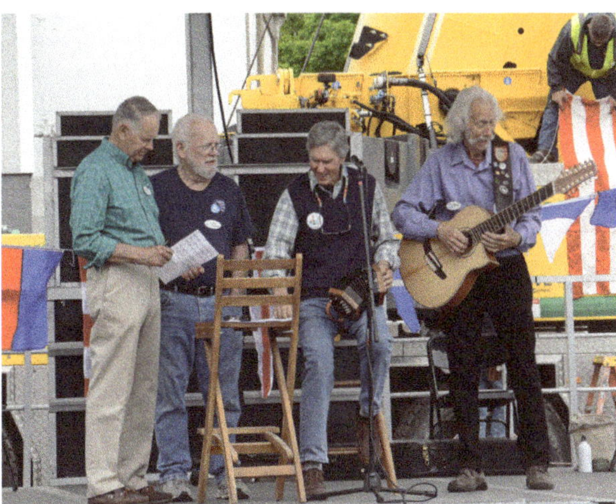

Music from our own volunteers.

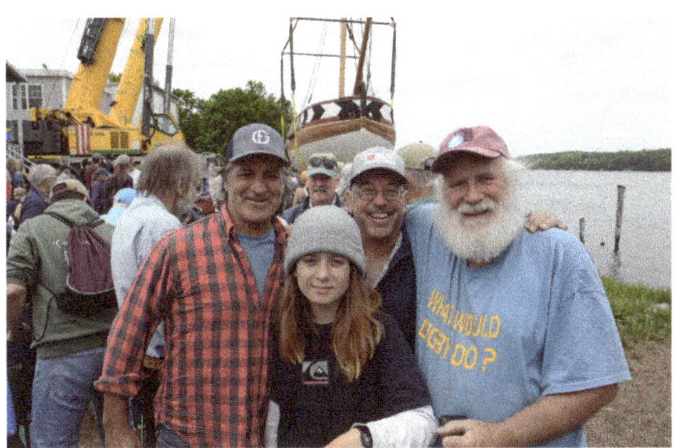

Rob Stevens and friends at the launch.

Volunteers

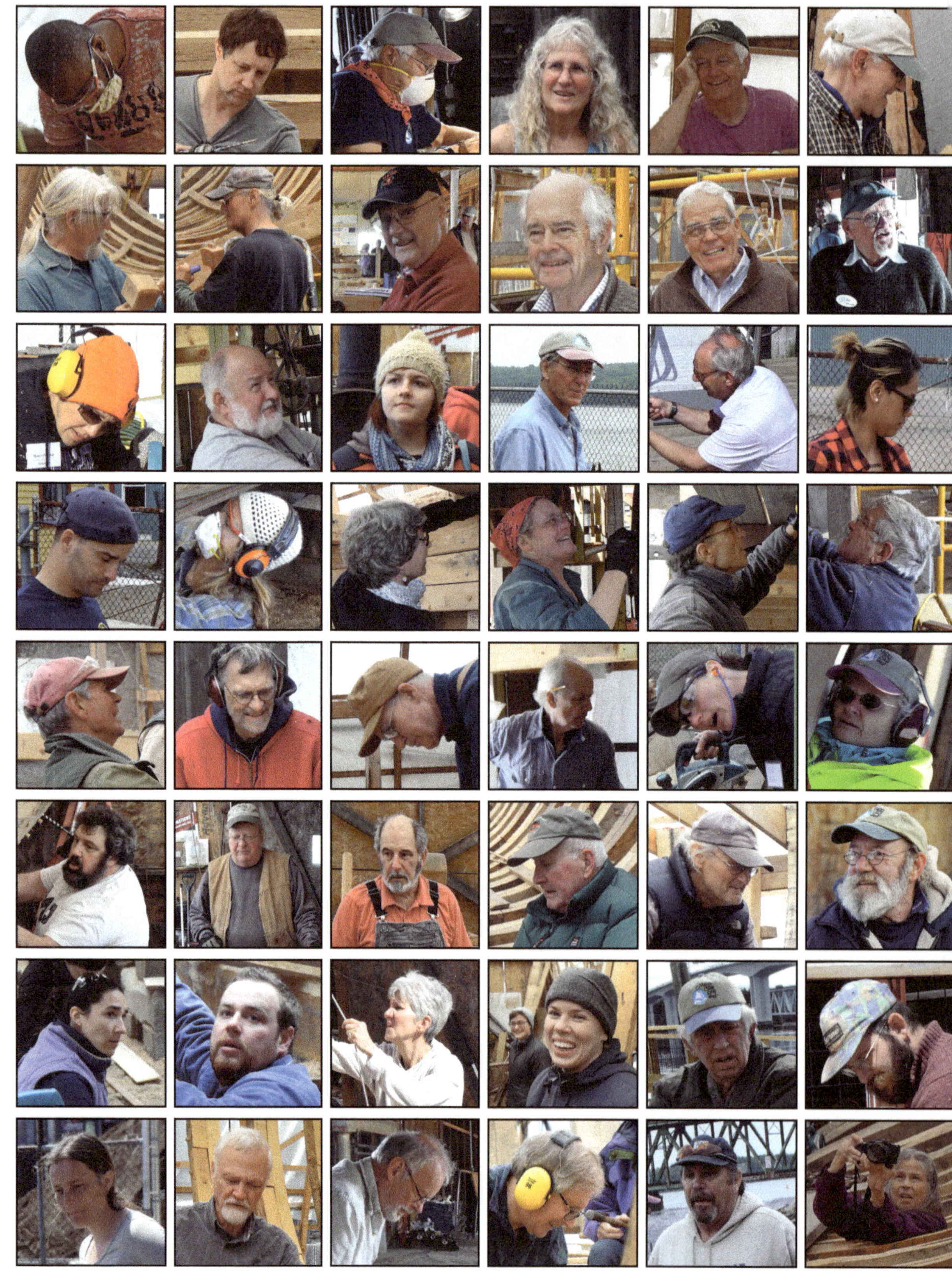

Volunteers

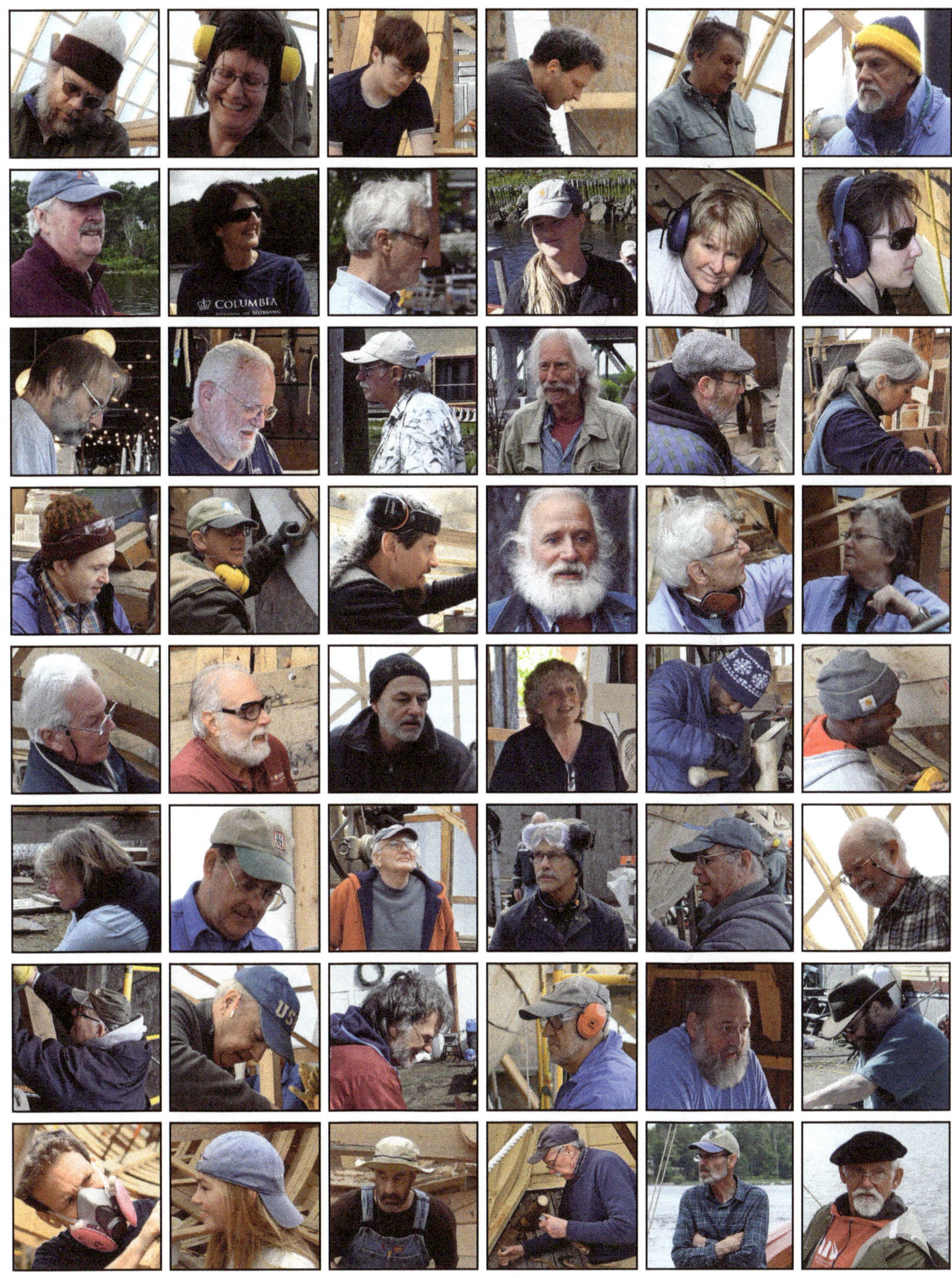

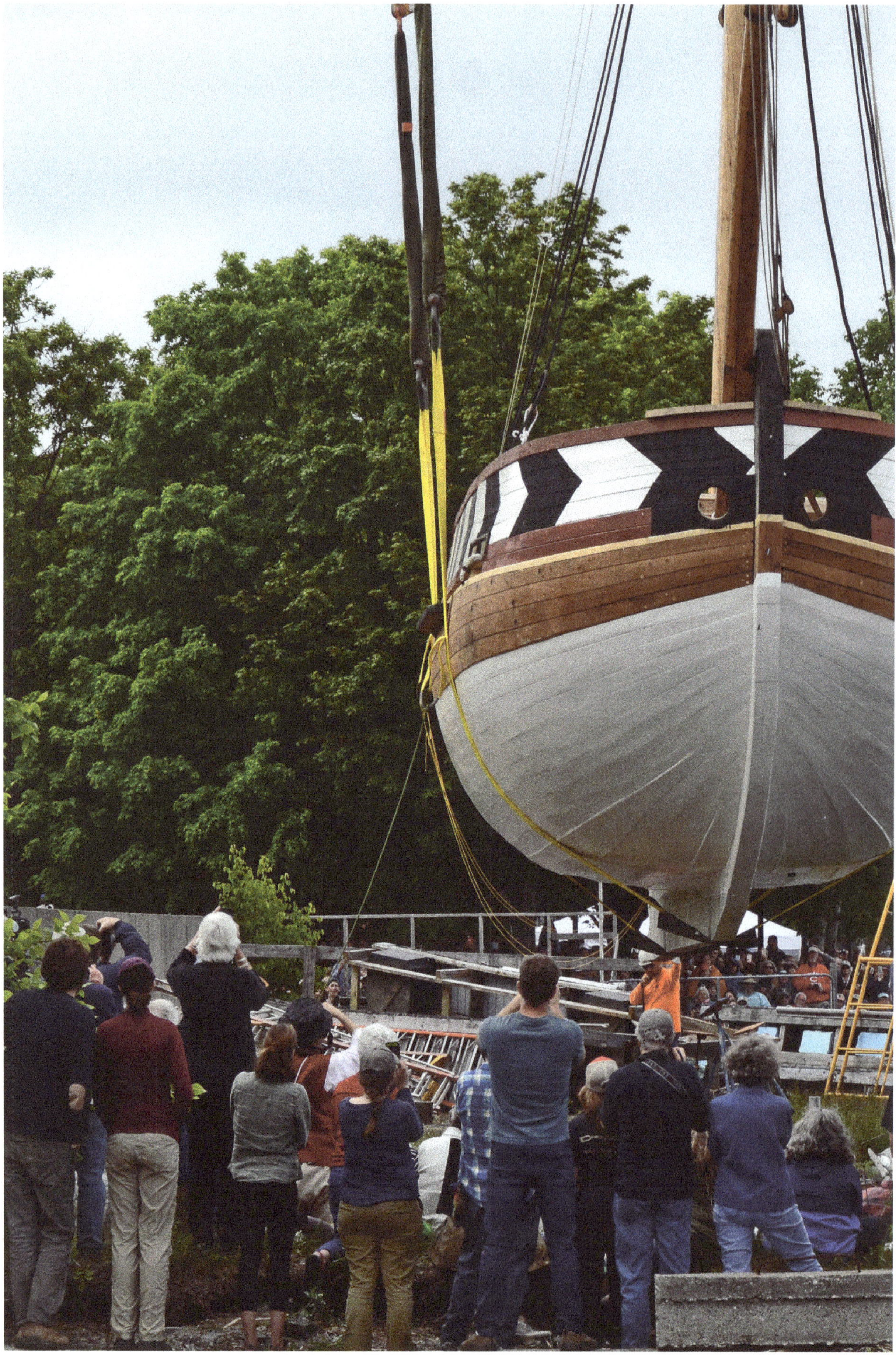

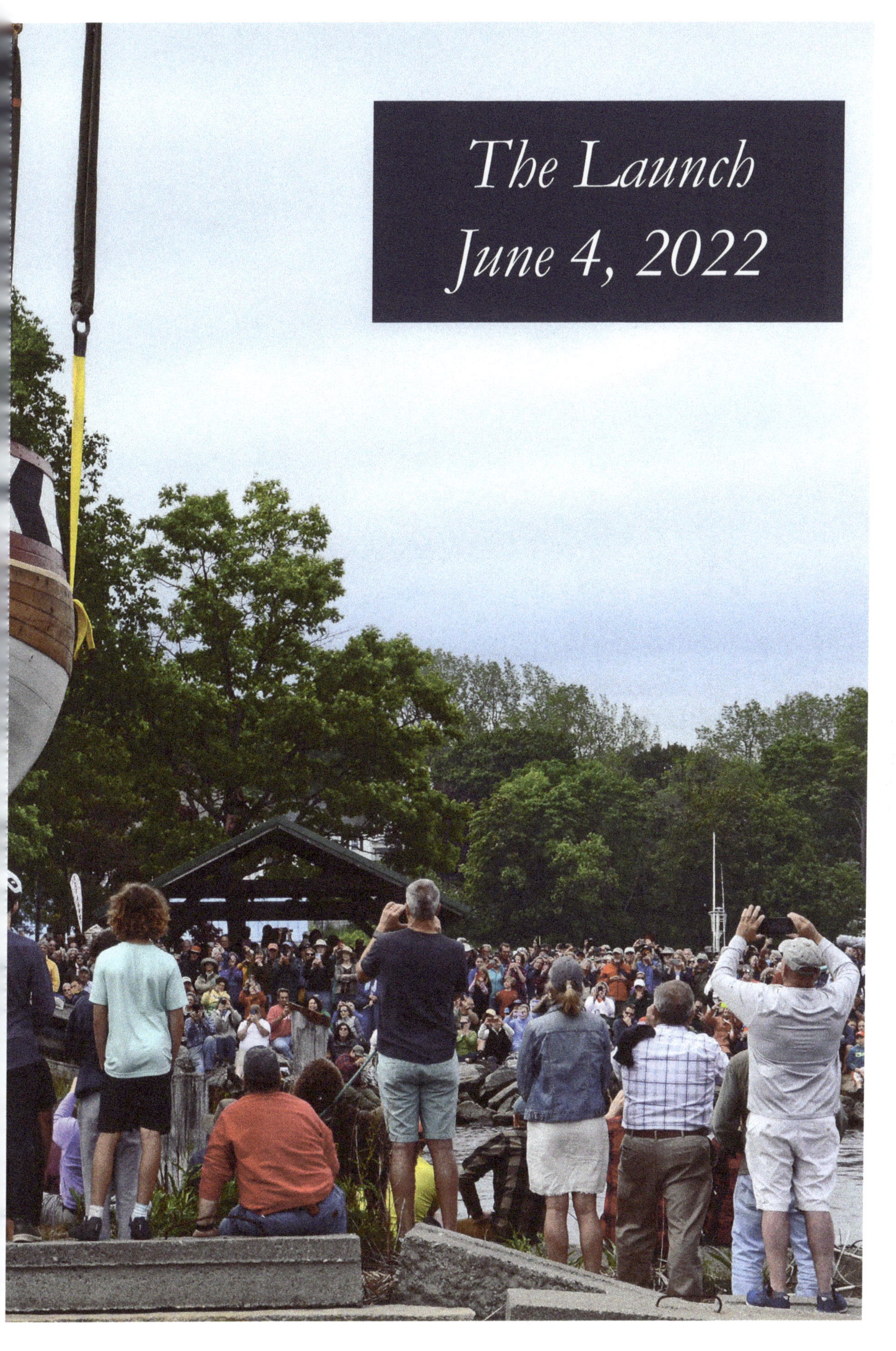

The Launch
June 4, 2022

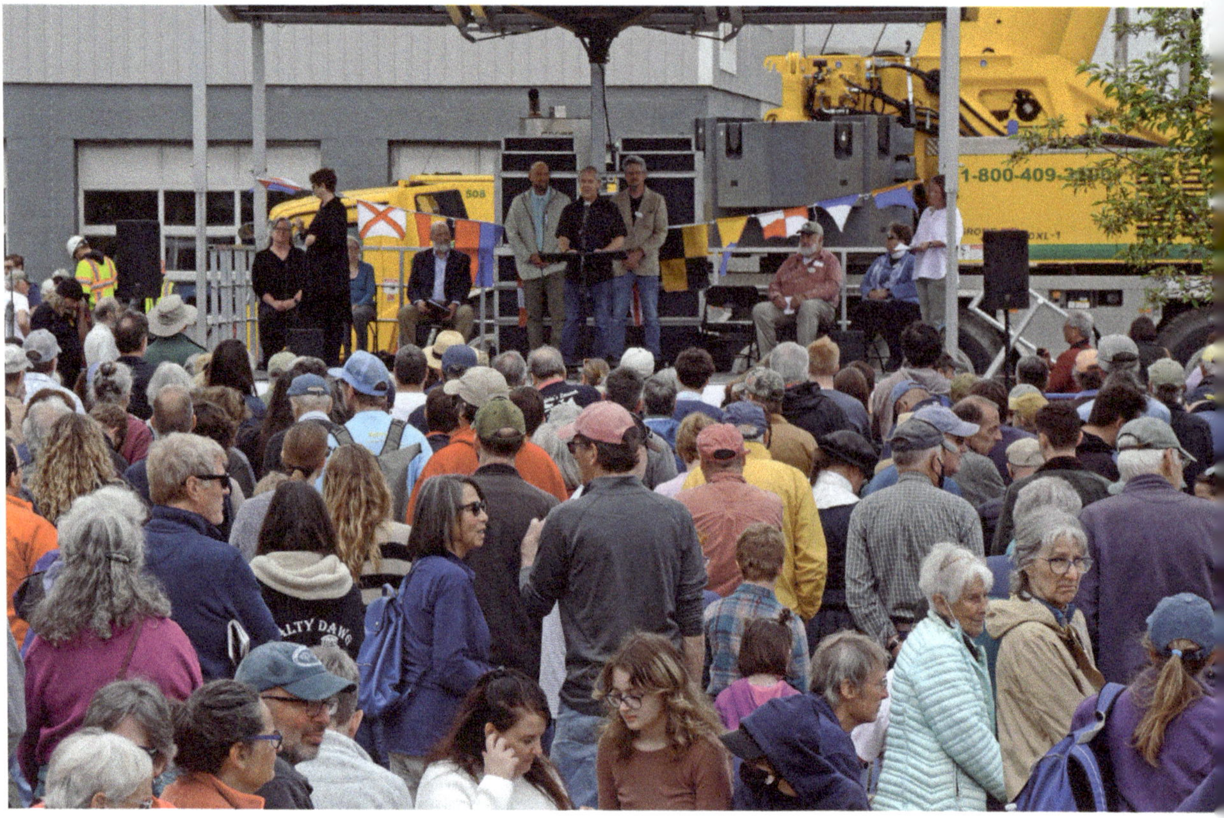

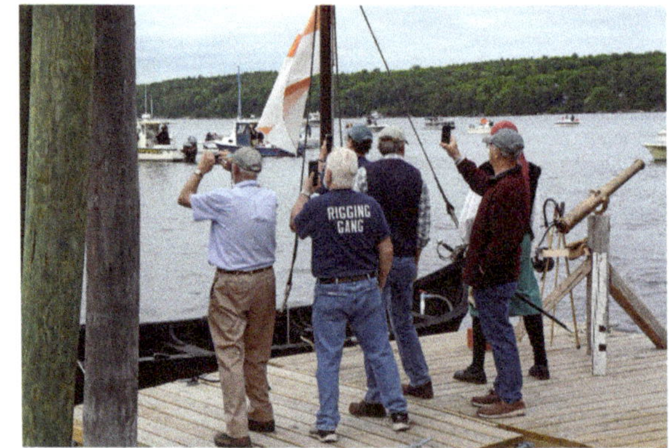

A crowd of spectators and volunteers gather for the launch ceremony.

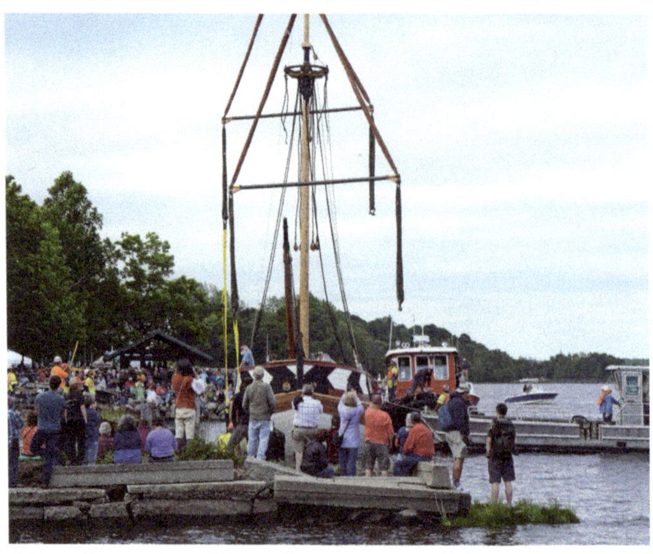

Virginia is released from the cranes, into the Kennebec.

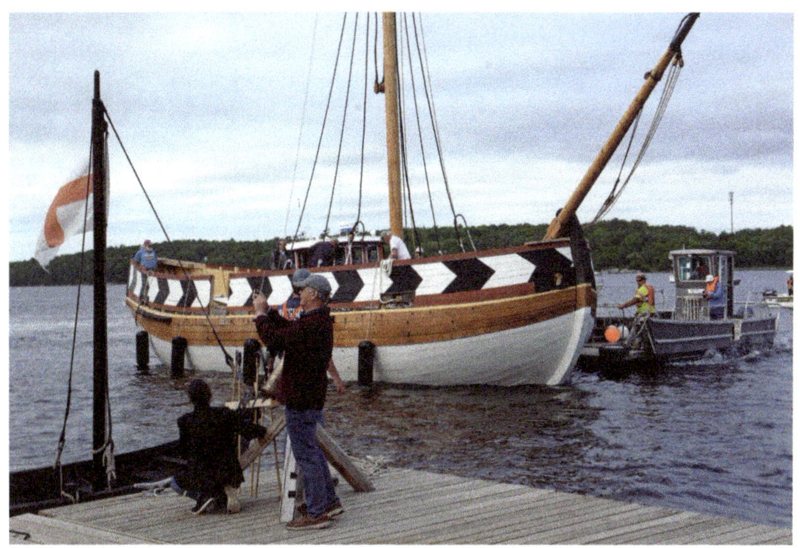

A tug moves the *Virginia* to her dock.

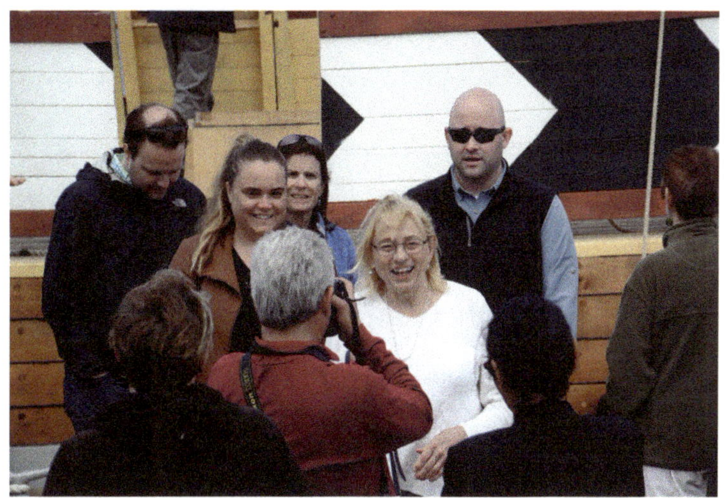

Governor Mills joins the celebration.

The people approve!

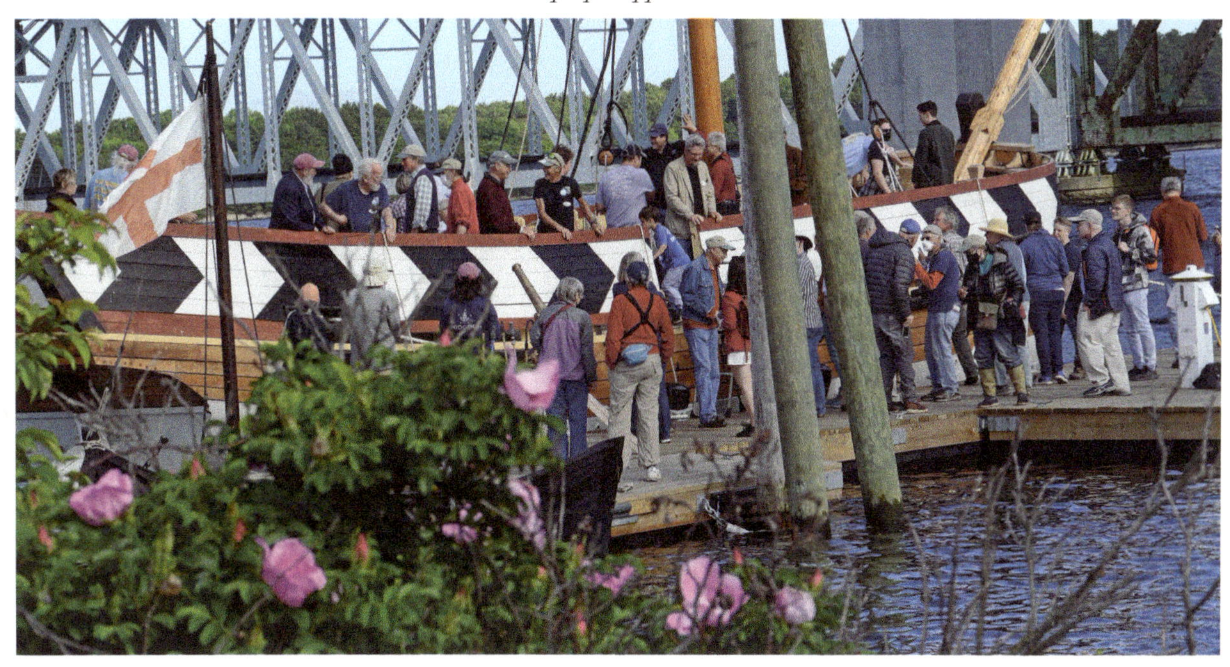

After the Launch

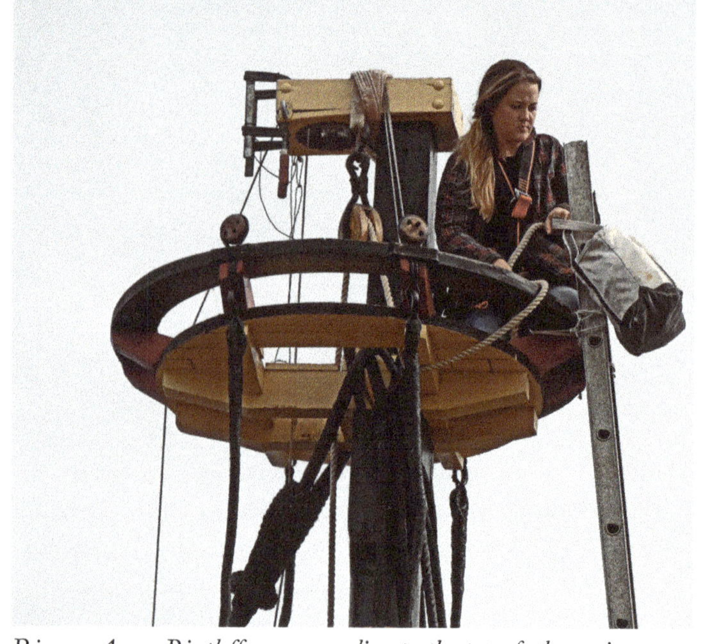

Rigger, Avery Bintleff, secures a line to the top of the main mast.

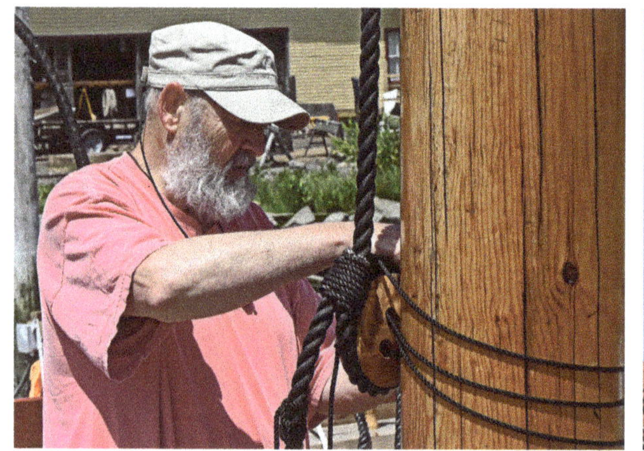

Head rigger, Jim Nelson, secures lines at the main mast.

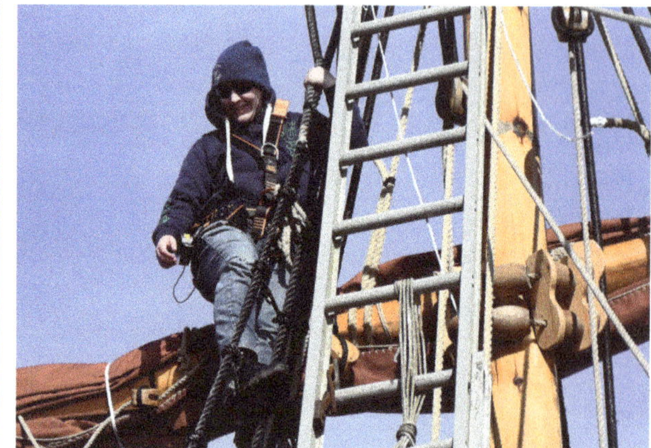

Rigger, Rowan Blaiklock, climbs the ratline.

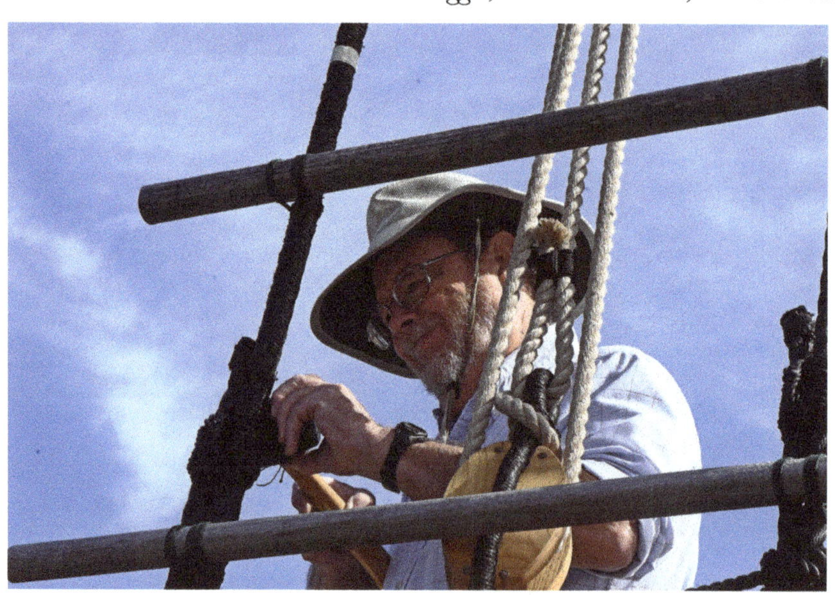

Rigger, Michael Foster, works on temporary ratlines.

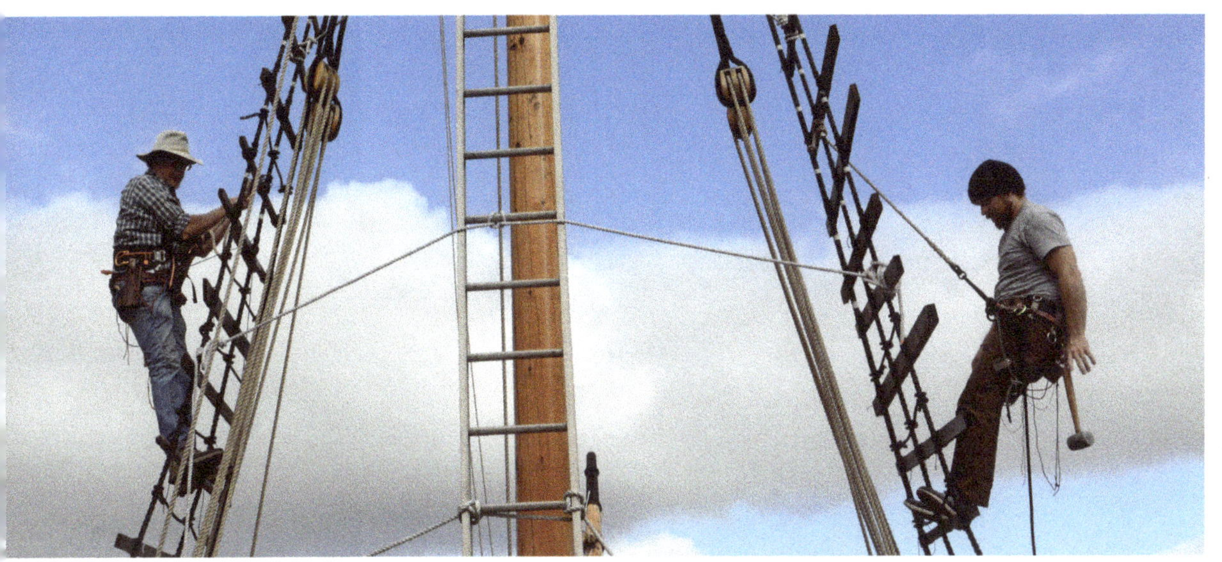

Riggers work on temporary wooden ratlines.

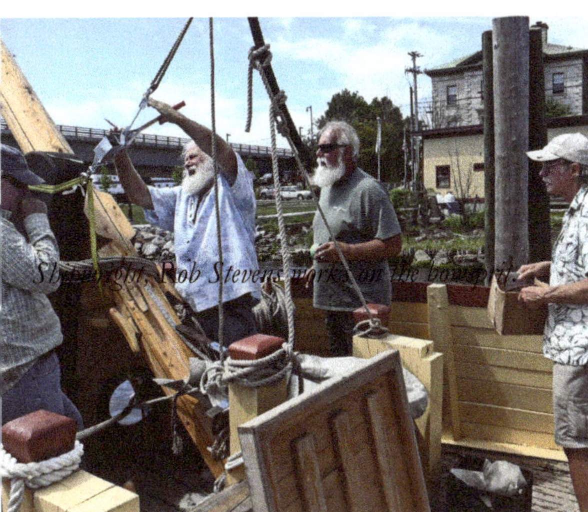

Shipwright Rob Stevens works on the bowsprit.

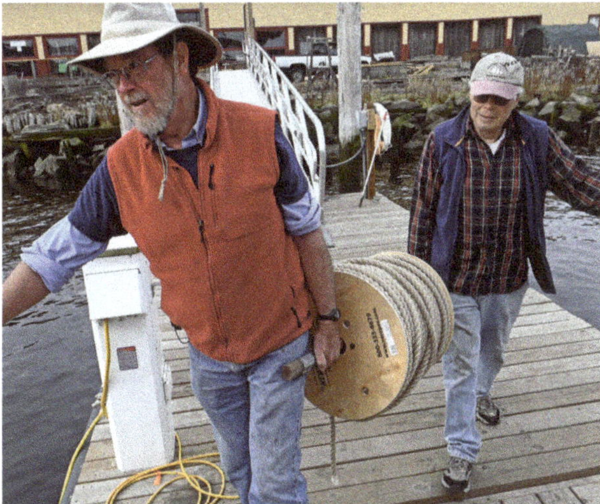

Michael Foster and David Bellows deliver line to the Virginia.

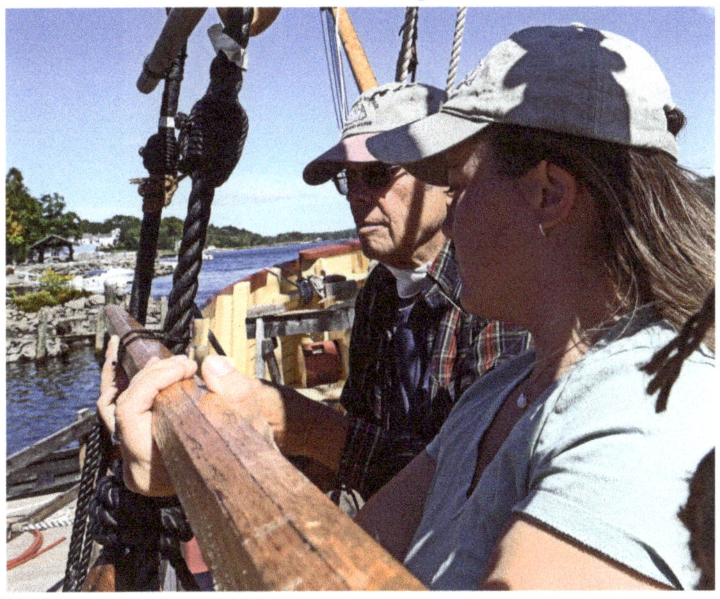

Avery Bintleff and David Bellows secure a sheer pole to the shroud.

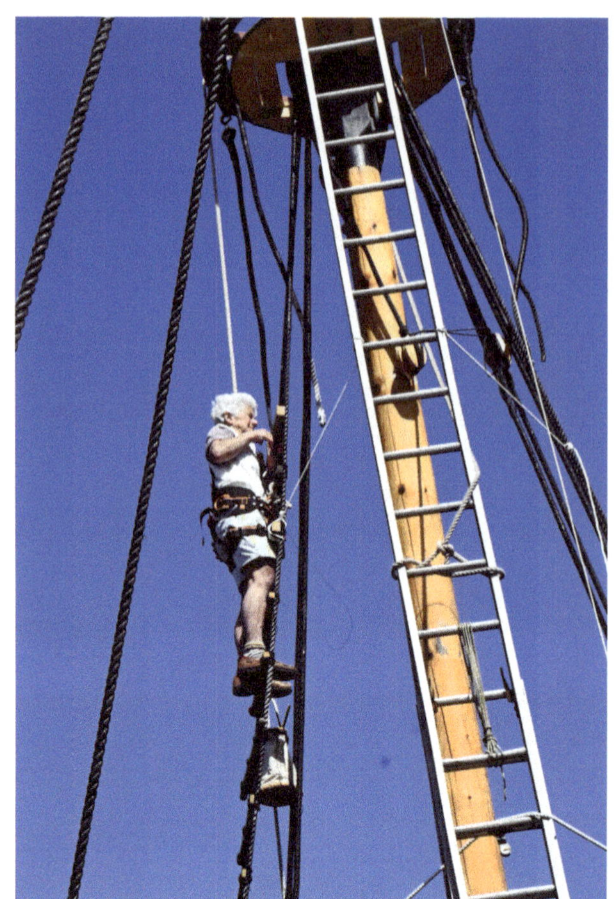

Eilse Straus-Bowers added rope steps to the ratline.

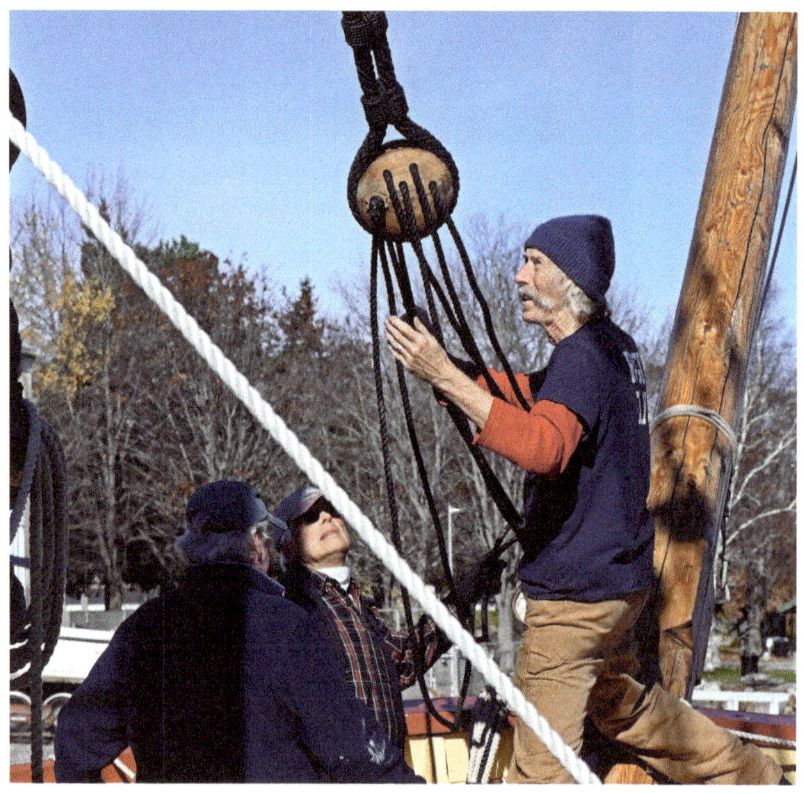

Fred Gosbee puts the final touches on a standing rigging at the bow.

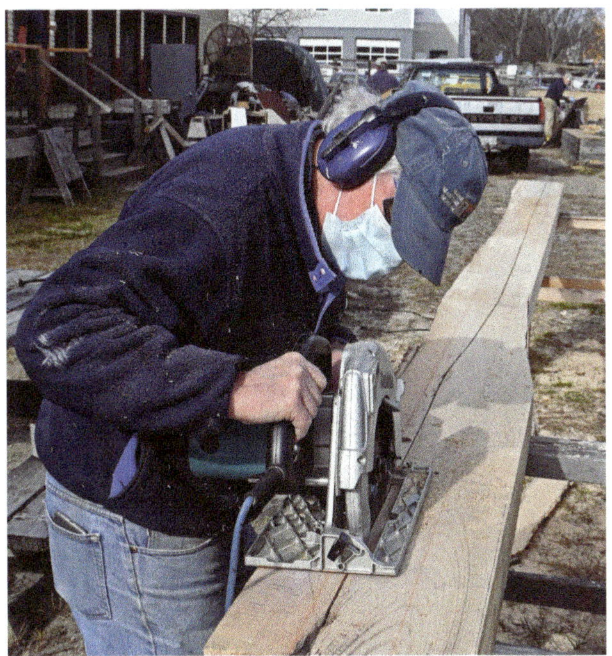

Paul King cuts an oar from a plank of ash.

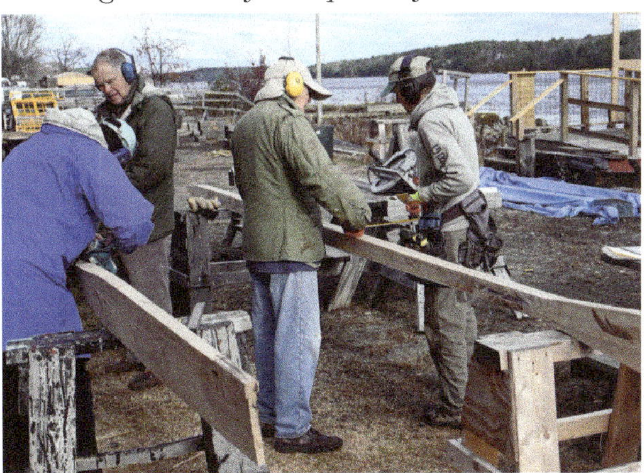

Volunteers shape oars using saws and planers.

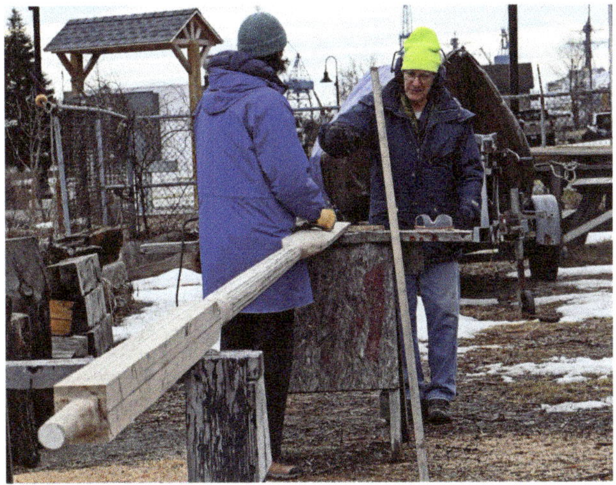

Francis South and Ewen McEwen add the final touches to an oar.

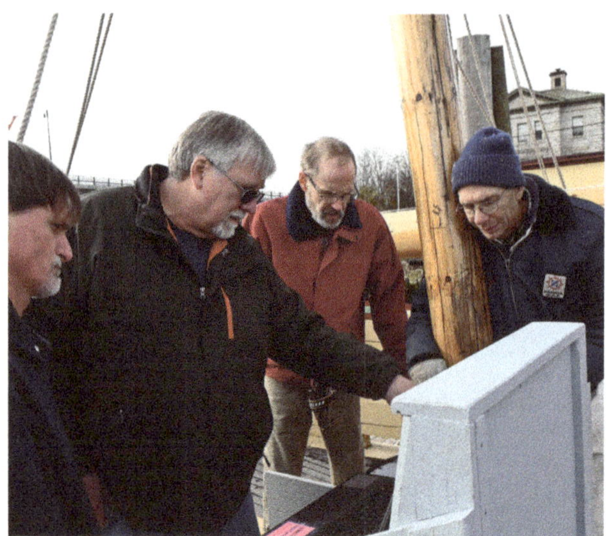

*Volvo-Penta representatives train Dana Leonard (right)
and Bruce Suppes (center) to use the onboard computer.*

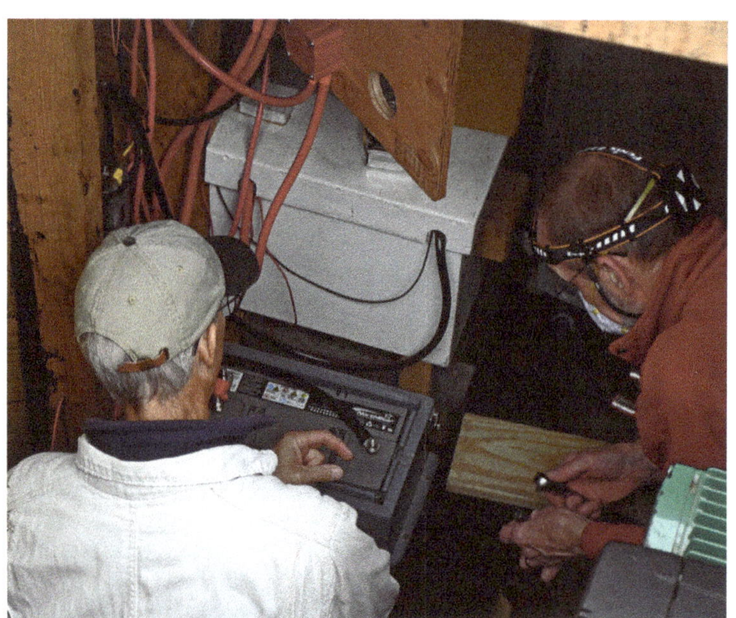

*Dana Leonard (left) and Bruce Suppes (right) check the batteries in
the engine compartment.*

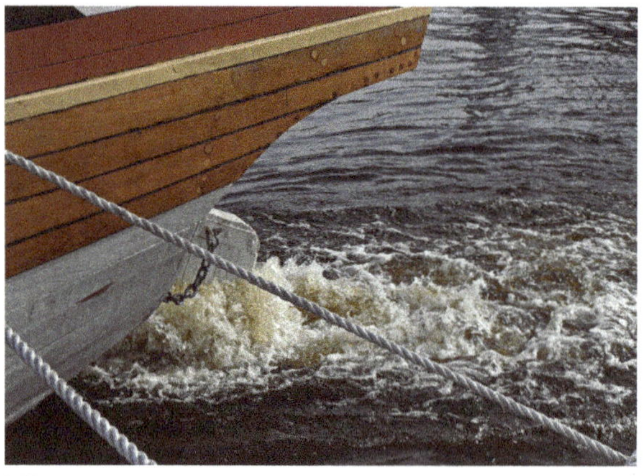

The engine starts and the prop turns. Success!

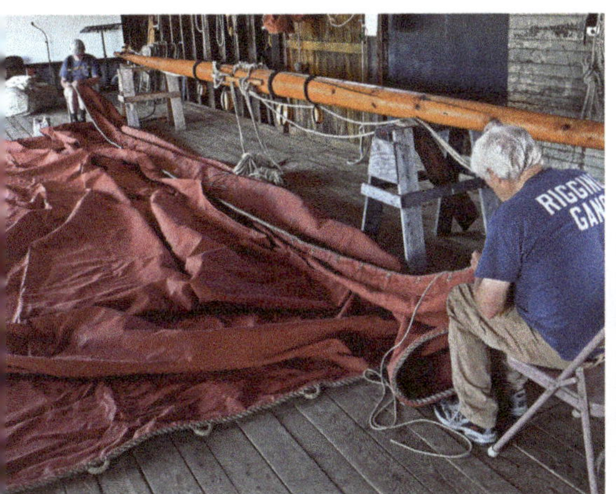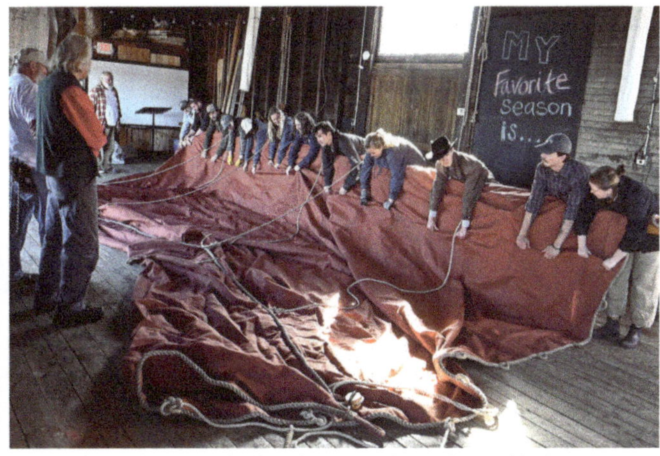

Volunteers rig the sprit mainsail in preparation to attach it the sprit yard.

Once the sail is attached, volunteers dress the sail before carrying it to the ship.

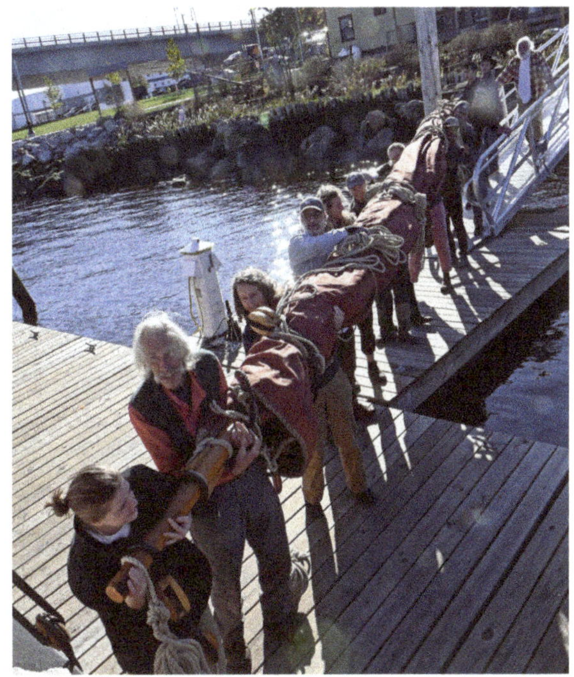

Eleven volunteers carry the sail and yard and load it onto the ship. (above and below)

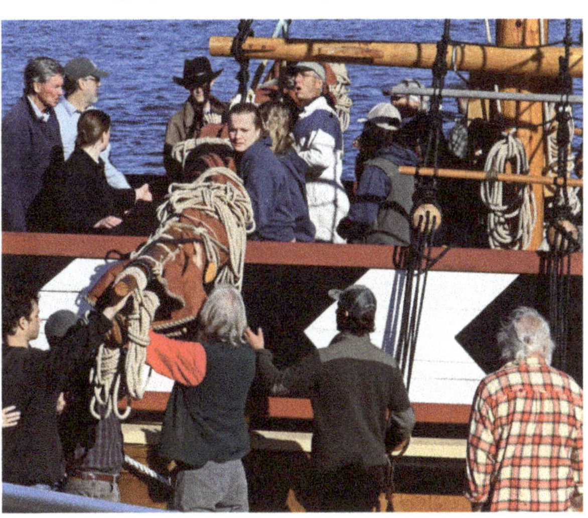

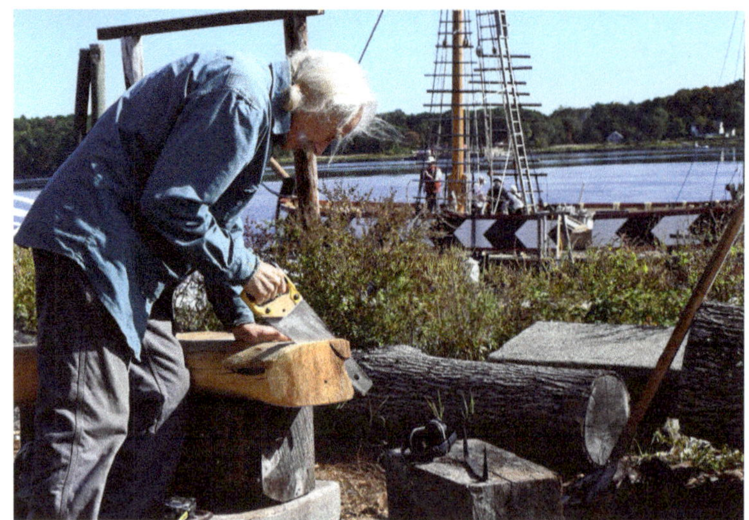

Fred Gosbee again uses his woodworking skills to create the gammoning knee.

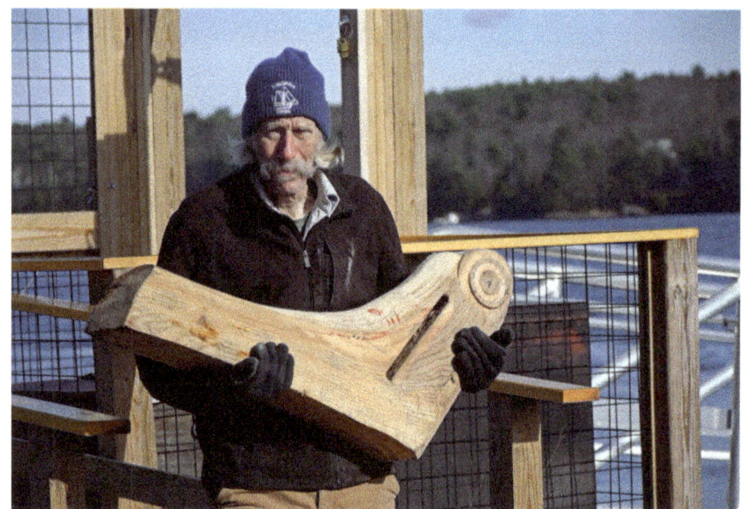

The finished gammoning knee.

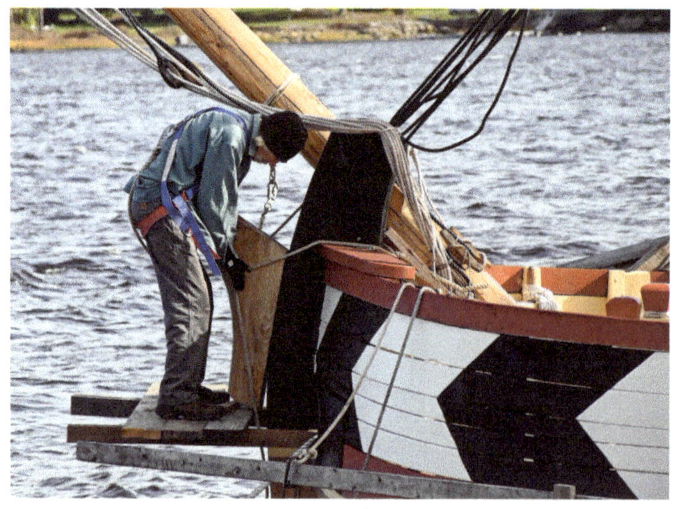

Gosbee attaches the knee to the bow of the Virginia.

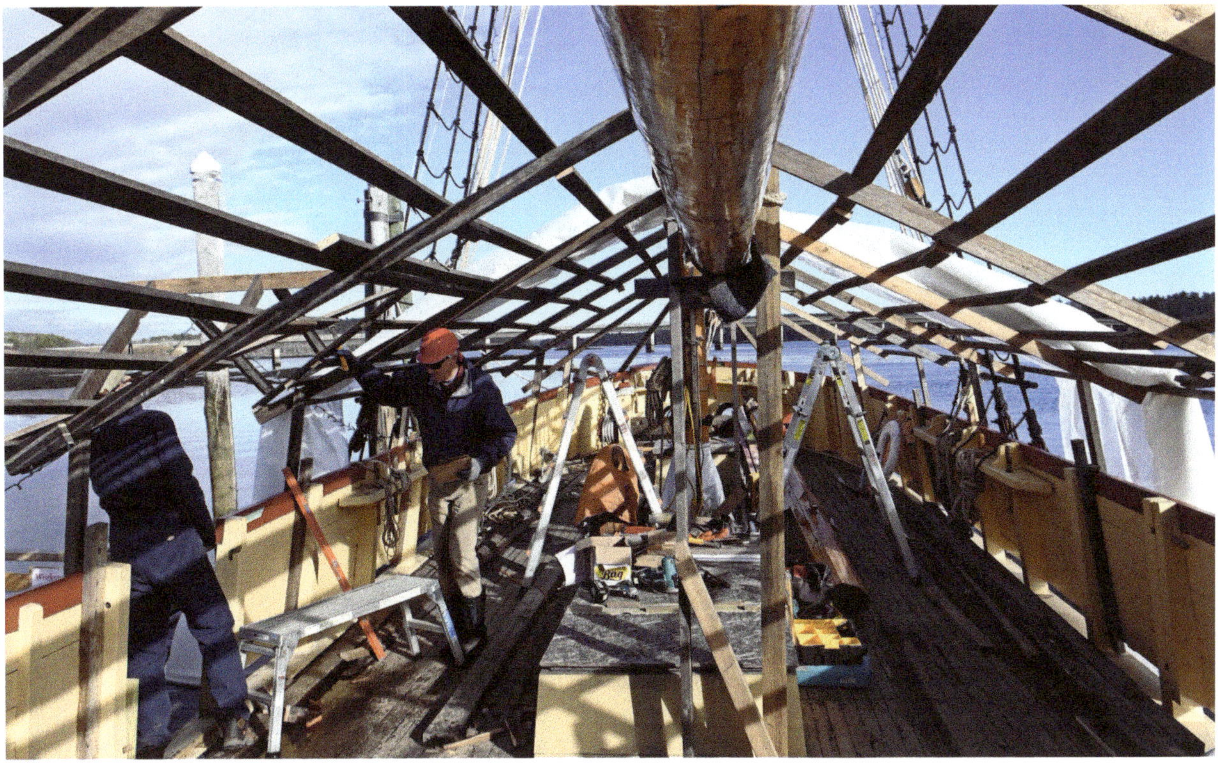

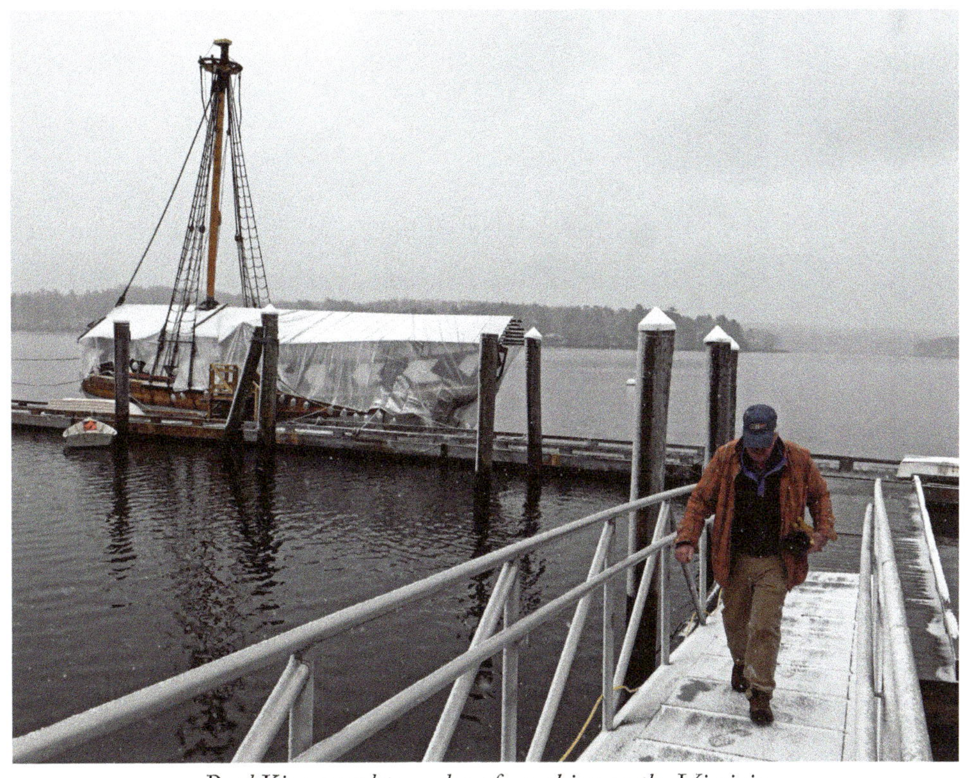

At its Wiscasset winter home, volunteers cover the Virginia for the coming weather.

Paul King completes a day of working on the Virginia.

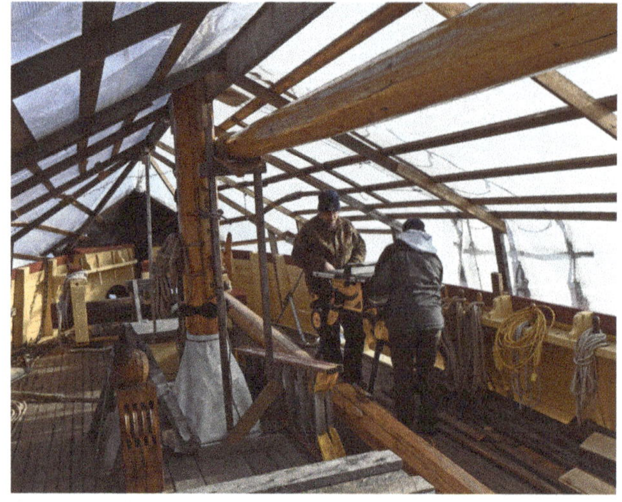

Jeremy and daughter, Rowan Blaiklock, enjoy the winter cover while working on the ship.

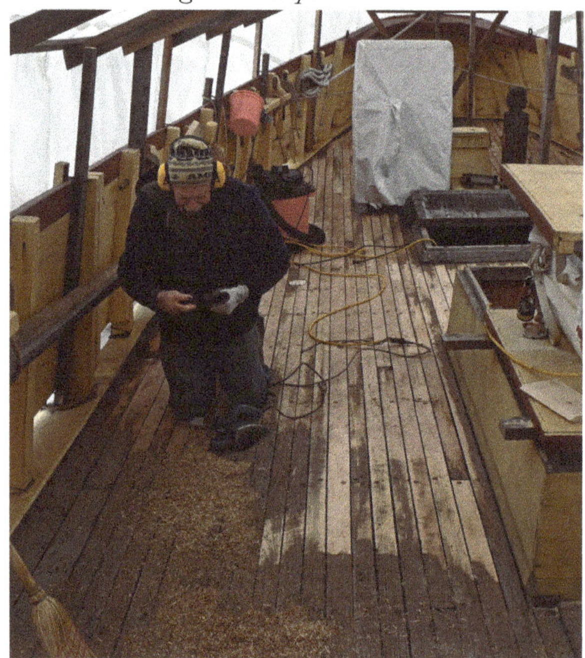

Captain John Foss cleans and recaulks the deck.

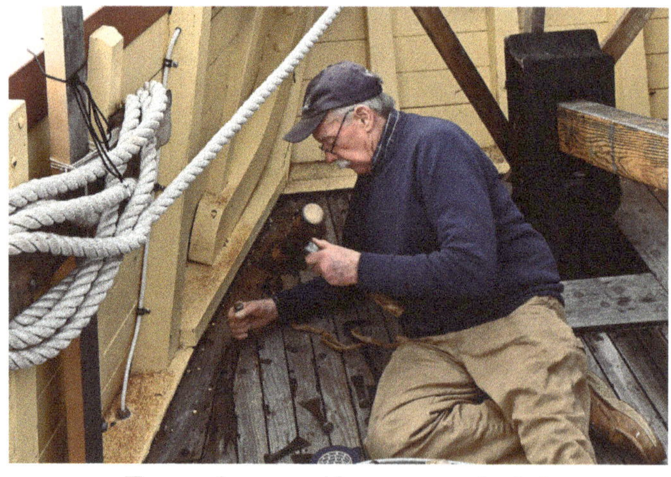

Foss touches up problem areas on the deck.

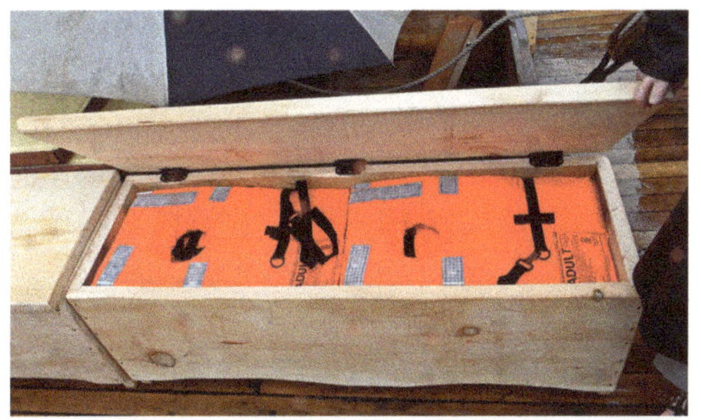

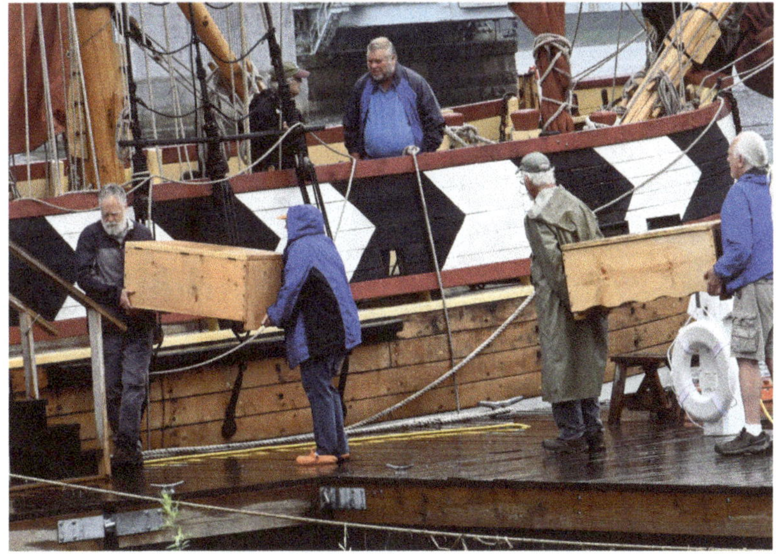

Volunteers load personal flotation device (PFD) chests.
PFDs are commonly called life preservers.

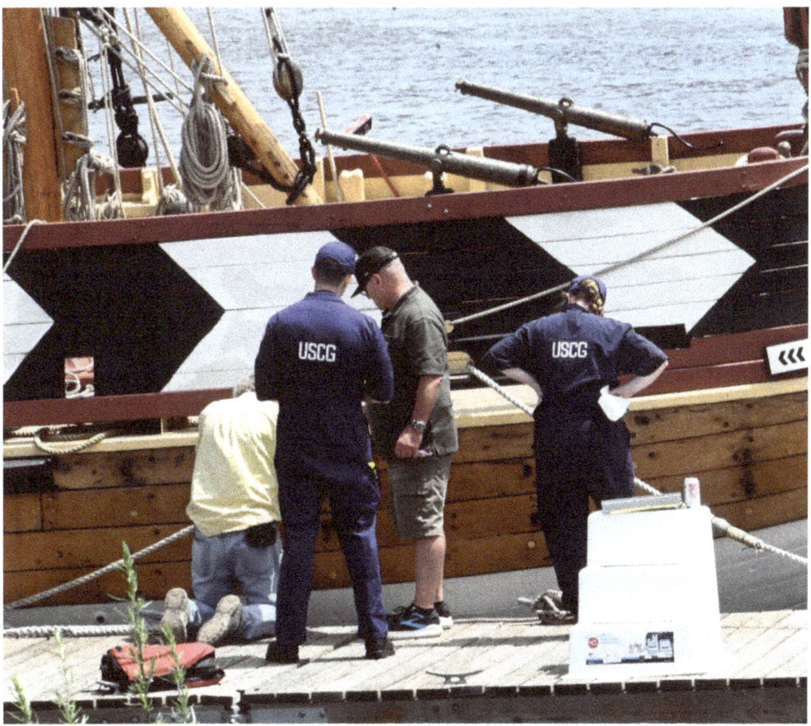

U.S. Coast Guard inspectors visit the *Virginia* performing the stability
test. The *Virginia* passed!

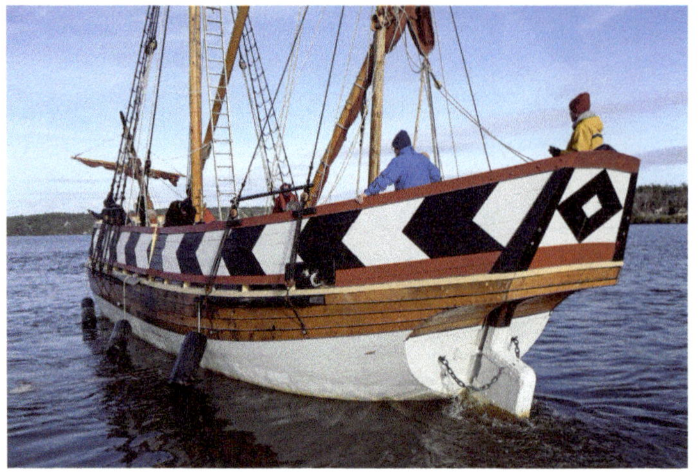

December 6, 2022, The Virginia leaves the dock in Bath for its first cruise on the Kennebec.

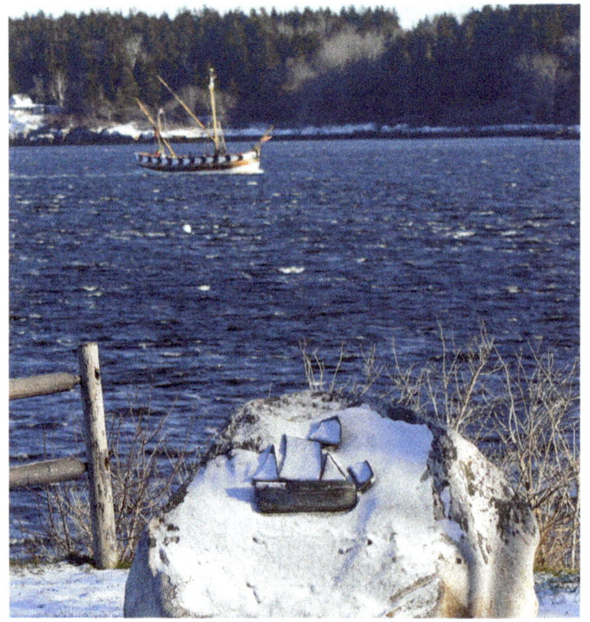

December 12, 2022, First trip downriver and off to Wiscasset for the winter.

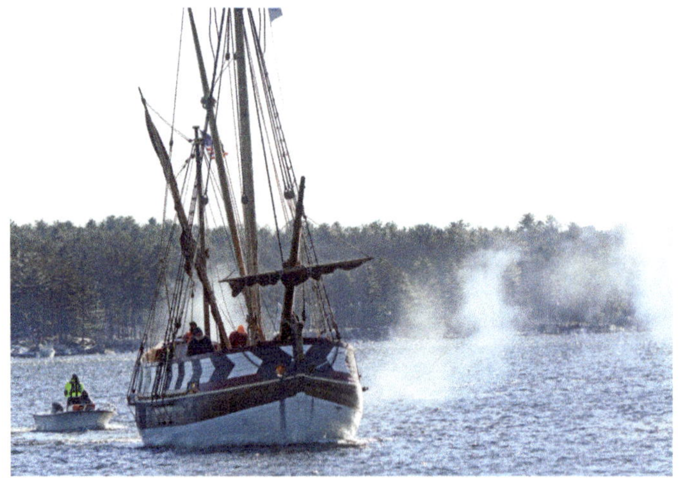

December 12, 2022. First sail to winter home of Wiscasset.

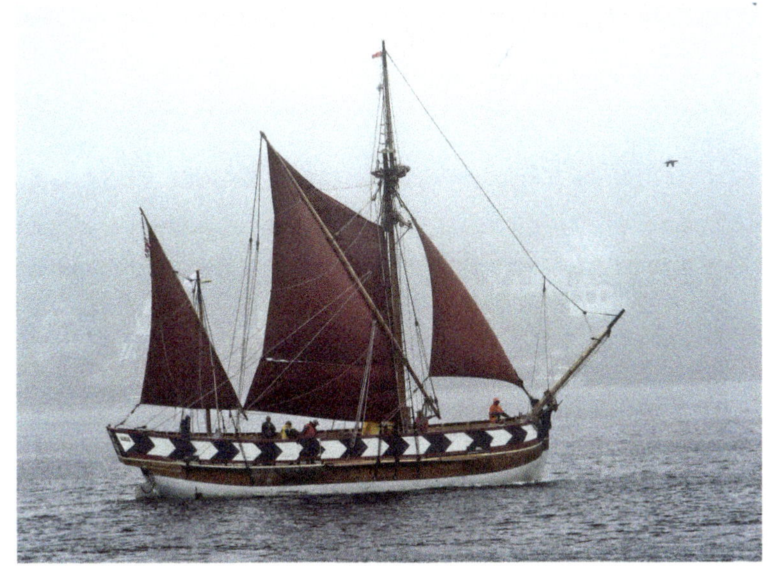

June 26, 2023. First cruise using multiple sails to Boothbay.

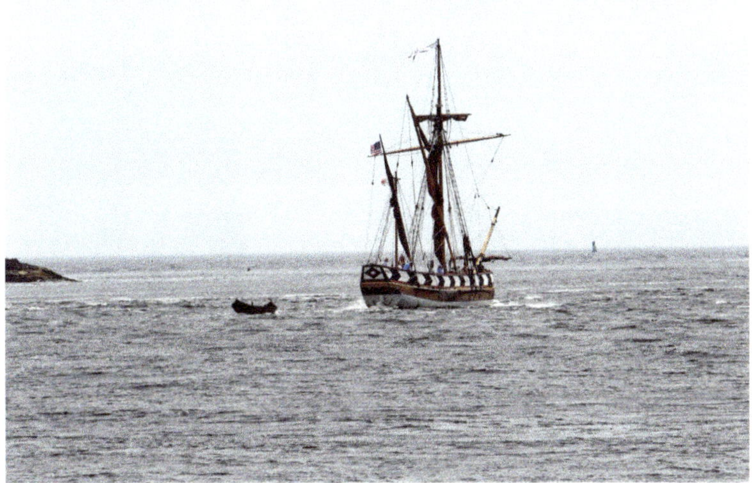

July 14, 2023. First cruise to Pemaquid.

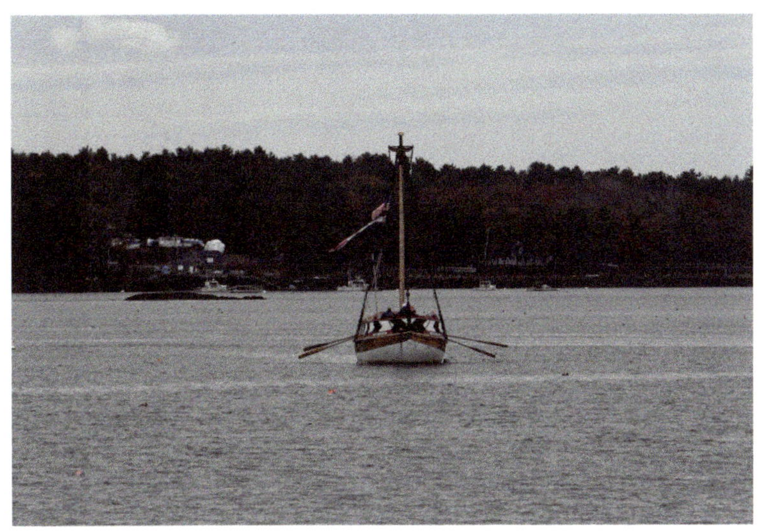

November 10, 2023. First use of human-power—with oars.

Volunteers Sailing

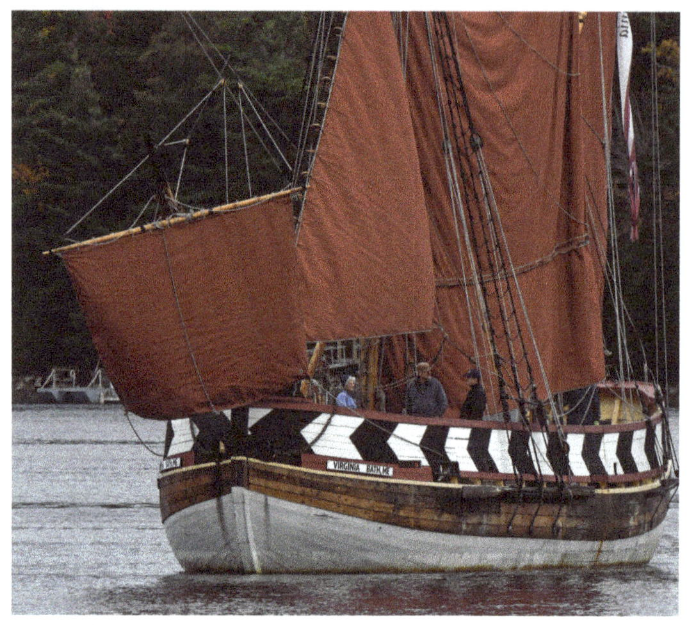

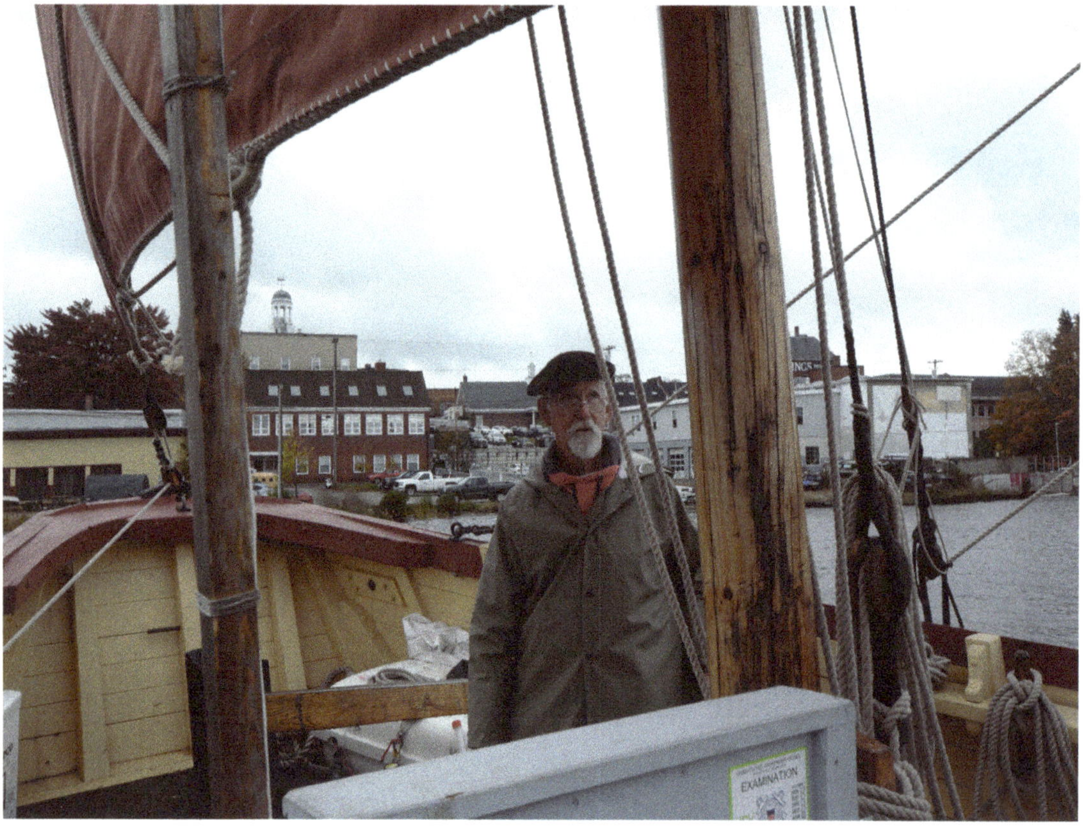

Captain J. B. Smith stears the Virginia away from the dock in Bath.

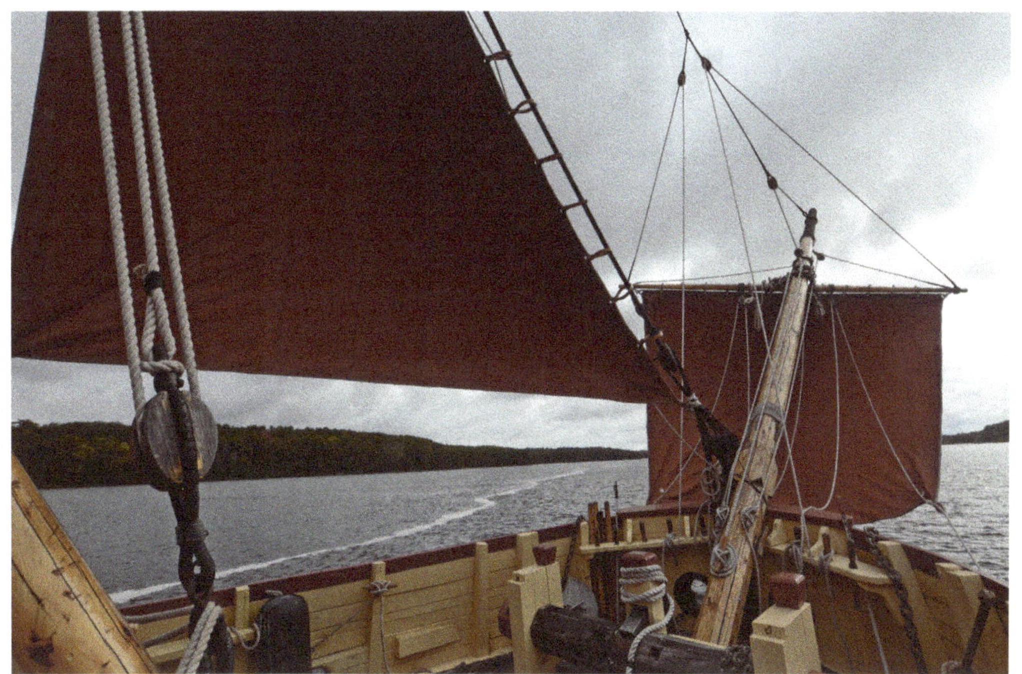

Heading up the Kennebec, showing off the tanbark (red) sails.

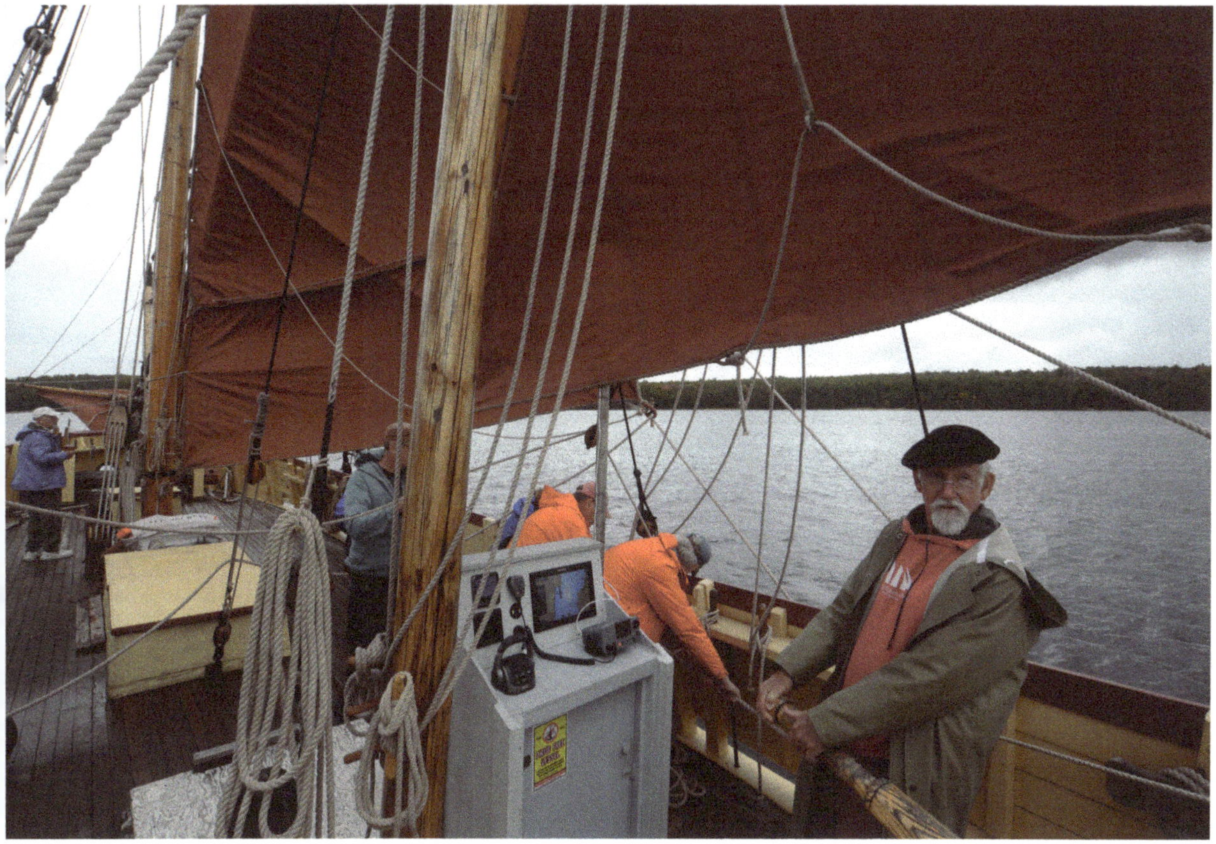

Captain J. B. Smith keeps an eye fore and aft as the ship sails.

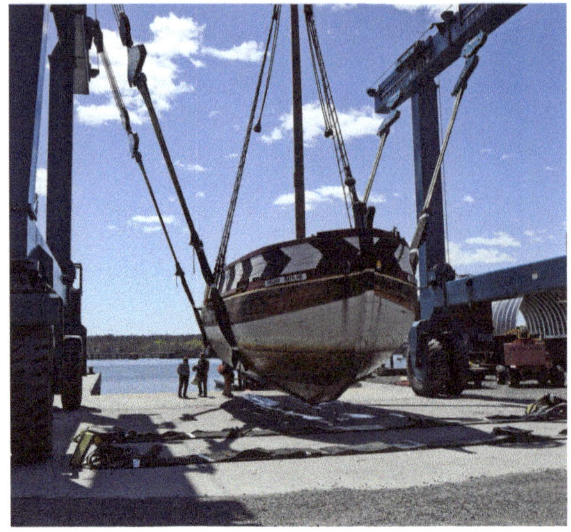

*After two years afloat, the Virginia comes out of the
water at Portland Yacht Services.*

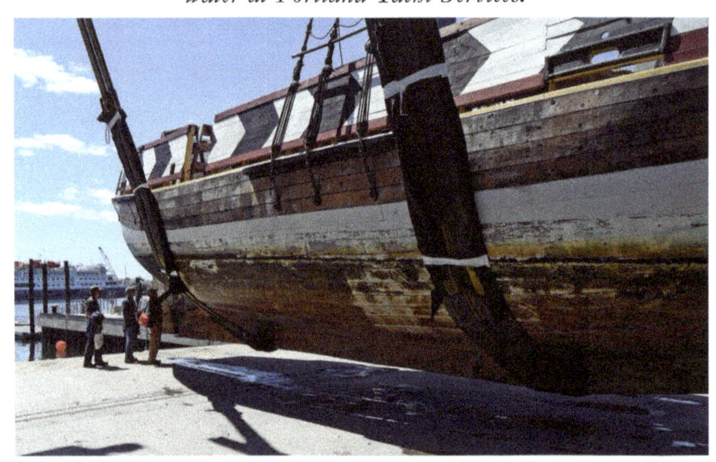

The Virginia crew inspects the hull of the ship.

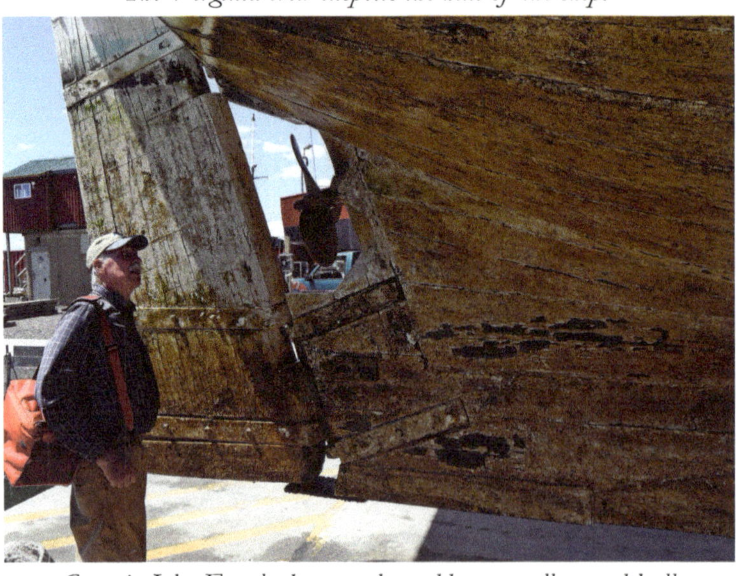

Captain John Foss looks over the rudder, propellor, and hull.

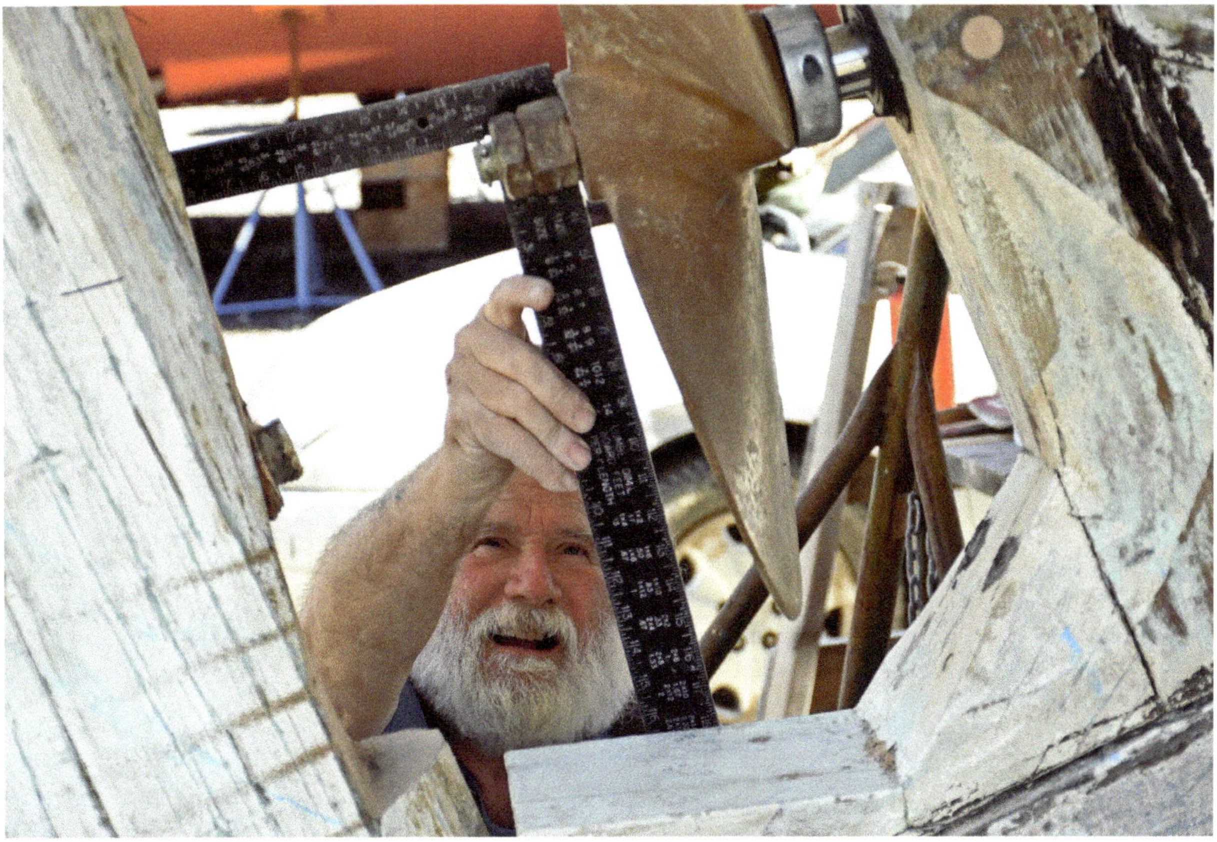

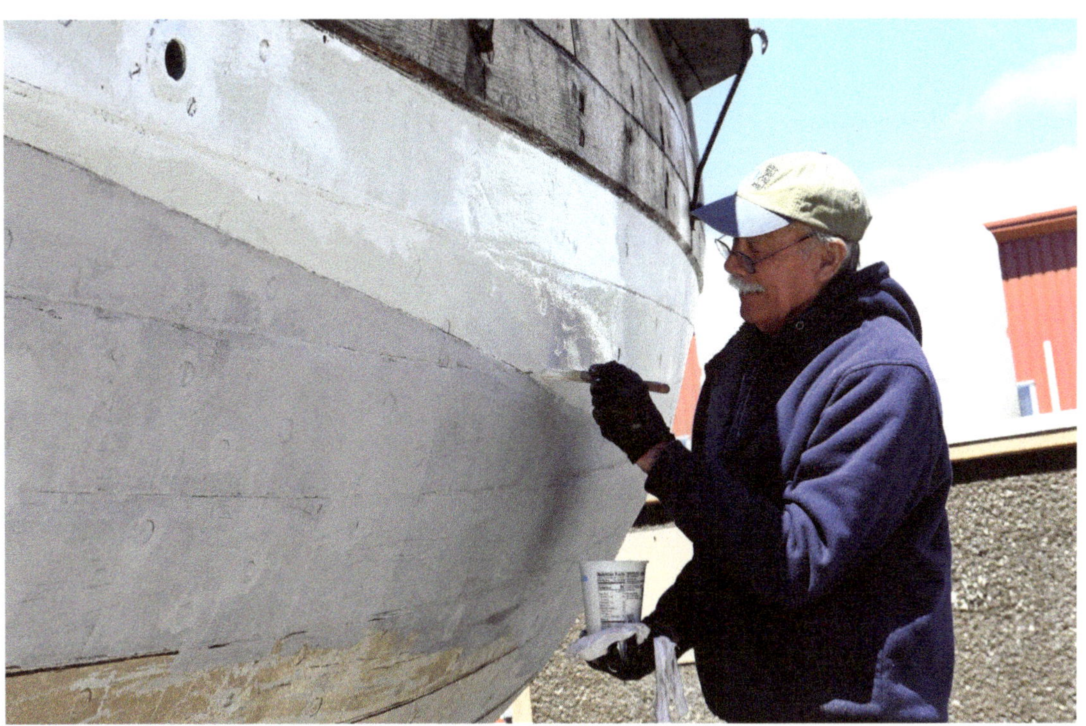

Boat builder Rob Stevens measures the propellor angle.

Captain Foss gives the hull a fresh coat of paint.

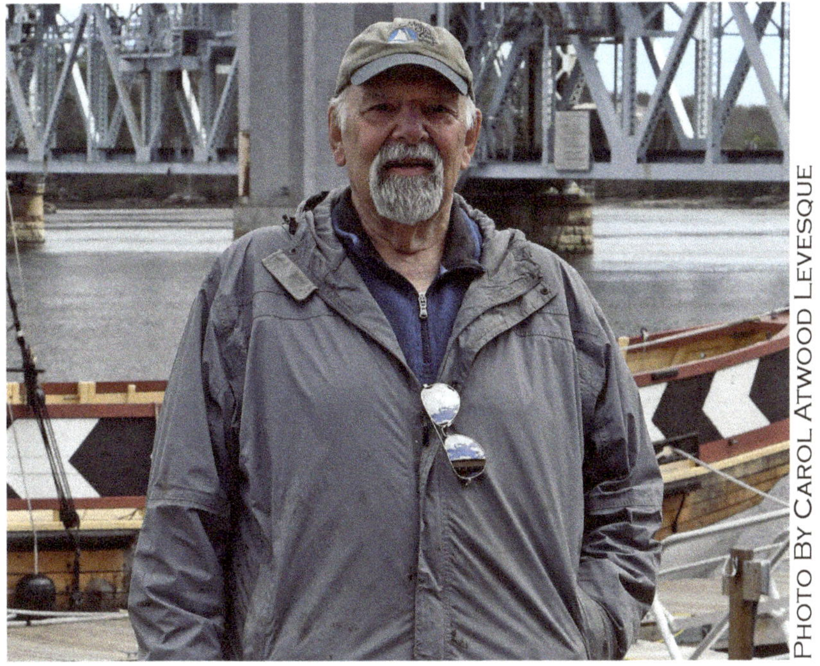

Paul T. Cunningham

Paul T. Cunningham grew up in Freeport, Maine. He earned a degree in Secondary Science Education at University of Southern Maine (Gorham State College). Subsequently, for nearly a decade, he taught elementary science in Gardiner, Maine.

Paul's love of photography led him away from the classroom. His first photographic job was with *The Shopping Notes* during the late 1980s. In 1990 Cunningham began his career as photojournalist at *The Times Record* and retired from there in 2008. Now Paul freelances, and follows Shipwright Rob Stevens on many of his exploits. The balance of his time is spent organizing the fruits of two decades of photography.